10.00 00
NO

THE CHRISTIAN WAY
IN RACE RELATIONS

CONTRIBUTORS

MARION CUTHBERT, Department of Personnel Service, Brooklyn College

ARTHUR W. HARDY, Personnel Services, The National Council of the Y.M.C.A.'s, New York City

GEORGE EDMUND HAYNES, Consultant for Africa of the World's Committee of the Y.M.C.A.; formerly, Executive Secretary, Department of Race Relations of the Federal Council of the Churches of Christ in America

J. NEAL HUGHLEY, College Minister and Professor of Social Science, North Carolina College for Negroes

WILLIAM LLOYD IMES, Director of Social and Adult Education, New York State Council of Churches; formerly, President, Knoxville College

GEORGE D. KELSEY, Professor of Philosophy and Religion, Morehouse College

RICHARD I. McKINNEY, President, Storer College

BENJAMIN E. MAYS, President, Morehouse College

WILLIAM STUART NELSON, Dean, The School of Religion, Howard University

HARRY V. RICHARDSON, Chaplain, Tuskegee Institute

JAMES H. ROBINSON, Minister of the Church of the Master, New York City

HOWARD THURMAN, Co-minister of the Fellowship Church of All Peoples, San Francisco

FRANK T. WILSON, Dean of Men, Lincoln University

THE
Christian Way
IN
Race Relations

Edited by

WILLIAM STUART NELSON

Essay Index Reprint Series

BOOKS FOR LIBRARIES PRESS
FREEPORT, NEW YORK

INTERNATIONAL STANDARD BOOK NUMBER:
0-8369-2004-X

LIBRARY OF CONGRESS CATALOG CARD NUMBER:
79-134121

PRINTED IN THE UNITED STATES OF AMERICA

CONTENTS

❧

PREFACE

THIS volume is the result of a co-operative enterprise on the part of the members of the Institute of Religion, not only in terms of authorship but in terms of conception, detailed planning, and criticism. The Institute is composed of men and women trained in the field of religion and is sponsored by the School of Religion of Howard University. For the past four years it has engaged in a study of Christianity and the problem of race relations in America, especially Negro-white relations. Members of the Institute have prepared papers on various aspects of the topic and subjected them to the criticism of the other members in annual week-long sessions. During the past two years the papers have been written in relation to the outline which forms the working basis of this book. Although names are assigned to the chapters and the primary authors assume complete responsibility for their contents, the chapters may very properly be regarded as the product of group enterprise. This is not to suggest that every idea or emphasis has the approval of all or even a majority either of the participating writers or of the total membership of the Institute. The writers have been permitted complete freedom under criticism.

In view of the critical problems which America now faces by reason of its race relations, the attempt is here made to set forth the central role which the members of the Institute of Religion feel the Christian way of life should play in the solution of these problems. The writers have set for themselves the task of describing these difficulties and of characterizing the Christian ethic with special reference to its promise as a solvent. Cognizance is taken of the obstacles confronting any effort to apply Christian principles to the problems of race relations, particularly as these difficulties manifest themselves in economic, political, and social areas. It is pointed out at the same time that the Christian community is not without resources for· implementing its ideals. There is the church, there are the Christian associations, Christian colleges, certain nonecclesiastical organizations, and there are individuals. The effort is made not only to describe the possibilities inherent in these agencies but also to point to past failings in their fullest employment. The volume concludes by drawing upon the genius of the Christian religion, upon history, and upon what we know to be the nature of man as a basis for such hope as we may entertain or such judgment as we may expect in our further wrestling with the problem of race relations.

Our readers, we hope, will be moved to sit in judgment on the profoundly important question of the practicability of Christianity in relation to social problems. A contest between Christianity and the world about it is being waged on many fronts— among them the economic, the political, and the racial. There are those who doubt profoundly the ability of the Christian ethic, as now embodied, to emerge victor in any of these struggles. Others have their faith. If the following discussion contributes significant light on this great question, it will have fulfilled completely the hope of all who have participated in it.

The first thanks of the authors go to those members of the Institute of Religion and to non-member consultants who have contributed so substantially to this volume. Publishers of the numerous volumes to which references are made have been gracious in their permission to use the passages quoted and we express to them our deepest appreciation. We are deeply grateful to President Mordecai W. Johnson and the trustees of Howard University and to the Hazen Foundation for their unfailing encouragement of this enterprise, as well as for substantial financial support. I wish to express my personal thanks to Professor Frank D. Dorey, Professor William A. Banner, and Professor Leon E.

Wright of the faculty of the School of Religion of Howard University for assuming important editorial responsibilities following my departure for India. They were ably advised by Dean Frank T. Wilson of Lincoln University, Pennsylvania, and President Richard I. McKinney of Storer College, members of the Interim Institute Committee.

THE EDITOR

Washington
   1947

I
THE ISSUES

1

Crucial Issues in America's Race Relations Today

WILLIAM STUART NELSON

FROM the moment Negro slavery was introduced to these shores the American people have been faced with the most serious problems which might conceivably issue from this form of human relationship. At few moments in our history, however, have these questions assumed so urgent and so important a position as they do today. America's role in international affairs is currently more intimate and critical than in any previous peacetime period. We face problems of internal adjustment of the most crucial order. Negroes themselves are at the point of grave decision in many matters affecting their relation with white Americans. No longer can a settlement in basic principle of the problem of Negro-white relations in this country be postponed without consequences of extreme seriousness to men everywhere.

I

In view of the race problem here, the first great question is whether America can succeed in the present world emergency in making the moral contribution to international affairs which is her responsibility and which has always been her dream. From the beginning America has hoped to stand as an example of something good in human relations and to influence mankind toward that for which she herself has stood. This role may not have been formulated precisely in the minds of a majority of Americans but it has always been broadly envisaged. The views of our intellectual and political leaders in the matter have been well defined. In spite of the warning against foreign entanglements which Washington so strongly uttered in his Farewell Address, the President expressed the eloquent view that "It will be worthy of a free, enlightened, and at no distant period a great nation, to give to mankind the magnanimous and too novel example of a people always guided by an exalted justice and benevolence." Henry Clay echoed Washington's hope by urging that this country keep its "lamp burning brightly on this western shore as a light to all nations," and President Fillmore declared our policy to be "wisely to govern ourselves, and thereby to set such an example of natural justice, prosperity, and true glory as shall teach to all nations the blessings of self-government and the unparalleled enterprise and success of a free people." Sumner Welles in our day sees millions asking what the aftermath of the recent struggle will hold for them and suggests that "those of us who are fortunate enough to be able to live as citizens of the free American Republics have our great responsibility in the forming of the answer to that question."[1] During the war, the voicing of our moral responsibility in world affairs reached a peak; in this time of peace the duty is felt no less sincerely and determinedly. Our conviction of mission is widespread and profound.

Of greater importance than our own dream is the world's need of democratic examples and its susceptibility to their influence. The sympathy America has expressed toward revolutionary movements in Europe and our welcome to political refugees have kindled high hopes in the hearts of the oppressed. "This is a good time to remember," says a current note in "Americans Whose Careers Are Relevant Today,"[2] "that Lincoln belongs as much to the democratic men of Europe as he does to us, to the working

[1] Hoover, Gibson, Wallace, and Welles, "Blueprint for Peace" in *Prefaces To Peace* (New York, 1943), p. 419.
[2] *Fortune*, XXIX (1944), 155.

men of the First International, to the French students who opposed Napoleon III, to the Russian peasants in the Caucasus who wept when they heard he was dead. It is important to remember that when Lincoln was mocked by slaveholders and monarchists, Italian democrats and Mexican revolutionaries and English liberals were united in praise and love of him." The hope men have in America burst into joyous expectation during the Wilson era. Its shattered fragments were gathered and laid at the feet of Franklin D. Roosevelt. It persists today in the midst of profound misgivings.

There are still hundreds of millions of people in the world, many of them men of color, who still do not know the real meaning of freedom. Their daily rounds and their destinies are in the hands of far-off and powerful minority groups. They are suppressed politically, exploited economically, and abused socially. Within European nations there are still minorities whose rights are entirely ignored or constantly in jeopardy. One of the most important questions raised in the hearts of these people today is the future attitude toward them of the government and the people of the United States.

Whatever may be the dream of America or the hopes of mankind, there can be no mistaking the urgent need of decisive contributions by some nations to a more equitable life among men. We have now for the third time even within the memory of young men the gathering of gigantic world forces on opposing sides and the admission by all informed opinion of the prospect of another and even greater world struggle. Immemorially men have enunciated lofty ideals relating to the world community, to which the world's great religious and moral codes bear testimony. History is also spotted with small bodies of men who have lived faithfully in the light of these high purposes. But now the world is not so much in need of new codes or the repetition of old ones. It will not be saved by token adherences to principles of equality in national or international terms. The need of this hour is that nations, great and strong, shall take a position so unequivocal in all of their internal and external relationships that mankind will recognize the real presence of a new dimension in human affairs.

If this need is clear, it is equally clear that America bears a peculiar responsibility for taking this role. America has a great creed which leaves nothing to be desired so far as creeds go. Her words and arms have been raised against foreign tyranny from her very birth. She is a young nation unfettered by the ancient ways and taboos which older peoples are either unwilling or too weary to renounce. She possesses commanding resources, human and material, and is thus able to match brute power with brute power if she chooses. A demonstration by America of an emancipation from ancient biases, a transcendence of opportunism, and a trusting of her fate to the ideals she has so long professed would perchance produce the miracle in human relations which this hour requires. This is not to encourage in America any messianic urge with its accompanying dangers. We have lived too long as civilized men to believe that a people can save mankind. Neither is there room for the glorification of the notion of "world leadership." The hopes which we as a people can rightly cherish and the responsibility which we clearly bear are to live our national life in such a spirit that men will see our good ways and be persuaded by them. The force of example is incalculably greater than moral propagandizing and its implied self-exaltation. Indeed, example often bears the mysterious power of miracle.

The great question which America must answer is whether she possesses the moral power to live by her creed. Does she really understand the creed which she professes? Or understanding it, does she profess it with her lips, eulogize it, but in her heart renounce it? Can we set an example before the world today of the freedom and equality to which we have borne such eloquent verbal testimony?

There is ground for a negative answer to this question in a catalogue easily made of our national offenses against the American creed. That offense which stirs the deepest doubt today is our unsolved racial problem. It is this which, as Gunnar Myrdal says, constitutes America's greatest failure. For more than three hundred years this problem has vexed her and cheated her. Even when she has made progress toward its solution it has often been a tainted progress to be credited to fortuity or compulsion, economic or political. It is a cancer in the body politic which must be removed before our own democratic health can be expected. It stands athwart the path which might conceivably lead us to a new world.

A knowledge of our unhappy situation is in no wise confined to ourselves. During the war German and Japanese propagandists made impressive use of our dilemma. The recent request of the National Negro Congress to the United Nations that this body take the necessary actions to check and eliminate the abuses from which Negro Americans suffer called the world's attention officially to our disordered house. Ilya Ehrenburg, Russian writer, raised a question worth pondering as he left for his home following a two months' visit in America. He was discussing American criticism of Russian-controlled elections in Yugoslavia. "I have been in the State of Mississippi," he said, "where half the population were deprived of their right to vote. What is better: To deprive of the right to vote a man who has a black conscience or one who has a black complexion?"[3] In the view of Pearl Buck, "The persistent refusal of Americans to see the connection between the colored American and the colored peoples abroad, the continued, and it seems even willful, ignorance which will not investigate the connection, are agony to those loyal and anxious Americans who know all too well the dangerous possibilities."[4]

The crucial nature of the problem lies in the further fact that time is running out on America. We propose in our national life to set standards but to achieve them in our own good time. We prefer a middle-of-the-road compromise to an extreme solution. Where time is of no account such a method has its strong appeal. But upon the scene of world conflict today, time is of the essence of importance. The most eloquent pronouncements on freedom ring in the ears of the world during its every waking hour. The United Nations Security Council has pledged "To achieve inter-

[3] New York *Times*, June 26, 1946, p. 81.
[4] *American Unity and Asia* (New York, 1942), p. 29.

national cooperation . . . in promoting and encouraging respect for human rights and for fundamental freedoms for all without distinction as to race, sex, language, or religion."

Meanwhile there are deep stirrings among the oppressed peoples of the world—stirrings of hope and of purpose. The people of India and of Indonesia have left no doubt as to their mood. Minorities in China, Greece, Belgium, and Yugoslavia have violently protested the old order. "People everywhere," declared Wendell Willkie upon his return from around the world, "articulate and inarticulate people are watching to see whether the leaders who proclaimed the principles of these documents [statements by Chiang Kai-shek and Stalin, the Atlantic Charter, the proclamation of the Four Freedoms] really meant what they said."[5] Or as Henry A. Wallace wrote in *The Century of the Common Man*, "The people are on the march toward even fuller freedom than the most fortunate peoples of the earth have hitherto enjoyed."[6]

There is further urgency in the fact that another great power is now in the thick of world affairs, a power with no such creed as ours and no such history but with a promise and a demonstration within her own borders that have stirred the deepest hopes in the hearts of forgotten men. Can it be that we who for so long have proclaimed freedom and equality and achieved them substantially in numerous areas of our life will, in part at least because of our attitude toward a minority people at home, sacrifice democracy's right to a fair chance before the people who are in need of a new and better way of life?

America must consider whether, with her democratic and Christian pretensions, she is prepared to resign herself to being a second-rate example of the basic principles of the Republic and permit others to offer a purer demonstration of what she professes. She must know that the oppressed people of the world have seen in other lands new solutions to their problems and have become enamored of them; she must understand that she faces the crucial

[5] *One World*, quoted in *Prefaces to Peace*, p. 127.
[6] *Prefaces to Peace*, p. 372.

issue as to whether she will present to the world now a compelling example of true liberty for all of her citizens or abandon the hope of proving a world-emancipating influence.

II

The second crucial issue which America faces because of her race problem involves the soundness of our national life. In spite of our great resources, actual and potential, we cannot meet successfully the demands of this bewilderingly changing world unless we can keep nearer the maximum development of our material and spiritual powers. We shall not soon forget the great depression. We hear now the cries of the hungry from many lands. Tomorrow some new, titanic need at home or abroad will burst upon us. We stand in need of our full strength.

THE SOUTH SUFFERS

In contrast to this need, America today, as a result in considerable measure of the unsolved racial problem, presents areas of critical weakness. One of the saddest commentaries upon the price men are willing to pay for their prejudices is the state of the American South. Here is a section comprising approximately one-third of the total land and nearly one-half of the water area of the United States. Its lands touch the sea, cross magnificent mountain ranges, sweep through fertile river valleys and across rich grazing plains. Its climate is excellent and its lands are among the most productive in the world. From its population, approximately one-fourth that of the United States, have come some of the finest spirits this nation has known.

But this southland has borne a curse, the curse of racial antipathy and exploitation. It is unnecessary to recall the spoilage to land and people inherent in the institution of slavery. It is of greater relevance to view the tragic cost of current prejudice to that great section and its people.

In the midst of a grave national crisis the President of the Republic felt it necessary to point to the South's great economic lag. Low wages and long hours have caused thousands of southerners to move from country to city, farm to mill and back again, always attempting to improve their lot a little. The willingness to accept low wages in industry rather than endure destitution on the farm has led to unwholesome competition among the unskilled laborers and made the agricultural worker a "threat to job, the wages, and the working conditions of the industrial worker."[7] Descriptive of the economic state of the South but illustrative also of a far too tardily emerging insight and determination is the pledge of Senator Claude Pepper of Florida in relation to higher minimum wages: "As long as I live, I will challenge the feudal tradition in the South and those who to preserve it would continue a kind of economic slavery."[8] Twenty-two million acres of soil once fertile have been forever ruined and another area as large as Oklahoma and Alabama has been seriously damaged by soil erosion due in part to the ignorance and poverty of tenant farmers and the greed of landlords.

Politically the South is a tragic picture today. Here is a section with a quarter of the nation's population, yet for all practical purposes with only one political party. In 1940, 76 per cent of all its votes were cast for the Democratic candidate for the presidency. In Mississippi 98 per cent of the votes went to the same candidate. This was not due, moreover, to so overwhelming a love for the man. In the South the majority of men are enslaved politically to their past and to their current biases. They think in terms of one party only and conceive its principal plank to be the determination "to keep the Negro in his place." This domination of the politcial mind in the South by this single consideration means that its vote is counted before it is cast. We see here the consequence of sectional political totalitarianism in a drugging of the springs of political thought, the producing of feeble statesmen, the robbing of the people of social reform. The campaign statement of one of its recent vote seekers is significant: "The present and future welfare of the South demands that the white race remain the dominant race. . . . I feel very strongly that certain social and socialistic activities sponsored by the New Deal and more particularly by Mrs. Eleanor Roosevelt are intolerable, detrimental, and an insult to the people of the great South."[9]

The totalitarian political mind of the South is accompanied by an explicit fascism with regard to the Negro. Although Negroes constitute one-third of the southern population, politically they are practically powerless. It would be difficult to find anywhere in the civilized world a more completely fascist state as regards the political treatment of Negroes than exists at this very hour in Mississippi. Likewise it would be difficult to find a political unit which has produced such puerility, demagoguery, and sinisterness in political matters. Recent Supreme Court decisions will alter this situation in time but it will be by no consent of the majority of southerners and the decisions may have come too late. Even now every resource is being employed to circumvent them. Expressed unblushingly is the determination to keep the Democratic party "an exclusively white party," whatever the cost.

Culturally the South is potentially rich but actually very poor. White men have frittered away their own creative powers and crushed the creative genius of the Negroes in their midst. It is obvious that in a land dominated by one great fear and one great obsession little cultural creativity can be expected. There is always an ax to grind, a dogma to defend, an honor to protect, a past to perpetuate. There is little time or mood for the writing of history, for science, for art, for poetry. Southerners have demonstrated creative ability but too often they have done so only after leaving the South. Almost one-half of the eminent scientists who were born in the South are now living elsewhere. Herein lies one of the region's greatest tragedies. It is a land of wasted people. In 1930, 3,800,000 of the South's native-born population had moved out of the section entirely. They left for jobs and they left for life, a fuller life. The man in whom the spark of genius glows flees the place lest this spark be smothered and never revive. Gerald Johnson points to a sudden recent flowering of southern literature

[9] *Afro-American*, June 23, 1945, p. 24.

but can find no southern music of distinction and no theater of national dominance. According to him, southern painting and sculpture are nonexistent and southern architecture has produced nothing of significance since 1848 when Robert Mills of Charleston designed the Washington Monument. "Southern scholarship," Johnson says, "is represented most largely and most brilliantly by the hordes of Southern-born professors who crowd Nothern universities." There is the shocking fact that the Far West spends $1.05 per capita on libraries and the Southeast 16 cents. The libraries of the Far West circulate more than five books a year for each person in the area; those of the Southeast circulate seventy-seven hundredths of one book per capita. In the entire country there are 3.20 people for each copy of a daily newspaper published; in Mississippi there are 18.11, in South Carolina, 12.44, and in Arkansas, 12.29.[10]

The relative poverty of the South is reflected in its support of education. Although it devotes a larger share of its tax income to education than the nation as a whole, it still spends only about half the average spent for the country as a whole and one-fourth of what is spent per child in New York State. The total endowments of the colleges and universities of the South do not equal the combined endowments of Yale and Harvard. Its medical schools do not have facilities to educate doctors to meet its own needs. And it may be recalled that in spite of these facts the South is attempting a separate system of education for Negroes and whites, one which the Supreme Court has ruled must be complete if it is to be at all.

The deficiencies of the South cannot be attributed wholly to the element of race, but it is clear to any with the most meager knowledge of the situation that the effort to keep one-third of the population "in its place" is in considerable measure responsible for many of the South's ailments. Edward Byron Reuter, writing in *The American Race Problem*,[11] leaves no doubt as to the influence of the race problem on southern life. He says:

[10] Gerald Johnson, *Wasted Land* (Chapel Hill, N.C., 1937), p. 81.
[11] New York, 1938, p. 86.

The present arrangements [of race relations] are demonstrably un-economic and morally stultifying; they retard the cultural advancement of the southern regions of the country, hence of the nation, and they make personally tolerable conditions of life impossible for large numbers of persons. They are an endless source of political corruption and governmental inefficiency; they perpetuate the educational backwardness of both the Negroes and the whites. In nearly every case, they operate to prevent the satisfaction of the real needs of the community life. Every consideration of economic, political, social, moral, and educational welfare calls for radical changes in the race relations.

The effort to keep one-third of the population poor, ignorant, enslaved politically can never fail to affect in the same manner the rest of the people. Fear—by whites of Negro political domination and economic competition and by Negroes of the ferocious hatred of the whites—is, says Gerald Johnson, "responsible for appalling waste of energies of both races."[12] "I do not plead for black more than I plead for white education," says John Graham Brooks. "The South cannot rise unless the white man is educated too. So long as the Negro is down, the white man will stay down."[13] What is said here about education can be said concerning every aspect of life in which Negroes in the South are treated unjustly. The prosperity, political freedom, education, culture of the entire South depend upon the extent to which these good things are made available to every man, Negro or white. An editorial on May 7, 1946, in the *Twin City Sentinel* of Winston-Salem, North Carolina, bears frank and convincing testimony to this fact: "If we are to build a great civilization in the South, we must make freer the capacities of men, both white and black, to exercise their talents, their skills and impress the integrity of their personality upon the regional life."

It is not difficult to understand, says William J. Robertson in *The Changing South*,[14] why there has been a dearth of great men in the South since the Civil War: "It is the old story: the Solid South and its adherence to one political faith."

[12] *Op. cit.*, p. 63.
[13] *An American Citizen: The Life of Henry Baldwin, Jr.*, quoted by B. Schieke, *Alien Americans* (New York, 1936), flyleaf.
[14] New York, 1927, p. 181.

The South with all of its magnificent possibilities in land and people is needed today in her full strength. She can never hope, however, to fulfill her great destiny until she leaves behind her "the ancient intolerances and narrowness which have bound her so long."[15]

THE NORTH SUFFERS

The presence of the unsolved race problem has its unhappy influence likewise upon the North. Northerners have not failed to capitalize on the weaknesses of the South to their own enrichment of purse but corresponding impoverishment of character. The North has refused to make full use of available Negro labor, which has resulted in a glutting of the labor market. The results in unemployment, in strife among laborers, and in the depression of wages and conditions of labor are too well known to require discussion.

The North has been victimized in no uncertain way by the political fascism of the South. Because of the disfranchisement of Negroes the South exerts a highly disproportionate, and generally unhealthy, influence upon national affairs. It is a matter of large importance to the North that in 8 southern states 24 million people cast 829,000 votes and elect 79 representatives with an average of 10,500 votes for each Congressman. In 8 northern states, on the other hand, 24 million people cast 7,738,814 votes to elect the same number of representatives with an average of 98,-000 votes for each. The people of Connecticut, to take but one state as an example, have a basis for concern in the fact that although in 1942, 560,000 votes in that state sent 6 representatives to Congress, the same number of votes sent 58 representatives from southern states. The North cannot help but note with alarm the powerful committee chairmanships in Congress lodging in southern hands by reason of the simple process of counting Negroes as citizens and counting them out as voters—an act not only of gross moral wrong but of violation of the Constitution.

The North increasingly has fallen victim to treating the Negro

[15] William J. Robertson, *op. cit.*, p. 301.

as a social pariah, as is the universal practice of the South. Abolition sentiment in the North fell an early victim to interest in
economic exploitation. This has been followed by the spread of
southern racial patterns to the North. It should be a matter of
deep shame to states which have contributed so much both to
the theory and to the fact of liberty and equality that they have
failed to carry forward with determination the work of emancipation and have permitted within their borders certain American
citizens to be subjected to proscriptions in employment, in housing, in the use of public accommodations, in election to political
office.

THE NATION SUFFERS

Said Julius Rosenwald, "I am interested in the Negro because
I am interested in America." The implications of this remark for
the nation as a whole are obvious. Our sins and our losses in relation to the race problem are ultimately national. If the economy
and the culture of one section suffer, the economy and culture of
the entire people suffer. If politically one section of the country
is fascist, the nation can escape, to that extent, neither the indictment nor the fact of fascism. How can America as a whole fail
to lose when bill after bill providing for the increased welfare of
the people is scuttled because, in large part, it promises a better
life for Negroes? We do not forget the opposition to the federal
ballot for soldiers, to unemployment insurance for veterans, to
the social reform proposals of the Farm Security Administration,
or the defeat of the bill providing federal aid for education.

The gravest loss from which the nation suffers as a result of
the unsolved racial problem is spiritual. What lofty sentiment
can she express, what high office can she attempt which is not
suspect? Upon what can confidence in her disinterested concern
for others be grounded? It is not too much to say that this failure
has raised a fundamental question concerning the great American creed. Has it been after all a dream of such liberty and equality as one can take for oneself or one's group or for one race
alone? Has it been a creed operative when consistent with eco-

nomic and political advantage and social heritage—and only then?

These questions take on deeper significance when it is realized how completely failure in race relations applies to American life. It is a failure of North and South, East and West, of the majority in the nation, of minority groups, of the state, the church, labor, management, men, women, the educated, the uneducated, the rich, the poor. Everywhere one finds some people, and usually a majority of the people, who victimize or are prepared to victimize the Negro. The race problem represents a national failure, and well might the question be asked whether it does not represent a basic denial in the American spirit of what our creed so eloquently proclaims. The answer to this question must be "no." But a verbal "no" will not suffice; it must be a "no" written in the acts of the American people.

The significance of this total picture is obvious; and the anxiety which it creates in the heart of every true patriot is great. We live in a moment of the world's history when the maximum resources of the nation are insufficient. Whatever America's vaunted power, she can ill spare any of it now. She is faced with new and graver problems; she is faced with new and stronger rivals. She needs her every material, intellectual, and spiritual resource. She needs her entire people. Wendell Willkie has spoken of the richness which minorities give to a democracy in normal times. What of critical times? We know that in the world struggle, which is now in the skirmishing stage, the alignment will be not simply of nation against nation but of ideas against ideas, of group against group, even within nations. At this hour enemies of the democratic way of life are searching for fissions in our body politic and are prepared to widen any they discover by every possible means. Why blind ourselves, asks Attorney General Clark, to the "deep-seated and vicious plot to destroy our unity—the unity without which there would be no United States?" The need for a united America is abundantly manifest, and equally manifest is the impossibility of achieving that unity without solving, in terms both of principle and of direction, the problem of Negro-white relations.

III

A third crucial issue facing America today in race relations stems from what is happening to the Negroes themselves. Volume after volume is written describing the inequalities which Negroes endure. It remains nevertheless a question as to whether either they or white men fully comprehend what is happening to them or the grave nature of the indictment which in consequence may be brought against the American people.

Life, in American eyes, is a precious thing and the taking of life a great crime. It is a crime with which the American people as a whole do not dream they can be justly charged. And yet let us examine the lot of the Negro at the hands of white Americans today. There is the story of a young Negro woman, greatly loved by Negroes generally, who was injured in an automobile accident a few years ago near Dalton, Georgia. She was in need of the kind of immediate treatment for which only a hospital is equipped. But the Dalton hospital did not receive Negroes and it was necessary to send to Chattanooga for an ambulance. The young woman died in Chattanooga shortly after her arrival there. The life of a young woman is a precious thing.

Stories of such brutality can be repeated for other communities, some of them farther north than Dalton. Not so dramatic but equally fatal to human life is the fact that in 1938 there were in Mississippi 0.7 beds per 1,000 Negroes as compared with 2.4 beds per 1,000 whites; and in the Carolinas there were 1.2 beds per 1,000 Negroes as compared with 2.1 per 1,000 whites. In 1928, one hospital bed was reported available for each 139 white persons in the total population of the United States, with one bed available for each 1,941 in the Negro population.

Death rides upon the fact, moreover, that Negro physicians are often denied the opportunities for normal growth in their practice. Throughout the state of Louisiana there is only one modern hospital in which a Negro physician can practice; in Mississippi there is none. A similar situation obtains in other southern states. Indeed, there are only a few hospitals in the whole United States in which Negro and white doctors work together on terms of equality.

Poor housing is an admitted source of disease and death. To whom then must the finger of condemnation be pointed when Negroes, crowded into ghettos, North and South, present the nation with high mortality rates? Who denies them fresh air and sunshine, play space for their children, sleeping space for all, protection against cold and filth? Who draws the line at the railroad track? Who signs the covenants? Who keeps the wages down and the ceilings on upgrading, so that even the ghettos cannot be sufficiently improved? It is the American people, North and South, rich and poor, Christian and un-Christian. These are they who preside over the still births, the infant burials, the premature deaths of many young men and women. This is a hard but incontrovertible logic. There are hands which the repetition of ancient formulas and the proclamation of future hopes cannot cleanse.

If Americans were informed that in some foreign land men possessed the magic power to inflict upon others the curse of ignorance or partial ignorance and deliberately exercised it, they could scarcely find terms sufficiently condemnatory of this practice. But is not this same cruel end achieved by the inequalities in our educational system? When one child in a state or county or town has one-third or one-fifth or one-fifteenth of the sum spent on his education as is spent on another child in the same community, he is the victim of a curse. How are we to characterize the fact that in many counties of southern states not a single high school exists for the training of Negroes? Or that Negro men were called up by Selective Service who not only had never seen the inside of a school but, removed as they were to the very fringes of civilization, had never seen money or heard a radio?

Americans are usually regarded as generous. In times of world crisis they have touched the hearts of men everywhere by their immediate and overflowing responses. Are we conscious of the fact, however, that Americans are saying daily to millions of their fellow Americans, "You cannot have bread, or if you manage to get bread, you can have no butter, or if butter, no cake"? Gunnar Myrdal[16] begins his chapter on "Economic Inequality" by these arresting words: "The economic situation of the Negroes in America is pathological. Except for a small minority enjoying upper or middle class status, the masses of American Negroes, in the rural South and in the segregated slum quarters in Southern and Northern cities, are destitute." This is explained by the distribution of Negroes in certain regions and occupations with low pay and high unemployment risks, and this, in turn, is explained by discrimination. "White prejudice and discrimination," says Myrdal, "keep the Negro low in standards of living, health, education, manners and morals." What name have we for the attitude of Representative John Rankin (D., Miss.), who attacks the free-lunch bill, designed to eliminate discrimination in the quantity of food served to minority groups, and who defends his actions by saying, "This program means trouble. It's dynamite, gentlemen. . . . I say it's poison"? "Democracy," writes Jonathan Daniels, in the *Virginian Quarterly Review* (1938, p. 482), "is bread." What, may I ask, is bread-snatching?

Liberty is a basic element in the American creed. What is it, on the other hand, when citizens who are subject to law are denied a voice in the making or administering of that law? This is the state of the great majority of Negro Americans today. In the general election of 1940 it is estimated that in 8 deep southern states only 80,000 to 90,000 Negroes voted out of a total Negro adult population of 3,651,356. In the primaries practically none voted. This is the result of disfranchisement enforced by such "formal" devices as the poll tax and a "satisfactory" explanation of state constitutions and by such "informal" devices as insults and threats. This is a species of slavery. It is a condition in which the political hands and feet of men are shackled and their gen-

[16] *An American Dilemma* (New York, 1944), I, 205.

eral welfare menaced in consequence. The authors of this evil are oppressors, whatever may be the flag they wave or the creed they recite.

There is deep solicitude in our land today because of mounting crime. Many good men are seeking for a solution. These good men would be outraged if it were suggested that some of them are at the root not only of this new crime but of crime of long standing. Everyone with the faintest knowledge of social conditions understands that crime thrives upon segregation, unemployment, ignorance. Who promotes these conditions also promotes crime. It is not an offense, to be sure, for which one is dragged before the court or loses one's standing in the community. This is the price which those who are the victims of the offense must pay. It is a wrong, however, which is extremely grave and which the American people must begin to ponder more deeply.

Of all the offenses from which Negroes have suffered, none is so tragic as that which has affected their spirit. Many things have happened to the Negroes' spirit since they became slaves. They have learned to hate, to accommodate, to dissemble. But the affliction that concerns us most in connection with the task we have set ourselves in this volume is their loss of faith—faith in their religion and in their country. It is not a complete loss of faith but it is a mounting one and a dangerous one. Said a young Negro minister to me some months ago in the midst of a discussion of the race problem, "I am becoming increasingly at a loss to find reasons why I should remain a Christian." Many Negroes have long ago abandoned the search for reasons. They have found in the inhumanity of their fellow Christians reasons abundant for their disavowal of the Christian faith. There are today in preparation for the ministry of 38,000 Negro churches a meager 327 college graduates. One of the reasons for this pitifully small response to the need for religious leadership is the irrelevance which young Negro men feel religion bears to the major concerns of their lives. They reason that there is money in business, healing in medicine, power in law; in religion, what? They do not want the patience of their mothers. Most of them were born and have suffered in the most religious section of our country, if churchgoing and Bible quoting can be called religion. A Negro minister, speaking at Howard University in June, 1946, to the largest graduating class of Negro college and professional students in America, declared that it was blasphemy to call the segregated church a church of God and urged its repudiation. I have yet to hear one dissent from his words. Another Negro minister, speaking in the same commencement season to the graduates of Atlanta University, declared: "Christian nations have furnished the world with its worst example of unbrotherliness, for no other people on the globe have singled out as many groups with which they are unwilling to work, pray, to be sick with in the same hospital, and to be buried with in the same graveyards as leading Christian nations."[17]

There is something very sad in the statement New Orleans Negro ministers made in an effort to secure play space for their children: "We are not allowed at the parks, although provisions are made for ducks and geese. It is hard for us as ministers to teach our children Christianity under such circumstances." It is a matter of grave concern when in service after service in Negro churches the theme turns on the abuses suffered by Negroes at the hands of white Americans, and the mood is one of unalloyed hatred.

There is tragic irony in a comparison of this loss of religious faith by Negroes and the missionary efforts of the American church at home and abroad. The literature of one church has only recently announced renewed missionary efforts among Negroes; and a great southern denomination in 1943 expressed the following purpose in making expenditures on a Negro program: "We believe that through this program we can and are making the best contribution for the Christianizing of the Negroes." There are, it is true, millions of Negroes in America who are candidates for conversion to high religion. It requires little imagination, however, to understand their resistance to those professors of religion at whose hands they have suffered so long. Ne-

[17] *The Atlanta University Bulletin*, Series III, No. 55 (1945), p. 5.

groes are feeling increasingly like the elderly Chinese gentleman quoted by Pearl Buck. Miss Buck's missionary father asked him whether it was nothing to him that to reject Christ meant to burn in hell. The gentleman answered: "If, as you say, my ancestors are all in hell at this moment, it would be unfilial for me not to be willing to suffer with them. Besides," he continued, "if heaven is only full of white men, I should be very uncomfortable there. I had rather go to hell where the Chinese are."[18] The day is not far away when Negroes may turn their backs completely upon the religion they have seen and seek another—perhaps the one they hear professed but of which they have witnessed so little.

It is a matter of great moment that Negroes' faith in their country is so often and so profoundly shaken. The story of their loyalty from the earliest days of the Republic and before, even as they were held as slaves, is a rare page in human history. As might well be expected, their increased sophistication has been accompanied by increased critical-mindedness and, alas, by increased cynicism. And there can be no great wonder when the facts are pondered.

There is little to inspire loyalty among Negroes, past or present, as a result of their relationships with the governments of the states in which the great majority of them live. The federal government is an object of hope for Negroes, but also of fear. They never know the hour when their enemy will come into power there. From day to day they see their cause suffer because in high office and in highest councils there are those who wish them ill. They have learned, moreover, that even their friends are friendlier when Negroes have votes and use them astutely. They have learned that in a democracy no office seems completely to transcend politics. Thus in the wars and in the peace of recent years the attitude of Negroes has been marked by a realism compounded of hope, of bitter complaint, of resignation when there was no recourse, and of deeply laid plans for the future reordering of their relationships with the government.

[18] *Op. cit.*, p. 75.

There is another, almost mystical, side of the relationship of Negroes to America. It is visible when they sing the national anthem or "America," singing words belied by the experience of their entire lives, or when they march behind the flag. It is love —love for the soil that gave them birth, love for a history which they have been taught, love for the creed which they have recited. They are caught up by an affection like that of a child for his parent, wrongs forgotten or forgiven.

The great and immediate task of America in relation to Negroes is to see that they are not only children of America but citizens of the nation in the truest sense. We cannot afford now to have in America any numerous, unhappy, cynical, belligerent minority. We must have an America united, strong, devoted. To permit less is to weaken critically our democracy and to endanger our nation. Nor can America be America and continue to subject thirteen million of her people, whose sweat and blood have been given prodigally to make her a great country, to the suffering born of their equivocal place in the commonwealth.

The question will be asked in deep earnestness by many Americans whether recent progress in American race relations does not suggest a less serious view of the situation than this account represents. There is no unanimity among Negroes as to whether there has been progress in a true sense. Although admitting certain improvements in external matters, there are those who feel that at the deeper levels the relationships have deteriorated. White men who are determined upon the *status quo* in basic relationships feel that they have about reached the last line of retreat and upon that line they intend to stand, come what may. Negroes, too, have girded themselves for a battle to the bitter end. The Columbia, Tennessee, riot or pogrom, both in its physical and in its legal stages, the Detroit riot, and numerous minor incidents indicate clearly that there is no disposition on either side to give quarter. Some people see this as marking a new and ominous stage in our problem.

In my own view, there has been progress but a progress which suffers from certain important limitations. In the first place, it has been in many instances peripheral. By the state, Negroes are still treated to a large degree as wards; by many in religion, as an object of charity; by industry, as a tool. Their past, their skin, the threat it is felt they offer to white men's security have in no wise been forgotten. They are still eating the crumbs of democracy and religion. In the second place, too much of what they have gained has been forced gain. During the war there was no alternative but to make certain concessions to them. Deference must be paid now to their political influence in the North. Even the worst oppressor cannot stand the importunities of the oppressed forever. Even tyrants must sleep. Progress which comes in these ways may widen rather than close the chasms between men. Finally, perhaps the progress which has been made has been too little and come too late. In so far as religion is concerned, it is a serious question as to whether Negroes have not already on the whole been converted to a power ethic and become almost entirely lost to the love ideal of Christianity. They have waited for three hundred years to see religion alter basically their relations with their fellow Americans. What they have witnessed has proved on the whole unconvincing. Now it may be too late. For a long time, too, Negroes have looked with hope to the American way of life in economics and in government. I should dare say that they are now in a mood to risk other ways. Each day the socialized economy makes a stronger appeal to thoughtful Negroes and there is significance in the fact that Negroes are primarily laborers and are rapidly becoming an integral part of the labor fraternity. As to government, the oppressed are always hopeful of what the new may bring. To know the attitude of Negroes toward Louisiana's Huey Long is to fear that they might be lured to the support of a benevolent dictatorship should the choice be presented. If, on the other hand, socialization in government should present itself as a live option it would, in my judgment, have predominant Negro support. If, as can happen, a combination of dictatorship and socialization should become a choice, Negroes, in the light of their experience, could not be counted upon in advance to support the kind of democracy they know.

It may not be too late to save the Negro people to the religion of their fathers and to the ideals of their country. It may not be too late to save America in the eyes of the world and to save her against the grave weaknesses she harbors within. There can be no question, however, but that the sands of time are running out. Americans bear the responsibility now of rising, as they can rise, to the will and the strength which marked the beginnings of this nation and which can mark her redemption today.

II

GUIDING PRINCIPLES

2

The Christian Way in Race Relations

GEORGE D. KELSEY

IN THE preceding chapter Dr. Nelson has made clear the fact that there is no area of American life in which the dynamic of the Christian religion is needed more than in that of Negro-white relations. Here the inner contradictions of human nature boldly lay themselves bare. Weaklings appear in their most pronounced weakness; and men of strong mind in the academic disciplines and of great spirit in other aspects of social living speak and act like disgruntled children. Obsessions, fears, anxieties, rationalizations, falsehoods, half-truths, and forced congeniality are, more often than not, the concomitants and tools of the relations. The problem of race is indeed America's greatest moral dilemma.[1]

In its highest expression, the Christian ethic is not an ethic of race relations. It is an ethic of the individual and mankind; it is not an ethic of a nation, class, or race. It is the theory of the Christian life, which issues from the union of the soul with God. This life is thus absolutely individualistic. Individualism here

---

[1] The idea that the system of racial caste set against the background of the American creed furnishes America a moral dilemma belongs to Gunnar Myrdal, Swedish economist. This idea is set forth in Myrdal's two-volume work on the Negro in American democracy under the title *An American Dilemma* (New York, 1944).

means the purehearted surrender of oneself to God. It means the
abandonment of the self to Christ, so that it is no longer the self
which thinks, feels, speaks, or acts, but Christ. It means one's
having the mind of Christ in him. Since the soul that is united
with God is inspired by the will and spirit of God, it must actively realize the love of God toward all people—strangers and
enemies as well as friends. All people are viewed as God views
them. Thus absolute religious individualism—the purehearted
surrender of the self to God—is accompanied by an equally absolute universalism: a fellowship of love determined solely by
the love of God.

Individualism and universalism are rooted in all that we know
of the divine activity and relation to man. They are principles of
creation. "So God created man in his own image, in the image
of God created he him; male and female created he them."[2] Every
individual being is a derivative being; he exists because God so
wills it. God creates man as a counterpart of himself. "He gives
His creature being, face to face with Himself—indeed, not an
independent but a dependent-independent being. God endows
the creature with the power to *be* 'over against' Him—indeed,
the power to keep his own being face to face with Him."[3]

God creates every individual for a purpose—to have fellowship
with him, to trust and obey him. This is the meaning of the
"image of God." "It is not that man as he is in himself bears God's
likeness, but rather that man is designated for and called to a
particular relation with God."[4] It is not that there is such a
thing as a divine substance of which man is made. Rather, it is
that man partakes of the divine image in a functional manner.
To the extent that man loves and obeys God, and allows his actions, thoughts, and feelings to be determined by God, he partakes of the divine image.

The concept of the image of God has significant implications

---

[2] Genesis 1:27.
[3] H. E. Brunner, *The Divine-Human Encounter* (Philadelphia, 1943),
p. 53.
[4] *Ibid.*, p. 128.

for race relations. It does not mean that men are created out of a divine substance. It is not a reference to the fineness or coarseness of the material out of which our bodies and minds are made. The concept does not refer to substantial nature. It means essentially *relation to God*. To partake of the divine image is to trust and obey God. There is, therefore, no room in the Christian doctrine of creation for the view that some races or groups have received a "higher nature" than others at the hands of God. The measure of a man's humanity depends wholly upon his functional relation to God.

Man has been so created by God that he can become man only by perceiving God, by receiving God's Word and—like a soldier repeating a command—repeating God's Word. . . . God created us in His image, as reflections of His image. That means that we are human in the degree we permit God to speak to us. We are man to the extent that we let God's Word echo in our hearts. We are not simply men as a fox is a fox. But we are men only when God's Word finds echo in us. To the degree that this fails to happen we are inhuman.[5]

Thus religious individualism is rooted in God's creative action and in the Creator-creature relation.

Religious universalism is likewise rooted in creation. God hath "made of one every nation of men to dwell on all the face of the earth, having determined their appointed seasons, and the bounds of their habitation; that they should seek God, if haply they might feel after him, and find him . . . for in him we live, and move, and have our being. . . ."[6]

Not only does the individual derive his being from God and stand face to face with him as his counterpart, but mankind as a whole has its being in God and stands face to face with him as his counterpart. All men in their creatureliness meet in the Creator. And just as the individual is called to a particular relation—fellowship—with God, mankind is called into subjecthood in God's Kingdom. The Kingdom of God is the image of God universalized.

[5] H. E. Brunner, *Our Faith* (New York, 1936), pp. 37–38.
[6] Acts 17:26–28.

God created man for a purpose. But man has not pursued this purpose; rather he has chosen his own course, asserted himself against and alienated himself from God. God's second great act is, therefore, that of judgment; and the relation between God and man becomes that of judge and sinner. Through sin man makes a caricature of the image of God in his heart. Sin is ungodliness; to sin is to turn away from God. Yet man remains bound to God even in sin. It is precisely this fact which makes his act sin. If, in asserting himself against God, man should entirely free himself from God he would no longer live as a sinner. But man is bound to God even in sin; he cannot get away from him. He staggers and stumbles but always against the holiness of God. This is the supreme isolation of the human soul; it is utter restlessness. Loneliness is most acute in sin.

Although the sinner must face God alone and is always individually accountable, he is not really alone in the sense of being the only sinner or in the sense that no one else is accountable for his sin. All men are sinners. Sin is both individual and universal. Christianity does not know of two camps, the one constituted of saints and the other of sinners. There is only one camp; it is mankind standing before God in sin and in need of redemption. Those who "hunger and thirst after righteousness" are not exceptions. "Then said I, Woe is me! for I am undone; because I am a man of unclean lips, and I dwell in the midst of a people of unclean lips: for mine eyes have seen the King, Jehovah of hosts."[7] For the very reason that a man strives toward God he knows that he is a sinner better than a man who does not. If we should like to think of two camps, even in this relative way, we shall have to designate the camp of saints as constituted of those who are sinners and more or less know it, and the camp of sinners as constituted of those who are sinners and more or less do not know it. Mankind is in a sinful state. While each individual stands in immediate relation to God as sinner to judge, he is also jointly responsible for the entire history of sin. This is

[7] Isaiah 6:5.

true because every particular sin is but an expression of the state of sin in which mankind stands, and for which mankind is responsible. Individualism and universalism are thus inherent in the Judge-sinner relation.

What does universalism in sin and under the judgment of God mean for race relations? It means that a Negro, as a victim of injustices practiced in the name of race, is not only an immediate sufferer but a fellow sinner with the perpetrators of evil. He is responsible jointly with them for their sin directed against him because he is jointly responsible for the whole history of sin. Similarly, when a white man looks with disdain upon a Negro in ignorance, poverty, and degradation, he looks with disdain upon himself. For he is responsible for this state of affairs even if no immediate causal relation can be traced to his actions. He is responsible as a fellow human being who is responsible for the entire history of sin. He is responsible for all the shackles which bind men. People, therefore, are incorrect in their judgment and are unconsciously pharisaical when they seek to free themselves from guilt in America's vicious system of caste by the simple declaration: "I do not personally have any race prejudice." All men are accountable for all sin. Sinful acts leap out of the state of sin. Mankind is in a state of sin.

God has not left man alone. He did not abandon his world plan because of man's self-chosen alienation. Rather, he manifests himself in his third act, as the Redeemer. He revealed his will to Abraham, Moses, the prophets, and at last "when the time was accomplished" he revealed himself in Jesus Christ, his "Word." God wills the redemption of every man. If there are one hundred sheep in the fold and one is lost, he searches untiringly for the one. He anxiously awaits the return of the prodigal and, when he sees him coming afar off, hurries out to meet him, embraces him, and has a great feast prepared for him. Religious individualism is nowhere more clearly and beautifully manifest than in the redemptive love of God. Religious universalism is thus clearly expressed in the idea of the Kingdom of God. God not only comes to the individual soul; he comes to mankind. He comes to restore his corrupt creation to its original goodness and to perfect it.

The Kingdom is now present; but it is present in only a small way. It is not here "in fullness of power." It is here as a little more than a "mustard seed." It is yet to become a full tree. We recognize the presence of the Kingdom wherever there is a "communion of saints," wherever men meet in God, and wherever love issues from faith. The Kingdom means union. It is the most thoroughgoing expression of universalism, for the principle of its union is God. All other types of union—institutions, clubs, and societies of all sorts—are oriented around some one or more particulars.

Now, what meaning has redemption for race relations? As stated, God wills the redemption of every individual. Every individual is supremely[8] worthful to God; his search for the lost soul is unceasing. Herein lies the worth of the individual. The value of man is derivative; it is value for God. We have seen that man is so created that he becomes a person only in relation to God. He does not have his value in himself; his value does not lie in the measure of his intellect, his racial origin, or his social position. Human value is wholly derivative; it lies in *relatedness to God.* It is functional. Since God wills the redemption of every man, since every soul is for God equally redeemable, since he maintains the relation between himself and every man from his side, every individual is of equal worth. There is no other universal basis for the measure of human worth. All other bases are finite and particular, and they themselves stand in need of redemption. Blood, power, intellect, and civilization are themselves finites and particulars which are often more or less arbitrarily selected from among other finites and particulars to indicate superior human worth. But once we have selected one, two, or more of these as measures of human worth we must refer them to the one universal criterion to justify their worth. They themselves are never ultimates. And they are always deeply mixed with the sickness of

[8] The word "supreme" as used here means highest in creation.

human existence. In short, they are among those finites which must be redeemed or must pass away; they, too, must be related to God to be of value.

In an effort to improve the attitudes of one racial group toward another, Christian teachers commonly point to the contributions to the literature, arts, and sciences of the group of poorer reputation. From what has been said above, it can be seen that such emphasis is irrelevant to essential Christian teaching. The worth of an individual does not lie in his writing a poem or making a scientific discovery. Human worth lies in relatedness to God. A human being or a group has value because he or it is valuable for God. Any other valuation is based entirely on human judgment and is, therefore, both selfish and from a particularistic point of view. On the other hand, it may be said that it is necessary to indicate the cultural contributions to arouse the interest of people since people are as they are. With this we should agree.

Christian teachers are dealing with people of hard hearts, limited horizons and perspectives. Some concessions have to be made to the "hardness of their hearts" in the endeavor to soften those hearts. But Christian teachers must not be misled into the assumption that an appeal to the cultural contributions of a people is itself Christian teaching. Christian teaching concerning human worth can be stated in the following manner: "Every human being is of supreme worth because, and only because, he is of supreme worth for God. He deserves, therefore, love and respect." In essential Christian teaching there is only one point of reference: God. Good, value, or worth are wholly derivative from God; they are not intrinsic.

The redemptive work of God has additional meaning for race relations. It was stated above that the Kingdom of God means union. The Fall is its opposite; it means disunion, cleavage, tension. Genesis tells us that man's self-chosen alienation from God produced a general condition of separation and disunion upon the earth. Prior to the Fall, man lived in a state of innocence, beyond good and evil. But as a result of the Fall, the distinction between good and evil was introduced. Tension and cleavage came into all relationships—human, animal, and natural. Henceforth, all physical life is lived at the expense of some other life; and man is set in a negative relation to animals and to nature, the source of his livelihood. He earns his bread in toil, by the sweat of his face; when he plants corn, thorns and thistles also grow. Cleavage and tension are set up between the sexes; man becomes ruler over woman. The Fall thus signifying disunion, cleavage, tension, to eat of the "forbidden fruit" is, therefore, to live in a negative relationship with others. It is to deny the principle of union, communion, and fellowship. The "racial element"[9] is rooted in the Fall. When the individual permits his attitudes and actions to be determined by race, he is continuing the Fall in life; he is maintaining cleavage, tension, and disunion; he is rejecting the clear voice of God which calls him to union, communion, and fellowship—to the Kingdom. The Kingdom of God is the only universal form of community. All other forms are partial and particular.

We have seen that man always stands in relation to God and has his person only in that relation. Whether God be thought of as Creator, Judge, or Redeemer, the life of the individual is related to him and the individual is what he is because of that relation. Likewise mankind is related to God, and human equality and community are found in this relation. The Creator-creature and Judge-sinner relations are different, however, from the Redeemer-saint[10] relation. In the Creator-creature and Judge-sinner relations only God intends the relation. As Creator he alone is active and as Judge he keeps man bound to himself, for man in sin intends *not* to be related to God. If he were great enough he would without doubt break the relation. But in the Redeemer-saint relation man *intends* to be in union with God. He knows his dependence, knows God's love, and surrenders himself to God in faith. The Christian life issues from this faith.

---

[9] "Racial element" is here used to mean the divisive element, the tendency of men to think of their connections in organic terms.

[10] As indicated above, a saint is one who knows that he is a sinner and has directed his life toward God in trust and dependence.

It issues when the union between God and man is *intentional from both sides.* No other life is Christian save that which proceeds from a heart that is united with God; there is no other spring, no other source. All else is sin. The Apostle Paul has succinctly stated it: "Whatsoever is not of faith is sin."[11] The Christian life issues from an absolute individualism. The Christian ethic, the theory of that life, is consequently individualistic. For the same reason the Christian ethic is universalistic. All men of faith meet in God. God is the foundation of their union and fellowship, the point of reference for their lives. No principle, no ideas, no interest makes them a communion; only union in God creates communion. Common interest, ideas, and principles are themselves derivatives from this foundation.

Religious individualism and universalism mean that the Christian life is lived entirely within one context: the Fatherhood-sonship-brotherhood context. The moment we step out of this context in any of our relationships and activities, we have deviated seriously from the Christian position. Let us suppose that we substitute the terms "Negro" and "white" for the terms "son" and "brother" in the Fatherhood-sonship-brotherhood pattern. Immediately the pattern loses its meaning. In the original pattern the son is son because of the Father; and the brother is brother because of the Father. The Father is the basis and determining factor in their relation. But in the pattern in which the terms "Negro" and "white" are substituted, the Negro is Negro because some particular, finite characteristic is singled out and the white man is white for the same reason. This particular, finite, and transitory characteristic becomes the basis and determining factor in their relation. And since it is a particular, finite, and transitory characteristic and is chosen for the purpose of pointing up difference, it is by its very nature a principle of disunion. It is rooted in the Fall of man; it belongs to the divisive element in life. The very term "interracial" is under Christian moral suspicion. It suggests two camps standing over against each other. It suggests the *we-they relation,* a relation in which *I and*

[11] Romans 14:23.

thou, two souls under God, can never meet. All Christian activity
and relations must submit to the Fatherhood-sonship-brotherhood
context.

This is the same as to say that Christian relations are essentially interpersonal, not intergroupal. John Macmurray throws
clear light on this idea in his book, *The Clue to History*:

> When therefore we say that Jesus denied that human life is organic,
> what we mean is that Jesus denied that human community can be based
> upon organic relationships. In other words, he denied that human com-
> munity can be based upon blood-relationship. This implies an attack
> upon the family, upon race, upon nationality, upon all the so-called
> "natural" relationships, as the basis of *human* relationship. He attacks
> the family basis of society when he says, "Who is my mother and who are
> my brethren? Whosoever shall do the will of my Father which is in
> heaven." He attacks the idea that race can be the basis of human com-
> munity when he answers the Pharisees who opposed him with the claim,
> "Abraham is our father," in the words, "If ye were Abraham's children,
> ye would do the works of Abraham." He attacks nationalism as a basis
> of human society when he says, "Many lepers were in Israel in the time
> of Eliseus the prophet; and none of them was cleansed, saving Naaman
> the Syrian."[12]

Human community is a community of persons. And since, as we
have seen, an individual becomes a person to the extent that he
is related to God, all attitudes, feelings, actions, and relationships
of persons in a truly Christian community must arise from the
persons' relationship to God. For example, a Negro who is a
Christian can never have a "white friend." He will have a friend
who happens to be white. A white man who is a Christian can
never have a "colored friend." He will have a friend who happens
to be colored. The whiteness and blackness can in no way determine the relationship. The determinants are sonship and brotherhood, which are what they are because they have their basis in
Fatherhood.

When two souls meet in God, love toward each other springs
out of their faith in him. Love becomes the bond of union between them; they become really personally related. We may in-

[12] John Macmurray, *The Clue to History* (New York, 1939), pp. 64–65.

quire into the nature of the really personal relation by seeking to understand the nature of the bond of union.

The criterion of Christian love is that it gives and sacrifices. Following Luther's description, Anders Nygren sets out a few of the most essential features of love: (1) "Christian love is *spontaneous in contrast to all activity with a eudaemonistic* motive. . . . It does the good not in order to gain or increase its own blessedness, but 'out of free love and for nothing, to please God, not seeking or regarding anything else, but that it thus pleases God.' . . . [2] Christian love is also *spontaneous in contrast to all legalism.* . . . The law is in essence unproductive; indeed, it is at bottom self-contradictory. It requires free surrender to God's will; but just because it demands, it is an obstacle to this free spontaneous surrender. . . . Man is completely won for the good only when he does the good spontaneously from inward inclination and would do it even if it were not commanded in the law."[13]

(3) Luther describes Christian love as overflowing love. It is not set in motion by something from the outside. Not even the desirable qualities of its object set it in motion. "It springs forth out of its own source, fellowship with God."[14]

(4) From this Luther draws the inference: ". . . that this love is 'round and whole,' the *same* to one as to another and without respect of persons. . . . Christian love is the same whether it be directed to the godly or the ungodly. . . . God does not allow His love to be determined or limited by man's worth or worthlessness. 'For He maketh His sun to rise on the evil and the good and sendeth rain on the just and unjust' (Mt. 5:45)."[15]

(5) Luther goes on to show that love toward the sinner is purely spontaneous and unceasing in character. "Even though again and again it finds itself deceived, that is no reason why it should become hesitant and reserved. 'For it is of the nature of

[13] Anders Nygren, *Agape and Eros* (New York, 1939), Vol. II, Part II, pp. 508–511.
[14] *Ibid.*, p. 512.
[15] *Ibid.*, pp. 512–513.

love to suffer betrayal.' . . . Only one of the ten lepers returned to Christ and thanked Him for His beneficence; it was lost on all the rest. Christian love is 'a divine, free, unceasing, yea indeed, a lost love,' which is prepared freely to find its kindness thrown away and lost as also Christ has found."[16]

The meaning of Christian love for race relations is so obvious that we need not dwell upon it. The fact may be repeated, however, that Christian love is not love "for something." It is not due to blood relation or to any particular connection which the object of one's love has with oneself. It is the unconditional will to community; it is not set in motion by any quality or function of its object. It is purely spontaneous, unmotivated, groundless, and creative; it is the love of God operating in the human heart.

There is another feature of Christian love not yet considered which has a special relevance to the American system of caste. It is the fact that in love, the other, the "thou," is given to one as a whole, as a personal whole. Many Americans seem to believe that they can meet the requirements of Christian love by loving the souls of members of other races while holding their bodies in contempt. But love does not see the other person from the point of view of one of his functions only: "Like the Ethos of reason she honours in the other person his higher destiny; but in this she also includes his psychophysical needs. She does not separate his rational nature from his bodily nature, since she regards personality as a whole; she is able to unite both because in the Divine Will in Creation both the bodily nature and the eternal goal of man are posited as a unity."[17] This means that it is impossible for an individual to love another's soul and hold his body in contempt. Christian love involves the acceptance and appreciation of the other person as he is, as God gives him to us. Otherwise, we reject the gift of God and borrow our love from some quality in the person. Our love is therefore not spontaneous, not unmotivated, not groundless, not creative, and not Christian.

Certain practical problems in the American caste situation call

[16] *Ibid.*, pp. 513–515.
[17] H. E. Brunner, *The Divine Imperative* (New York, 1942), p. 327.

themselves to our attention in their relation to the Christian ideal of love. The first of these is what may be called *racial strategy*. There is a certain estrangement, distrust, and defensiveness in all human relations. This is due to the basic sinfulness of human nature. The love of God never operates fully in any heart. Even the best of us are enclosed in a shell which is never completely penetrated. We never let our lives flow freely into the lives of our neighbors, nor do we open our lives completely to them. On the contrary, we at best resort to some measure of stratagem and defense. The psychology of strategy and defense especially characterizes the relation between strangers. When people are both strangers and members of two hostile castes, this psychology is likely to become the whole of the relation. If it does become the whole of the relation and continues to be so, obviously Christian brotherhood is impossible. A white person and a Negro, after having become acquainted, must not go on indefinitely having doubts and suspicions about each other, employing techniques of mutual adjustment, and generally staying on the defensive. The relation of strategy must gradually pass away, and the persons must ever increase in their achievement of the state of mutual frankness, trust, and respect on all matters. As has already been pointed out, "whiteness" and "blackness" must pass away as determinants in their relations, and "son" and "brother" must be substituted and reciprocally applied to the persons involved. Let us illustrate how the system of caste makes the employment of abnormal strategy necessary even for persons who at the outset wish to be friendly. A Negro and a white man meet and set in motion contacts which are to be frequent and indefinite. They find a certain reciprocal congeniality, but the Negro must hold back; he cannot be the aggressor in the potential friendship for he is operating under the handicap of a racial stereotype which says that Negroes are aggressive and therefore socially undesirable. The white man must then be the aggressor in developing the friendship. Again, a Negro and a white man meet and frequent contacts are begun, leading to more and more congeniality. They go on addressing each other as "Mr.—." How is the barrier which "Mr." establishes to be removed? Here the Negro must be the aggressor. He must be the first to make use of the given name because the white man is operating under the handicap of the widespread lack of civility on the part of white people toward Negroes. Admitting then that the system of caste imposes this extra handicap on Christian love at the start, it is nevertheless the responsibility of every person who claims Christ as his leader to move on into personal relations with all people—in short, to make all relations submit to the Fatherhood-sonship-brotherhood context.

A second problem of race relations for the Christian ideal of love is that of protest. Can protest be squared with the Christian ethical ideal, the essence of which is sacrifice and self-giving? In a world of sin the Christian ethic has a dual nature; it issues in an ethic of redemption and in an interim ethic.[18] It has a negative direction toward sin and a positive direction toward the sinner. In its essential and normative nature, the Christian ethic is one of redemption. To keep the work of redemption uppermost is its peculiar task, but in a world of sin it must also be concerned with the restraint of evil. It is not only interested in the great Revolution but also in those for whom the great Revolution is desired. Wage laws and lynch laws will not be necessary in the new age. But the new age has not yet come; we live amid the continuing conditions of the present, which cry out that something be done here and now. As an ethic of redemption, the Christian ethic is concerned with cleansing the sources of life. But no matter how clean the heart is, sin is always there; we are never completely reconciled to God in this life. An ethic of redemption is not adequate in a sinful world without restraint. Restraint, however, must never be separated from redemption, but must be limited by and subordinated to redemption. Restraint

[18] The ethic of redemption is the Christian ethic in its absolute and normative aspect. It consists in the absolute ideals and principles of Jesus. The interim ethic is the ethic of the Christian churches. It consists in the ethical ideas and achievements of the historic Christian community wrought out of efforts to apply Gospel demands and values to nature and history.

can never be determined in terms of itself but only with reference to redemption.

If protest or any form of restraint would be Christian, it must possess certain features. First of all, the protester must be self-critical and self-restraining. When a Negro protests against undemocratic practice directed toward himself, he must take that very occasion to examine himself and see whether he is democratic in the places and relationships where he has control. It ought to serve as an occasion for sober thought and inner reconstruction. When a Negro makes a needed appeal for justice or engages in action leading thereto, he ought to examine all his relationships and see if they are just from his side. Whenever he is the object of criticism from white men, even though that criticism be maliciously directed and mixed with half-truths and falsehoods, he ought to pick out what truth there is in the criticism and make it the basis of a really creative reconstruction. Self-criticism and self-restraint must always be the first step in the application of the ethic of restraint. Secondly, the method of protest or restraint must be such as not to injure. This does not mean that one should avoid arousing the antagonism of the perpetrators of evil. This is inevitable. The very fact that protest is needed at all makes it obvious that the opposition of the perpetrators of evil will be forthcoming. What we mean is that whatever methods of restraint may be used, they ought to be based on truth, legality,[19] orderliness, and good will. This leads us to a third observation. The goal of restraint must be the good of all. The protester must be sure of his goals. He must be sure that in his effort to gain justice he does not seek to leap over from a position of disadvantage to one of advantage, thus subverting justice. He must be sure that it is democracy which he seeks and not the substitution of one tyranny for another.

In the same category with the ethic of restraint belongs the ethic of alleviation. Both restraint and alleviation are a part of the

[19] The term "legality" as used here does not exclude the "higher law"; rather, it refers primarily to the "higher law."

Christian interim ethic. In a world of sin something must be done to alleviate injury and suffering; something must be done while the system which imposes injury and suffering is in the process of passing away. The ethic of alleviation is especially applicable to the system of segregation. In any situation, even in a bad one, there is some room for moral maneuver. It is the duty of the Christian to maneuver to the highest moral position in a given situation. But he must not be satisfied with this position; he must endeavor to change the situation itself. It is obvious, in the case of segregation, that the greater responsibility falls on the white man. For he is the one who possesses what little measure of freedom segregation leaves. In most situations he alone can maneuver. It becomes his duty, therefore, to use all the privilege and power at his disposal to eliminate discrimination from segregation. For example, in the South he must lend himself to the program of equalizing educational institutions and opportunities. When he has met with some measure of success in this venture, he must understand, however, that he has only moved to a higher moral position in a bad situation. His job is not yet complete; he can never be satisfied until segregation itself passes away; he must not separate the ethic of alleviation from the ethic of redemption. He must see that segregation is itself utterly un-Christian. It is established on pride, fear, and falsehood. It is the very nadir of human relations. It is unbrotherly, impersonal, a complete denial of the *"I-thou"* relationship, and a complete expression of the *"I-it"* relation. Two segregated souls never meet in God. Their relation is determined by pride, fear, force, hatred, and falsehood; it is completely without love and the Holy Spirit. The Christian ethic, founded as it is upon religious individualism and universalism, is wholly rejected as a guide and inspiration in the relation.

Some of the evils of segregation are summarized by John LaFarge in his book, *The Race Question and the Negro*:

(1) Segregation, as a compulsory measure based on race, imputes essential inferiority to the segregated group. . . . "Segregation imposes a definite stigma upon the segregated group."

Such an imputation causes a cheapening of the human personality in the mind both of the author and of the object of segregation which opens the way towards violence or exploitation on the part of the one and towards moral irresponsibility on the part of the other, resulting in objective injustice, or even crimes against the human person.

(2) Segregation, since it creates a ghetto, brings for the segregated group, in the majority of instances, a diminished degree of participation in those matters which are ordinary human rights, such as proper housing, educational facilities, police protection, legal justice, employment, etc. Hence, it works objective injustice.

(3) In the fields of industry, segregation makes possible the exploitation of Negro labor, while it spreads fear and distrust. At the same time, it is a threat to white labor since it divides its forces and makes unionization impossible.[20]

Segregation is commonly defended on the ground that the removal of its disadvantages will lead to social equality. Unfortunately, the term "social equality" is as often as not surrounded by a vapor of vagueness. It is necessary, therefore, to consider the whole range of its possible meaning.[21] Social equality may mean equality of basic human rights. This meaning harmonizes with the Declaration of Independence, which claims life, liberty, and the pursuit of happiness to be the inalienable human rights. Social equality may mean the participation of all the citizenry in the ordinary civilities of human intercourse necessary for normal living in American civilization. These involve equal respect and courtesies toward the women of all races, the equal application of the titles Mr. and Mrs. to the members of all races, and equal courtesies to the members of all races in educational, legal, business, professional, and ecclesiastical affairs. Social equality may also involve the liberty to choose one's own friends, wife or husband, and private associations in home, recreational, and club life. In the light of what has already been said it is superfluous to discuss social equality in relation to the Christian ideal of love. It has been pointed out that all human relations must harmonize with the Fatherhood-sonship-brotherhood pattern. Suffice it to say that

[20] John LaFarge, *The Race Question and the Negro* (New York, 1943), pp. 159–160.
[21] Cf. *ibid.*, chap. xv.

the relation of social equality is the only relation that can harmonize with that pattern. The alternative to social equality is either social contempt or social fear. Two souls cannot enter into social fellowship by way of social contempt or social fear. They cannot meet in God.

Another common fear is that the breakdown of segregation will lead to intermarriage. Here, as elsewhere, the dual nature of the Christian ethic must be taken into account. When marriage is viewed under the aspect of the Christian ethic of redemption, the question of the racial affiliation of the marital partners becomes wholly irrelevant. Christian marriage is a physical and spiritual union of two souls under God. When such a union takes place the marriage is Christian and sacred, and it is "blessed in heaven." The Christian life is grounded in an absolute religious individualism and universalism. From its point of view the limitations and barriers of our present sinful existence do not count. In speaking of the unlimited and unqualified individualism of the Gospel ethic, Troeltsch says:

> It is clear that an individualism of this kind is entirely radical, and that it transcends all natural barriers and differences through the ideal of the religious value of the soul. It is also clear that such an individualism is only possible at all upon this religious basis. It is only fellowship with God which gives value to the individual, and it is only in common relationship with God, in a realm of supernatural values, that natural differences disappear. Where this kind of individualism prevails, all earthly differences are swallowed up in the Divine power and love which reduce all other distinctions to nothing.[22]

In the Christian life the love of God is the determinant of action and attitude, for the soul has its being in God and there meets other souls. Barriers, therefore, of defense, pride, and fear which man has erected are cast down.

We have seen that the ethic of redemption taken alone is not adequate for a world of sin. All problems must be dealt with in the light of the dual nature of the Christian ethic. In applying

[22] Ernst Troeltsch, *The Social Teaching of the Christian Churches* (New York, 1931), I, 55.

the interim ethic to the problem of intermarriage, the issue of the social inconvenience of intermarriage at once presents itself. The interim ethic cannot be separated, however, from the ethic of redemption. The absolute demands of God and the ideal of love must remain normative for action, else one's ethical behavior becomes purely pragmatic. The issue reduces itself to the following: The question of intermarriage ought to be decided on the merits of individual cases. Marriage is an individual matter. Properly speaking, races do not marry; individuals marry. This is not to deny the social ramifications of intermarriage, but to assert that, in a free society in which people can live, grow, and enjoy relationships that are really personal, no artificial and arbitrary lines can be drawn in human relations. Restrictions upon intermarriage, whether imposed by law or custom, are like segregation, directed against the disadvantaged group and established upon pride, fear, force, hatred, and falsehood. Such restrictions belong to an atmosphere of ill will and sickness. Furthermore, they belong to an atmosphere of hypocrisy. Many people who lose all emotional control when facing the issue of intermarriage wink at miscegenation if the male participant is a member of the dominant group. In much of our American experience, intermarriage would be the only decent thing. And certainly the women of all races ought to have equal protection against the offenses of all men and equal redress in the wake of such offenses. This is a practical minimum of decency, honesty, and fairness.

One finds it difficult to discuss the American system of caste against the background of ethics without referring to the need of prophecy. The problem of caste in America must soon make hearts burn so that prophets will rise up saying, "Thus saith the Lord. . . ." Surely the "people are destroyed for lack of knowledge. . . ."[23] Their priests and pastors have rejected knowledge; they and the people stand under the judgment of God. America must act now; her prophets must speak. The well-known clichés, "the time is not ripe," "this will do more harm than good," "Negroes are satisfied," are a stench in the nostrils of God. He hates

[23] Hosea 4:6.

them. The "wine offerings" of rationalization, self-deception, and opportune ignorance do not please God. His prophets must speak and they must be prepared to be stoned, for Jerusalem always stones her prophets. But at length the people will hear the voice of God saying, "Let judgment roll down as waters, and righteousness as a mighty stream."[24]

[24] Amos 5:24.

III

BASIC DIFFICULTIES

3

Economic Forces and the Christian Way

J. NEAL HUGHLEY

THE FAILURE OF SOCIAL CHRISTIANITY

WHEN Walter Rauschenbusch electrified America by publishing in 1907 his *Christianity and the Social Crisis,* it looked as if a new day were dawning for the Christian cause. This stalwart prophet of the social gospel was at once received as a leader and spokesman for the new social program of the church and for the coming Christian order in practical affairs. He was heralded before theological groups, churches, colleges, forums, and conferences. Between 1907 and his death, in 1918, a succession of works poured from his pen, attacking our "semi-Christian social order" and proclaiming that the Kingdom of God demands a destruction of the old competitive capitalist system. A day of judgment and justice was at hand. People were thrilled and shocked as he roared: "We rebel against God and repudiate His will when we set our profit and ambition above the fellows and above the kingdom of God which binds them together."[1] The features of a truly Christian order, he declared, are justice, co-operation, good will, social solidarity, democracy—which ideals

[1] Walter Rauschenbusch, *A Theology for the Social Gospel* (New York, 1917), p. 182.

demand that the people rule in politics and industry. Away with greedy, parasitic capitalism, he charged, this "last entrenchment of autocracy." Sharing this passion for a Christian society were other outstanding figures, among them men like Harry F. Ward and Charles Stelzle, the former taking leadership in the formulation of the well-known "Social Creed of the Churches."

Then a curious thing occurred, a phenomenon which is summed up in Hopkins' chapter heading: "Social Christianity Becomes Official."[2] The various Christian bodies began to endorse this social emphasis. They called conferences, passed resolutions, published literature, and set up committees, commissions, and councils. This was true of the Protestant Episcopal church, the National Council of Congregational Churches, the Methodist Episcopal church, the Northern Baptist Convention, the American Unitarian Association, the Federal Council of Churches, and the Student Christian Movement. Hopkins notes that between 1900 and 1914 there was a "widespread acceptance of social Christianity throughout American Protestantism."[3] A deeply rebellious mood seemed to possess the churches in regard to the social front. They were outraged at the evils of child labor, at the "sweating system," poor wages, un-Christian competition, industrial strife, and the spirit of greed. They demanded recognition of the rights of the worker, better wages, protection from disease and accident, freedom from excessive working hours. Indeed, the widely accepted "Social Creed" summed the matter up in its first proposition: "For equal rights and complete justice for all men in all stations of life."

A general feeling prevailed that American democracy was on the verge of becoming genuinely Christian. Rauschenbusch himself had the notion that the lofty ideals of the Master had already largely conquered in the church itself, as well as in the Christian family and school. Even the political order, which tended more and more to exalt democratic principles and procedures, was set

[2] Hopkins, *The Rise of the Social Gospel in American Protestantism* (New Haven, 1940), chap. xviii.
[3] *Ibid.*, p. 298.

in the right direction. The only truly pagan area remaining was the industrial world, which tended to spill over into the Christianized areas its poisonous influences. If once the "mammonistic organization" of capitalism could be broken, labor exalted and strengthened, "industrial democracy" achieved, and the profit motive replaced by the "Christian spirit of love," then the battle for the Kingdom of God would be completely won.

All this development took place on the eve of World War I, with which began a visible process that has led to the almost total disintegration of Western Christian civilization. Between 1914 and 1946, in less than a generation, the entire framework of capitalist culture suffered shock. In Russia, Marxism triumphed completely; in Italy and Germany, a nihilistic fascism pulverized the existing order; in England, the Labor party with its policy of the socialization of industry grew until its present political triumph. In America, the only country in which a *laissez-faire* state was ever seriously attempted, there was an artificial boom of the twenties, followed by a catastrophic depression of the thirties. But in all, through all, and over all came the total war, whose effects, like a cosmic earthquake, have shaken our culture to the foundations.

It can now be seen that the outlook of American Christianity in the first two decades of our century was little more than a sentimentalized dream which obscured the ugly, harsh nature of our democratic-capitalistic society. An analysis of the churchly pronouncements, resolutions, and "social" literature of that era would show that the overwhelming majority of leaders and organizations were unaware of the gigantic, pervasive political and economic forces which ruled their world and which were destined soon to tear it to shreds. In the first place, there was no realistic understanding of the nature of the social struggle, with its inescapable conflict element and its inevitable contest of power, especially between capital and labor. There was virtually no development of strategy or tactics beyond conventionalized evangelism, educational work, and interchurch co-operation. Save in isolated cases, there was no awareness of the growing bourgeois character of the church—a tendency which went on despite the professed ideals. There was little or no understanding of the implications of Christian sentiments and principles for a formulated, coherent social theory. Hence, despite all the protest and all the holy horror, there was no effective, clear-cut challenge offered to the basic tenets of a corrupt and corrupting capitalist system.

The churches attempted to convert the financiers and speculators, to evangelize wealth seekers and status seekers in schools, government, business, and labor. They sought through conferences to do away with conflicts between parties possessed of passion and self-interest reinforced by fanatical convictions on both sides of "right" and "justice." They prayed that men with property in opposition to men without property would submerge their desires for power and security on behalf of "public welfare." They would eliminate economic waste, business depressions, deceitful advertising, cut-throat competition, monopolistic prices, and illegal trusts by proclaiming to men who believe that profit seeking is a high virtue the beauty and practical values of the "Christian ideal." Above all, they hoped, apparently through discussion and preaching and pious resolution, to exorcise from the body politic one of the most deep-seated, pervasive, and powerful of all socio-historical forces, the ethos of capitalism.

Let us pause to note one typical instance of our intellectual and moral bewilderment. A great international missionary conference was held at Jerusalem in 1928. This conference dealt realistically with many social problems, such as disease, race friction, denominational rivalry, and poverty in oriental countries. Bishop McConnell says, however, that the "most serious and vexing economic problem" was that of "forced labor." He testifies proudly that such a body of outstanding Christian leaders from many lands "called for those safeguards around the labor system which experience has shown to be necessary if any regard is to be paid to the human values involved."[4] And he concludes, no doubt echoing the general mood of these fellow Christians, that such a

[4] *Human Needs and World Christianity* (New York, 1929), p. 73.

problem can be met only by the "pressure of an informed American and European public opinion," evidently not being vividly aware of the fact that such an opinion is not merely "Christian" but *capitalist* Christian. Incidentally, the conference itself was against disregard of "human values" involved in forced labor, but not against *the system of forced labor!* Not having renounced the basic presuppositions of a capitalist order, the conferees stood unconsciously confused even when possessed of earnest evangelical zeal.

CHRISTIANITY AND THE CAPITALIST ETHOS

When Karl Marx set forth his arresting critique of modern bourgeois culture, he laid major emphasis upon the division of labor, presenting capitalism as essentially a struggle between the owners of the productive resources (the capitalists) and the workers, who incidentally were regarded as the real producers. Not only by implication but by direct argument Marx interpreted economic forces as impersonal, as "materialistic," as a dialectical process by which society moved from feudalism through capitalism to socialism. The primary mechanism of this historical movement was the conflict of economic classes whose interests were irreconcilable. The social order is evolving by its own inherent necessity, and force, he declared, is the midwife of history. But the theory was an oversimplification, leaving out of account not only numerous complexities, political, economic, and moral, but also psychological and religious forces which played a vital role in the shaping of the constellation of institutions and ideas known today as Western civilization.

Although he talked much of the profit motive and of "capitalist accumulation," he failed to perceive the germinal factors which created the all-conquering capitalist ethos. Some of these factors have been laid bare by the penetrating analyses of Max Weber, Ernst Troeltsch, Werner Sombart, and R. H. Tawney. Sombart explained that the spirit (*Geist*) of capitalism consisted of rationality, acquisitiveness, and competitiveness, laying great stress upon the factor of rationality as the primary creative element.

Weber and Troeltsch sought to point out the dominant role played by the religious ethics of ascetic Protestantism in the triumph of this *Geist* in modern industrial society, Weber himself opposing Sombart's emphasis on rationality. Tawney, in England, carried the Weber-Troeltsch thesis further, showing how its truth is illustrated in British social history but making corrections in the details of the hypothesis.

One momentous thing uncovered in all these researches, analyses, and arguments is the fact that historic Protestantism, at least large and important branches of it, became intimately allied with the rising technology, industrialism, and bourgeois democracy of the eighteenth and nineteenth centuries. Western democratic-capitalist civilization became a "Christian" civilization. Here was born a culture whose basic spirit was supported by the discipline, idealism, and inspiration of Christianity.[5] The economic doctrines of the free market, risk, private property, free wage labor, self-regulating competition, *laissez faire,* business for profit were infused with the moral ideals of hard work, thrift, honesty (that is, faithfulness to contracts), punctuality, and devotion to business responsibility. The gospel of success became both an economic aim and a Christian moral ideal. In due time most Christians lost their ability to conceive of any other economy as possible for society, despite the fact that both the Marxian and the Weberian hypotheses assumed that capitalism is not an expression of original human nature but a specific historico-cultural product. In America, so deeply entrenched is the ideology of capitalist culture that few Christians have ever been seriously moved either by the older body of argumentation or by the more recent American anti-capitalist critiques such as those of Henry George, Thorstein Veblen, and numerous lesser figures.

[5] Weber, *The Protestant Ethic and the Spirit of Capitalism;* Troeltsch, *The Social Teaching of the Christian Churches* (2 vols); Tawney, *Religion and the Rise of Capitalism.* For an illuminating description of the history of the vast controversy carried on over Weber's theory see an article by Fischoff in *Social Research,* XI (1944). Unfortunately, space does not allow us here to enter into the details of the pros and cons, but this is not essential to the point we emphasize.

One of the ironies of the contemporary situation is to see the rising resentment against the capitalist ethos alongside a refusal to reject categorically the capitalist system. A few theological thinkers today see that the implications of a Christian ethos for political and economic reconstruction involve the quest for an order radically different from an economy based on private property and competition for profit. Professor H. E. Luccock of Yale, driven by the logic of the Kingdom of God ideal, attacks not only the profit motive but the business system itself. Speaking of the ominous juxtaposition of poverty and wealth, he declares: "Not even the structure of profit-seeking business can be kept erect on such a slanting foundation."[6] He further charges: "A Christianity which balks either from fear or inertia at a real transfer of power, one which ties itself to any status quo, has betrayed itself."[7] He is finally led to go all the way to socialism, affirming that implementation of the gospel of love includes "the social ownership and control of the principal means of production."[8] Powerful Christian leaders like Reinhold Niebuhr, Kirby Page, and Harry F. Ward likewise have broken with the capitalist order decisively and unequivocally. But these are rare spirits. The majority of Christian leaders and writers, despite their vociferous outbursts against the diabolical wastes, injustices, and inequalities, the greed and selfishness at the heart of our society, still hope in desperation and confusion that somehow capitalism can be reformed on its fringes or can be melted away by individual conversion to the "way of the Cross."

For it becomes quite evident that a Christianity which does not repudiate the whole framework of selfish, profit-seeking capitalism, whatever its value in the past as a producer of wealth and machines, remains an ally of an order alien to its ideals. The agonizing fact is that the ethos of capitalism must be rejected as a diabolical enemy of the Christian spirit; and in the quest for a higher social ideal a new culture pattern must be found. To

[6] *Christian Faith and Economic Change* (New York, 1936), p. 36.
[7] *Ibid.*, p. 97.
[8] *Ibid.*, p. 99.

seek a fresh and nobler ethos for our society, a more truly Christian social morality, is the great demand of our times, becoming increasingly imperative as the ill effects of a decadent culture become more and more unbearable to its victims.

CAPITALISM UNDER ATTACK AND DEFENSE

We can see at last that every endeavor to achieve a more decent order, a more just and co-operative economy, a more Christian society, if you please, in one fashion or another, leads back to the basic issue of the nature, processes, spirit, and destiny of capitalism. No social group, no political, economic, or religious movement can presently escape the task of facing this question and defining its position in regard to it. Capitalism is no longer a matter of academic textbooks, of a mere abstract economic or social philosophy; it is a living, burning, imperious problem around which are being fought out the issues of modern life. The church can no more ignore this matter than it could ignore fascism, communism, race conflict, or war. If the Christian movement stubbornly refuses to think vigorously here, and refuses to define its attitude, judgment, and center of loyalty, it will either be rendered progressively more impotent in the social chaos or perish blindly at the hands of enemies known and unknown. As Professor John C. Bennett has written: "We live in a world in which large-scale changes in the structure of society are inevitable. It is *possible* now to overcome poverty. It is possible now to think of organizing the world for peace. It is a commonplace that this is a revolutionary period and it is our responsibility to make decisions which will affect the course of the revolution for good or evil."[9] To this we would subscribe heartily, and would add that "to make decisions" such as these is being forced upon us increasingly.

Now, it is in the United States that the acquisitive spirit, without limitations of feudal traditions and possessed of a vast continent of seemingly limitless resources, reached its fullest development. The story of the "triumph of American capitalism" is a

[9] "Enduring Bases of Christian Action," *Social Action*, IX (1943), 21.

fascinating one, full of awesome ventures and conquests of which any people might well be proud, at least in some respects. But such industrialism and its individualistic spirit mastered not merely an economy but an entire culture, filling the country on the one hand with goods and machines, on the other with a fever to compete, to strive for first place by any hook or crook, to succeed legally or illegally, to get ahead of one's neighbors even by "conspicuous consumption" and "conspicuous waste." These last two phrases have been made current coin by Thorstein Veblen, whose epoch-making studies first laid bare in deadly detail the unlovely aspects of our "free enterprise system." His earliest book, *The Theory of the Leisure Class*,[10] now regarded as a classic in culture analysis, showed how the capitalist ethos, as it conquered in America, has molded our fashions, tastes, morality, education, politics, and religion. His later works[11] all pointed out with telling effect, not merely the moral and spiritual evils of uncontrolled capitalist industrialism, but the ever increasing menace of inefficiency, business stagnation, and economic waste. If such analyses are basically sound, then at last, even in the United States, the capitalist spirit has run its period of greatest creativity and henceforth must become a fetter upon genuine social progress. A huge mountain of scientific facts available today has tended to confirm the general contention of this master social analyst.

Such considerations, plus a serious glance at the present scene, lead us to the conviction that American Christianity must center its attention in this area. Our established economic order is trembling under the deepening struggle between its defenders and its opponents. It is true that all critics are not violently and positively anti-capitalist, like Sorokin, Lewis Mumford, or Harry F. Ward, or positively socialist, like Norman Thomas. There are various shades of opinion and criticism among the most eminent investigators, writers, and thinkers. Yet whole organized bodies of

[10] First published in 1899.
[11] *The Theory of Business Enterprise*, 1904; *The Engineers and the Price System*, 1921; *Absentee Ownership and Business Enterprise*, 1924; and others.

economists are utilizing considerable time, energy, and resources in describing the evils and maladjustments of our economy—groups like those associated with the T.N.E.C. monographs, with Consumers Union, the Twentieth Century Fund, the Brookings Institution, and the Public Affairs Committee. Although most of these social scientists do not use the words "capitalist" and "capitalism" in contemptuous fashion (these are words over which our feelings are immediately aroused), they did not hesitate just before the outbreak of World War II to decry the weaknesses and abuses of the business system—the mounting concentration of control, divorce between management and ownership, wasting of labor and natural resources, restriction of output, abuse of the patent system, inefficiency, inflexible monopoly prices, the reckless scramble for dividends and executive salaries, and the irresponsibilities of high finance. The more militant critics, those fearlessly anti-capitalist, without hesitation cast aspersions upon the "economic royalists," the "industrial and financial oligarchs," the "pecuniary order," "the bookkeeping economy," "monopoly capitalism," and the "economic anarchy."

On the opposing side champions of capitalism have taken up arms. Under the slogans of "liberty," "free enterprise system," "the American economic system," the "American way," a never-ending campaign has been carried on. The depression tended to lower the morale of these "free enterprisers," but the boom occasioned by wartime conditions has inspired them. They are not only bitterly opposed to the European "isms" but suspicious of all internal reforms, of suggestions for enforced competition, modifications of corporation and inheritance laws, steeply graduated income taxes, minimum wages, full employment bills, wider application of social insurance, increased legal security for labor, and the like. A few years ago they were firmly set against even minimum political controls such as those of New Dealism; and of course the very phrase "economic planning" stirs them to wrath, even to fanaticism. In 1945 a vast movement got under way for the popularizing of a book by an Austrian economist, F. A. Hayek, because the book contains a strong plea for "freedom," at the same time warning that the struggle for a socialized economy leads inevitably to totalitarianism.[12] Among their latest victories are the tax reductions on corporate incomes, the elimination of the program of price control, and the passage of an antilabor bill in Congress. Thus, the battle is on. With the rise of labor and the increasing passion for economic reform and social security, there is on the horizon in America a "coming struggle for power."

What makes the impending struggle a desperate one is the new illusion of general prosperity, combined with a natural complacency and optimism created under war conditions. How else can one interpret the wholesale scrapping of the New Deal, the trend toward decentralization of power in the federal government, the resentment of Big Business toward any type of criticism, hesitation, and confusion over "full employment" bills, and the widespread clamor for general tax reduction? For the time being we can easily forget the economic ills which were in bold and unmistakable evidence before the global war, with the result that another and more terrible breakdown is assured. No amount of fanatical zeal displayed by reactionaries can eliminate that strange, fearful, ominous feeling that the basic problem of economic justice and security has not been solved. Moreover, there is not even a guarantee against an early capitalist collapse.

AMERICAN CAPITALISM: A CRITIQUE

A distinction must be made between American capitalism as an evolving complex of economic behavior and as an abstract

[12] *The Road to Serfdom*. Manifestly this economic essay has been widely misunderstood, not least by the "free enterprisers," who have used it as propaganda for *laissez faire*. Though it is true that Hayek fears socialism, or rather collectivist planning, he is not against regulation or even "planning" within the institutions of capitalism. He rejects *laissez faire*, calling for an over-all "legal framework" to guarantee competition. His program could be carried out only by some kind of New Dealism, which would be anathema to his American capitalist admirers and their camp followers in the circles of politics and journalism. The whole chain of events surrounding the popularizing of this "sad and angry little book" is a revelation of the desperation and fears of the economic royalists now presiding over the last great outpost of uncontrolled capitalism.

body of doctrine. Untold confusion has resulted from a failure to understand this distinction. It is granted of course that economic life, like every other phase of society, does not present us with rigid separation between theory and practice. Doctrine is more often than not a rationalization of contemporaneous attitudes, laws, traditions, and institutions. Social behavior is the material out of which economic philosophies are made. At any given time the complex of such behavior is a reflection of opinions, abstract ideas, and overt action. It is necessary, nevertheless, for a distinction to be made between capitalism as a system of economic thought and capitalism as a mode of living or social structure.

The theoretical basis of our present order, as is well known, goes back to the great English economists of the late eighteenth century and the early nineteenth—Adam Smith, David Ricardo, T. R. Malthus, Jeremy Bentham, James and John Stuart Mill, W. N. Senior, J. R. McCulloch.[13] These men gave to political economy the broad framework of ideas and attitudes which prevails, by and large, in the democratic countries. Despite the influence in ever widening circles of socialist views, and despite the criticism of the details of classical theory, this framework has persisted. Even the school of so-called "institutional" economics has not modified appreciably the dominant patterns of thought in our part of the world, particularly in America. As an heir of classical or "orthodox" theory, American capitalism has been characterized by the following seven basic assumptions:

1. That the principal if not the sole aim of an economy is the production of wealth (goods and services);
2. That private property in all types of goods is the essential foundation of a progressive society;
3. That economic self-interest is the socio-psychological drive which motivates individuals to produce;

[13] France also produced a crop of political economists, known as physiocrats, who held many of the fundamental ideas taught by the English school. Chief among the former were Quesnay and Gournay. But the English classical economists (particularly Adam Smith) exercised overshadowing influence and are taken for granted as the most important exponents of modern capitalist theory.

4. That the unhampered quest for profits is the legitimate aim of business and the key to general prosperity;
5. That competition is the fundamental process by which all types of economic activity sustain themselves in ever increasing production;
6. That adjustment of conflicts or restoration of equilibrium is gained by natural, automatic forces or processes operative in free economic activity;
7. That government is primarily a negative police force, serving as a referee for justice, a guarantor of contracts, and as protector of property rights.

We are not implying, of course, that these assumptions are coherently worked out and deliberately held, even by the majority of conservative economists, to say nothing of the rank and file of businessmen, political leaders, journalists, and other men of affairs. Nor are they a consistent expression in ideology of American economic behavior, past or current. Rather, they are the manifestation (to use Pareto's phrase) of a "rationalization of non-logical conduct." They reveal the basic attitudes, sentiments, and points of view which continue to express themselves in attacks on the government's endeavor to correct industrial abuses, in sneers at suggestions for national planning, in warnings against "communism," "bureaucracy," and "undemocratic" and "un-American" ideas, plans, policies, and methods. To be sure, the professional economists have given these notions some degree of logical formulation, but even their theories and principles do not have a sufficiently realistic connection with contemporary American practices and institutional trends. The words of Professor Frank D. Graham fit the situation perfectly: "Not only have postulates which originally represented an approach to reality, been progressively 'refined,' and thereby made less real, but the persistent trend of economic institutions has been away from the forms for which the doctrines were, in the first place, cast. Economic theory and economic fact have been marching in opposite directions." Indeed, these "preconceptions of economic science" are held so tenaciously and are so reminiscent of anachronistic patterns of political and economic behavior that Thurman Arnold refers to them as "the folklore of capitalism."[14]

Let us point out briefly some of the serious limitations in this inherited ideology of the American businessman. The notion that the economic system is concerned with little else than the creation of goods rests in part upon the false premise that an economy is self-contained, autonomous, and possessed with clearly defined, delimited goals. But there is no way of completely separating economic institutions or functions from other social structures and processes. The very phrase "political economy," used widely by the older writers, is the offspring of a situation in which political and economic functions were instinctively regarded as intertwined. Business goals cannot be isolated sharply from political or social objectives. Nor is this seriously attempted in practice. Everyone is aware of this fact in the emergencies of war or depression. It is only in relatively "normal" or so-called prosperous days that we can afford to indulge in this shortsighted interest in the undirected making and selling of things.

Even if the business system were segregated and self-contained in its structures, it would be forced sooner or later to consider a whole range of wider objectives. In order to benefit by discovery, invention, and research it would be obliged either to give encouragement to educational institutions or to set up (as it often does today) huge, expensively equipped laboratories. It would be led continually to seek new sources of raw materials, which involves the pre-emption, utilization, and transformation of lands, both mineral and agricultural. Moreover, business under conditions of modern technology is extremely dependent upon expanding domestic markets deliberately created, the conservation of many natural resources, international trade, vast reservoirs of consumer purchasing power, sustained employment of industrial workers, and a stable credit-currency mechanism. All of these conditions are now seen to be necessary for the very maintenance and stability of the system. The so-called "new capitalists" are reluctantly acknowledging that attention must be centered on all those problems which create a crisis for the economy, particularly

[14] *Social Goals and Economic Institutions* (Princeton, 1942), pp. 16–17.

unstable prices, labor-management disputes, bottlenecks in foreign trade, unemployment, and war.

The second assumption, namely, that unlimited private property is absolutely essential to human welfare and progress, is an exaggerated idea, not to mention its haziness. The phrase "private property" is often used very loosely in reference to intangible rights like patents, copyrights, and franchises, as well as to corporate-owned institutions. Yet the fact is that the most significant business property today is *group property*, whether possessed by corporations, co-operatives, or government agencies. This is true even in America; and in some other parts of the world, either the government or the co-operative society has taken a long step toward the destruction of the old fragmentary economy of small units. In Scandinavia, it is the co-operative; in Russia, the strong arm of the Soviet government has created a collectivist system. In our country, most of the recent studies of the corporation point not merely to a "managerial revolution" but to a property revolution as well. We listen daily to the mouthings of men who shout defense of "free enterprise" and "private property" while they continue to build empires of collectivist, corporate property whose only right to be called "private" is that no effective social controls have been erected to safeguard consumers, workers, and small enterprisers. What our business and political leaders mean by "private" is simply "non-governmental."

In fact, much of the so-called progress in American industry is due to this very tendency to destroy "private," that is, more or less personalized, property. The basic structure of our economy has been altered by the multiplication of colossal commercial and investment banks, monster super-corporations, giant, pyramiding holding companies, and interlocking directorates. The policy of the federal government, in attempting to eliminate monopoly conditions through "trust busting" and trust prevention activities, has been largely a failure. Although the old trustee and pool devices have been outlawed, the trade associations, mergers, holding companies, and gentlemen's agreements have marched apace, not only engaging in "reasonable" restraint of trade, but also annihilating *privately-owned* property. In manufacturing and mining alone there were over 1,200 mergers in the decade of 1919–28, causing a net destruction of 6,000 independent businesses. Two thousand others disappeared in 1929 and 1930. In the aforementioned decade there were nearly 1,800 bank mergers, with thousands of small financial enterprises being absorbed. At the same time at least 4,000 utility enterprises lost their existence or their independence. There were 15,006 banks, with loans and investments amounting to 51 billions, in 1940. One one-thousandth (or one-tenth of one per cent), that is, 15 banks, had 19 per cent of these 51 billions. Of the New York City banks, each of the three largest had more loans and investments than all the banks in any one state with the exception of six. The three together had more than any one state with the sole exception of New York State itself. Even in Chicago the two largest banking institutions combined had more loans and investments than all the banks in any one of forty-one states.

The classic study of the corporation in its effect on the structure of the American economy was made by Berle and Means.[15] The principal facts revealed in this work are widely known, but their full implication perhaps has not dawned upon the rulers of Congress and the rulers of business, nor perhaps even upon the mighty justices on the Supreme Court bench. We call attention to a few of these facts only to remind ourselves of what is happening to the "private property" so religiously defended by the champions of free enterprise. Berle and Means showed us that in 1929 there were about 300,000 nonfinancial corporations in the United States, the 200 largest of which controlled nearly 50 per cent of all corporate wealth. In only 11 per cent of these 200 corporations was the management based on personal ownership of stock, that is, ownership of all or of a majority of stock. In 44 per cent of the companies the management held only a small fraction of the stock. Moreover, in 1932, forty-three of these giant institutions had more than one-half billion each in assets;

[15] *The Modern Corporation and Private Property* (New York, 1933).

and these forty-three giants (with the exception of Ford Motor Company) were controlled through interlocking directorates by ten banks and three insurance companies. Let us ponder the utterance of Berle and Means when they say concerning the American Telephone and Telegraph Company: "100 companies of this size would control the whole of American wealth; would employ all of the gainfully employed; and if there were no duplication of stock-holders, would be owned by practically every family in the country."

In what meaningful sense can one brand as "private property" huge, statelike institutions which not only control incredible masses of tangible wealth, but are organized and operated with the resources of tens and hundreds of thousands of stockholders, bondholders, managers, and workers? Gone are the days when America was a pioneer country, characterized by a great mass of single enterprises and partnerships, with opportunity for all, whether for labor, agriculture, gold-hunting, or manufacturing enterprise. Gone is the time when individual initiative and "rugged individualism" would be a fair guarantee of economic good fortune or power. Free enterprise, in the orthodox sense, is rapidly passing into history, like the glorious free land of the western frontier.

Even careful students are sometimes misled by the complex, contradictory structure of the American economy. Such is true of Mussey and Donnan when they make so much of the fact that the "small business unit" will persist in the face of the great growth of "corporate behemoths." They were greatly impressed to find that of about forty-nine million "gainfully occupied" in 1930 nine and a half million (about one-fifth of the total) "were running small businesses of their own." A close analysis of the situation reveals, however, that outside of agriculture, the service trades and professions, and merchandising, the small business is of less and less importance. Even in wholesale and retail businesses, giant chains have appeared. Mussey and Donnan acknowledge that out of the nine and a half million who were running "small businesses of their own," there were some "six million farms," about two and a half million "retail stores" and "service industries," whereas there were only "a million more in transportation, finance, manufacturing, and mechanical pursuits."[16]

Bowman and Bach estimate that, though there "are still some nine million individual proprietorships," nearly seven million of them are farmers, including tenant farmers. Interestingly enough, some 43 per cent of the agricultural proprietorships are tenants. They maintain further that, in 1936, of the two million non-agricultural individual proprietorships, "over half a million were in retail and wholesale selling and over half a million in service enterprises."[17] Bowman and Bach affirm that the small proprietorships "are of little importance in manufacturing, transportation, communications, mining, construction, and the utilities, which together account for roughly two-thirds of the total employment and of income paid out in our economic system."[18]

It is difficult to ignore the disturbing conclusion of the economist, Theodore J. Kreps, when he wrote: "By seeking and being able to influence and control prices and production so as to maximize their own net profit and advantage, American business men controlling so large a segment of the economy historically as is constituted by the railroads, the utilities, the gigantic steel, aluminum, copper, cigarette, chemical, automobile, sugar, machinery, meat-packing, food-canning, petroleum, rubber-tire, cement, baking, and dairy products concerns, have themselves brought about a decline in the effectiveness of the profit system and laid the groundwork for a corporate, cartelized, dictatorial state."[19]

In 1934, Professor A. N. Holcombe of Harvard wrote that "measured by the value of business property, incorporated business was three or four times as important as unincorporated business. Private businessmen, operating alone or in partnerships with others, were a minor factor in the management of business. The system of individual proprietorship, envisaged by Adam

[16] *Economic Principles and Modern Practice* (New York, 1942), p. 150.
[17] *Economic Analysis and Public Policy* (New York, 1943), pp. 62–63.
[18] *Ibid.*, p. 62.
[19] *Economic Problems in a Changing World* (New York, 1939), p. 290.

Smith and the early individualists, can no longer furnish the basis for an acceptable economic and political philosophy."[20]

And Frank D. Graham, of Princeton, a strong defender of capitalism and of what he calls "classical liberalism," admits that "the corporate pattern is so obviously the dominant type of business organization, and its portent for the modern economy so great," that it has become the "medium through which a 'bigness,' quite out of proportion to the requirements of efficiency for anything except purposes of exploitation, is more readily achieved."[21]

Thus the real issue in twentieth-century America is not "private property" *versus* "collectivism," but how any private business property can be maintained against the organizing, collectivizing genius of the American businessman. Looked at from another angle, in the light of the continued failure of all "trust-busting" campaigns, the question is Who shall own and run the trusts?[22] The business oligarchs apparently are not interested in the preservation of an atomistic economy, or of any particular structure, so long as they remain in unhampered control of the resources and economic institutions of society. Thus we have the curious spectacle of an industrial and financial elite building economic empires and defending them in the name of the preservation of "private property" and "liberty." In further defense of such an "American system," many of them propose postwar "industrial planning," which if sponsored by the government is "fascism" or "communism" but if promoted by themselves is the protection of free enterprise.

The upshot of the matter under discussion in the last few para-

---

[20] *Government in a Planned Democracy* (New York, 1935), p. 105.

[21] *Op. cit.*, p. 207.

[22] Note that we use the word "trust" not in the technical, legalistic sense of the courts, as any institution or activity which in the courts' judgment engages in "illegal" or "unreasonable" restraint of trade. We mean by "trusts" all those vast, apparently legalized, businesses and business combinations which for all practical purposes, inside or outside the law, monopolize resources and markets and control prices. We see no essential difference in economic or social effects, for instance, between trusteeships and holding companies, or between "pools" and "oligopolies" engaging in monopolistic competition.

graphs is this: "Private property" systems are disappearing in all advanced industrialized countries, being replaced by various types of *group* property, so far as capital goods are concerned. In Russia, most of such property is completely nationalized, having become either a government enterprise or a "collective" under government supervision. In the fascist countries strict political supervision and control were exercised over the business system, with only a shadow of the "private property" system remaining.[23] But in the United States vast segments of the economy are collectivized under the control of impersonal super-corporations with the exercise of monopoly powers. What we are witnessing in America is the old, old story of pronounced institutional change being carried out unconsciously by continual modifications and accretions, effective control over such change being prevented by an antiquated ideology cleverly used by the ruling classes in the interest of the preservation of their social power.

Moreover, economic self-interest and the quest for profits have done as much as anything in recent years to prevent the smooth functioning of the economy. In the depression the profit motive added to our difficulties, creating idle plants, unemployment, rigidity of industrial prices, and greater dislocations in flexible price areas. Let all who doubt this read the Brookings Institution's publications, especially *America's Capacity to Produce* and *Industrial Price Policies and Economic Progress*. Let them consult Means's report at the 74th Congress, titled *Industrial Prices and Their Relative Inflexibility*. Or let them ponder the thesis of Ware and Means in *The Modern Economy in Action*, or the shocking facts recorded in *Economic Problems in a Changing World* (1939), edited by Willard Thorp.

Competition may be the life of trade, as Adam Smith dearly believed, but the evolution of the American economy since his time has virtually destroyed the conditions necessary for effective competition. Such necessary conditions are the existence of many

---

[23] In Britain, also, the triumph of the Labor party is the symbol of a fairly widespread public recognition of the end of the era of uncontrolled "private property."

buyers and sellers, general flexibility of prices, small business units, small-scale production, finance, and marketing, and reasonably accurate knowledge of market conditions by consumers. Such conditions have virtually disappeared in every area of our economy save in agriculture, merchandising, the professions, and the service industries. Even in merchandising the growth of the chains offers ominous forebodings for the future of single proprietorships, partnerships, and small corporations. The attempt to enforce competition by anti-trust laws and by intermittent campaigns of "trust busting" has given the government one long, unrelieved headache, thanks to the energy and ingenuity of our "entrepreneurs"! Even with the indefatigable zeal of Thurman Arnold, after four years of prosecution, 155 witnesses, and 40,-708 pages of testimony, the giant trust known as the Aluminum Company of America stood like the Rock of Gibraltar.

Even after the coming of World War II, with a skyrocketing of demand schedules, the profit motive made big companies producing aluminum, copper, magnesium, steel, automobiles, machine tools, and the like hesitant in expanding plant capacity. Elizabeth Donnan notes that it was not until January, 1942, that the automobile industry, "on the insistence of the Government," began to produce trucks, tanks, and planes, although as far back as 1940 the National Defense Advisory Council urged the making of airplane parts.[24] In an article in an issue of *Common Sense*[25] Aaron Levenstein reminded us that the federal government built so many war plants and financed so many others through the Reconstruction Finance Corporation that Uncle Sam for a time held a strategic one-fourth of the nation's productive capacity—which phenomenon was forced upon the government because of the fear and sluggishness of private industry, with its gaze centered on long-time, postwar profits. And as a most amazing phenomenon, we have seen our postwar American economy virtually paralyzed not mainly because of a wave of la-

[24] *America at War* (pamphlet, a supplement to a recent economics text, New York, 1943), p. 17.
[25] See a reprint copyrighted in 1944 by *Common Sense* publishing company, New York. The pamphlet is titled *"What Kind of Economy After the War?"*

bor strikes, but because of a general producers' "strike," designed
to break all governmental controls, particularly the O.P.A. Thus
whether in peace, war, or postwar reconstruction, we can no
longer rely upon "risk-bearing entrepreneurs" and the profit motive alone to sustain the processes of production. In both depressions and war booms there has appeared what Ware and Means
call "the distortion of the profit motive."

Our final observation in connection with these so-called rational capitalist "principles" is that the role of government can
no longer be a negative one. It cannot even content itself with
tactics designed to break up "trusts" and to enforce competitive
conditions. The indiscriminate effort to destroy monopolies is a
virtual failure; moreover, in many segments of the economy
large-scale operations and even monopolistic conditions are desirable from a standpoint of efficiency. From now on effective government in a highly technological society must involve strict
controls in the interest of widespread justice, business prosperity,
and co-ordination of increasingly complex economic institutions
and processes. The issue is not necessarily between economic
license and dictatorship. More control, along with increased
government ownership, we must have sooner or later, as an
alternative to chaos. Our problem in America, the Hayekites to
the contrary notwithstanding, is to build and maintain governmental structures, traditions, and processes which insure us on
the one hand against desperate fascist or communist methods,
and on the other against gross injustices and recurring dislocations inherent in unplanned, parasitic American capitalism.

THE NEGRO'S PLIGHT UNDER AMERICAN CAPITALISM

Employing a familiar military symbol, one can say appropri-
ately that the American Negro is caught between the arms of an
unconscious pincers movement—the operations of an unethical
competitive economy co-ordinated with the endless discrimination and denial of opportunity occasioned by American racism.
Economic exploitation is of the essence of a system of increasing monopoly and unbridled, publicly-sanctioned profit seeking.

Labor is looked upon primarily as a factor in production, as a mere item in the costs of business operation. The objective of efficient management, therefore, is to reduce the cost of labor, to utilize to the full the cheapest available workers, to seek ways and means of continually checking proposed advances in wage rates.

Hence the Negro has always been a source of cheap labor and a victim of a business technique committed to the maximization of dividends and managerial salaries. Prior to the Civil War, of course, the slaves were "sweated" under a cotton plantation system which offered neither compensation nor civil rights. Since his emancipation the colored American has continued to suffer under an essentially unreconstructed economy. He was freed without land or legal protection, was driven early from political influence and even basic citizenship rights, was made an outcast entitled only to the most menial jobs. Even the federal government refused to work out any consistent, long-range policy designed to guarantee economic resources and political freedom to a previously enslaved people as much entitled to the land they had built as were the slaveowners. Hence the expropriation and exploitation of the Negro population persisted through the Reconstruction even to our own day and generation. Indeed, anti-Negro sentiment—a sentiment manifesting itself in opposition to practical policies designed to correct these historic evils—has become virtually a national phenomenon in American culture.

A recent study reveals perfectly the desperate economic status artificially forced upon a tenth of the country's citizenry. We refer to a work titled *Negro Labor*, by Robert C. Weaver, who formerly served as Adviser on Negro Affairs in the Department of the Interior and later (during the war) as Director of Negro Manpower Service in connection with the War Manpower Commission.[26] Perhaps the most frequently recurring term used in this volume to describe the over-all position of the Negro in the economy is the phrase "occupational color-caste system" or the "color-caste system in occupations." The appalling facts remind

[26] The book is subtitled "A National Problem" (New York, 1946).

us of the merciless powers driving the black American to the margins of sheer survival. Technological changes, like modernized building materials and devices, electric welding, mechanical stokers, and the Diesel engine have destroyed old occupations while erecting barriers to entrance into the newly created ones. Employers, nearly always yielding to the well-known anti-Negro public sentiment, and always in quest of cheap labor, repeatedly relegate most of those employed to what Weaver calls the "heavy, dirty, lower paid jobs." The national government, vacillating, compromising, ever ambiguous and uncertain in policy, has been incapable of or unwilling to tackle the issue even in the midst of tremendous shortages in a wartime labor supply. The F.E.P.C., hurriedly established and generally resented by employers and southern politicians, was finally scrapped by the 79th Congress and the Truman administration.

In fact, organized labor in the past, tempering its demands to short-range goals largely pleasing to the oligarchs of the profit system, and governed by the racist ethos, has made a not inconsiderable contribution to the degraded economic status of the Negroes. The craft unions especially have been discriminating. Often they have barred Negroes from membership, denied them apprenticeship training and vocational education, erected over numerous categories of jobs (figuratively speaking) clear-cut signs "For Whites Only." An instructive instance of union policy is that of the railroad brotherhoods, especially the Locomotive Firemen, who have sought persistently for more than fifty years to drive Negro firemen from the railroads. As far back as 1899 a convention of the four brotherhoods urged their constituency to support a program designed to clear "our lines of this class of workmen." Weaver says that as recently as 1941 "agreements had been effected which would eliminate all Negro firemen in less than two decades."[27] Although the C.I.O. organizations are showing much more liberalism than has been characteristic of

[27] *Op. cit.*, pp. 102–103. The author cites as a source of his information on this item the report of H. R. Northrup at the railroad hearings of the F.E.P.C., as well as the latter's book, *Organized Labor and the Negro* (New York and London, 1944).

the historic racial policy of A.F. of L. organizations, the racist spirit continues to be one major determining factor in the general behavior of organized labor. Millis and Montgomery wrote: "In 1943 there were seven A.F. of L. and six non-A.F. of L. internationals that excluded Negroes by constitutional provision. A few other internationals, such as the Boilermakers and the Machinists, were accomplishing the same result by ritual pledging of members not to present for membership any one who was not of the white race. Furthermore, there have been numerous instances in which local unions have kept their doors closed to Negroes in violation of the international rule."[28]

Exploitation bears extremely heavily upon the brown American because it is at once an economic and a social force. The attempt to keep him from so-called social contact with a "superior" race involves necessarily wholesale denial of most opportunities for remunerative employment. To serve as clerk in a store, as secretary in an office, as teller in a bank, as radio announcer, as foreman or manager, as driver of a city bus or streetcar, as member of a government board or committee—all these and many other categories of work inevitably involve "social" contact with others engaged in responsible tasks in connection with "white" institutions. Booker T. Washington's famous figure of the two races living together as separate as the fingers in all matters "purely social" and "one as the hand" in all things essential to "mutual progress" may sound sweet and consoling to the die-hard conservatives; but it has no correspondence with objective social realities. To maintain rigid separation in all things "social" means that one group must be driven from participation in all kinds of opportunity—educational, religious, political, economic. If we may be permitted here a divergence from the principal argument, let us call attention to the fact that separation of the races "socially" required a rigid "religious" separation into white church and Negro church. The upshot of our conten-

---

[28] *Organized Labor* (New York, 1945), p. 262. This massive volume is the third in a series by the authors on the general subject of the "The Economics of Labor."

tion is that the ruthless denial of the Negro's chance for full participation in economic enterprise in the name of the preservation of a "pure" race or in defense of "white men's jobs" combines with an exploiting business system in the maintenance of institutions, policies, and tactics which tend to keep him in perpetual poverty and subjection.

The persistent and flagrant persecution of these loyal Americans under the double impact of profit-seeking business and a peculiarly blind labor force victimized by racism creates an embarrassing set of circumstances confronting the Christian forces. The economic plight of the Negro has become one of the most vivid symbols of the failure of modern social Christianity in this part of the world. Gunnar Myrdal's American "dilemma" is a dilemma for a Christian nation, a country proud of its world mission on behalf of "democracy" and "Christianity." For the same people who are the militant champions of a spiritual way of life and a people's government also, in the name of "free enterprise" and "American institutions," stubbornly perpetuate a decadent capitalist culture, as well as a type of racism which may become one main seedbed for the dreaded specter of a war too horrifying to conceive.

4

Political Forces and the Christian Way

ARTHUR W. HARDY

ANY discussion of political forces and the Christian way of life must recognize the effect that religion has exerted on the secular affairs of men throughout the various periods of history. Nearly all institutions, social, educational, economic, and political, show the influence of great religious leaders. As the essence of the great religions is reviewed, the common problem that emerges from the total picture is the contrast between the spirit of religion and the practices instituted by its followers. At this point it should be noted that organized religion has developed like any other institution serving men and is therefore subject to the same limitations and errors. But the claims of religious institutions have been greater than claims of other institutions. Thus men are less patient with the shortcomings of religious institutions. The universal tendency to rationalize one's acts in accordance with his desires contributes much to the inconsistencies between theory and practice. Referring particularly to this period of history, Mahatma Gandhi emphasizes the point that religion has become an inexcusable example of hypocrisy and insincerity. He says, "Men to whatever religion they may belong call only for the external facts of religion, and give the go-by to all its fundamental principles."

Despite the variance that exists between precept and practice, many of the world's great religions have brought into the lives of men and nations clean-cut ideas of the unity of men, the importance of the individual, and social justice. Even though men and governments of men may ignore these principles, they remain unshakable, and constantly crop up in history to plague and to challenge us on the validity of our acts.

Christianity's emphasis on the collective betterment of man would stand high in any evaluation of its many gifts to civilization. Its position through the ages has been one of drawing men together, in order that as a group they might work toward a common goal. Examples of this community concern in our modern life are numerous. The provisions for child welfare; humane treatment for the aged and mentally deficient; modern labor legislation and social security; recognition of the rights of women; public health work and the setting of safety standards in hazardous occupations—all reflect Christianity's recognition of the fact that the reconstruction of society is a twofold problem and must be attempted both individually and collectively.

The major social institutions in Western society had their origin in the church. The necessary differentiation in function has led men to claim for a particular institution independence to the point of confusion. This denial of interdependence has caused frequent failure in the rendering of effective service through many particular institutions.

The following paragraph, on "A Sixfold Democracy," briefly calls to mind a few of the implications that religion, and Christianity in particular, has had in the developing life of mankind:

For the purposes of this discussion it is suggested that a sixfold democracy be interpreted in terms of the six major social institutions, previously used as types, through which the individual may be developed and rendered justice and equal opportunity. These instructions, stated in dual terms of local form and generic value, are: the home and family; the school and education; the church and religion; the state and government; industry and work; and community and association. The sixfold democracy will therefore be: organic, educational, religious, political, industrial, social. It seems clear that each and all of these aspects of democracy are essential. Industrial democracy can no more be taken for the whole system than can work be interpreted to be the whole of life. Religious freedom will be worth little if organic democracy be not safeguarded so that children may be born well, grow in health, develop in mind and stature; if mothers and wives in isolated or congested areas must perform hard labor unequally divided between men and women.[1]

The factors cited above are important as we come to our consideration of the American scene. If we are to consider democracy in its manifold make-up, then none can deny that the Christian way of life should be a part of that process.

While there is no state religion in America as it is known in other parts of the world, Christianity is generally accepted throughout the nation. The ethical standard of the average man is the Christian standard, modified somewhat by the circumstances of American life. The average American citizen has never thought of any other religious instruction, and to him Christianity is the source from which he believes he has drawn his ideas of duty and conduct.

The modifications, however, embodied in the American's idea of Christianity are of interest to our discussion. The average American is anything but a pious individual. His concern with the dogma and philosophy of religion is superficial. Yet despite this the United States considers itself a religious nation and its citizens consider themselves a thoroughly Christian people. To the citizen of the United States the word "Christian" has come to have a special meaning that is somehow closely connected with democracy. Being a Christian, as the average American understands it, embraces a hopeful outlook on life, which includes observing all of the demands of citizenship and strict loyalty to the family. There is a strong indication that the average American attributes much of the material development of this country to the Christian character and moral fiber of the American people as a whole. Some substance attaches to this belief because, although it is freely admitted that the church in the past

[1] H. W. Odum, *Man's Quest for Social Guidance* (New York, 1927), pp. 387–388.

few years has lost ground as a force holding people together socially, yet by some intangible means it has managed to maintain its place in the institutional life of the nation. The whole conception of Christianity is a much-bracketed system of moral and religious ideas which are so simple, though interwoven, that they can hardly be distinguished from the conception of Americanism. In fact, hearing an American talk about Christianity and the American way of life, a listener unacquainted with the American rationalization of Christianity would hardly be able to distinguish between the two. It was during the twenties that L. P. Jacks visited America. It may perhaps be recalled that when he returned to England and was asked what he thought of American democracy, he replied: "I didn't investigate it. I don't like to disturb people at their devotional exercises."

However confusing or inconsistent this American idea of Christianity may be to an outsider, it has had a vital and significant place in building a democratic society; and the responsible use of the freedom that has been achieved has come about as a result of the application of these nebulous principles and unique rationalizations of the Christian way of life. There has never been in the United States any misunderstanding as to the separation of church and state. Half of the wars of Europe, and a majority of the internal troubles that have vexed European states, have arisen either from theological differences or from rival claims of church and state. This type of conflict or concern has never existed in the United States. There is no established church, and all religious bodies are equal before the law. The separation of church and state in the United States is accepted as a sound principle. It means only that the church and state are mutually free and that neither may control the other. It does not mean, however, that because there is no legal or organic relationship church and state may not co-operate to bring about desirable democratic objectives; nor does it mean that people who constitute the citizenry of a state are exempt from the spiritual insights and moral laws that set the standards of right and justice for communities and nations.

This separation of church and state in the United States does not mean that religion and the church do not get into politics and the government, or that the government and politics do not get into religion and the church. In practice, the politicians and statesmen do not hesitate to use the church and religious bodies to further their own individual political or social ends, and the great religious leaders through the ages have taught a way of life instead of a creed. The teachings of Jesus, indeed, have to do with every phase of man's activity, whether secular or spiritual.

Any attempt, however, on the part of politicians to exercise control over religion or the program of the church through political pressure or otherwise is certain to be resisted by religious leaders. On the other hand, the concern of religious leaders over public questions, economic, social, political, and international relations, considered to be secular and thus outside the province of the church, is very likely to meet strong opposition. Most industrialists, business leaders, and employers in general do not welcome the examination of their business practices, labor relations, wages, prices, syndicates, and monopolies. They do not want them to be publicly discussed and evaluated in the light of Christian principles. As a matter of fact, it must be admitted that unadulterated Christianity is a dynamic, revolutionary element in an un-Christian social order, and the controlling forces do not want to be disturbed. This "let us alone" attitude has come down through the years. It has played an important part in keeping Christian missionaries out of India, China, and Africa, until they "learned" how to keep Christianity out of secular affairs and thereby to render it inoffensive and ineffective as an instrument of social reconstruction.

In this connection, the following statement by Stanley High is interesting:

When in 1789 William Carey announced his plan to go to India as a missionary, the wrath of India's British traders was kindled against him. The English East India Company, on behalf of all exploitive interests, raised a hue and cry. The Directors were hastily assembled and resolved that: "The sending out of missionaries into our Eastern Possessions is the maddest, most extravagant, most costly, most indefensible project which has ever been suggested by a moon struck fanatic. Such a scheme is pernicious, imprudent, useless, harmful, dangerous, profitless, fantastic. It strikes against all reason and sound policy. It brings the peace and safety of our possessions into peril."[2]

Mr. High further states that

A Japanese official in Korea, when I asked him about the influence of Christianity upon the Korean people, declared, with something less than the customary diplomatic circuitousness:—"We are very happy to have the missionaries come here. We cannot deny that they do a great deal of good for the Korean people. But we are obliged to believe that their Christian teachings, misunderstood perhaps, were responsible for the unfortunate Korean independence movement in 1919."

The struggle for freedom and equality in India, Africa, Asia, Europe, and in the United States of America, among all peoples, has justification in the principles and tenets of the Christian religion. Notwithstanding this, the vested secular interests the world over, including the United States, do not welcome the insistent advocacy of the application of the teachings of Jesus in secular affairs, especially in business, industry, and politics. Leaders in the field of politics and business do not always consider it good and proper for Christian ministers and leaders to take an active part in politics and governmental affairs. There is always the fear that the ethical teachings of Jesus may be brought in as criteria for evaluating business and political practices.

Too often political forces are directed toward certain goals that are not worthy of Christian support. And frequently the means and methods of achieving these goals do not square with Christian practices. When the Christian way of life is held up as a guide or standard of acceptable practice, the sponsor, be he layman or clergy, is usually turned upon and ruled out on the grounds that it is the function of the church and Christianity to minister to the "inner man" and develop the "spiritual life" of man, and that secular matters are entirely outside the province of Christian responsibility.

[2] Stanley High, *The Church in Politics* (New York, 1930), pp. 106–107.

Another tactic employed by political forces is their use of institutionalized Christianity to further their own ends. There is considerable evidence to show that this approach has been used with amazing success. Either organized Christianity and its leaders actively co-operate with political forces in the accomplishment of political ends, or the Christian forces assume an apathetic attitude and have nothing to say against the methods, means, and goals which the political forces are using. Surely this passive acceptance is a form of co-operation.

An outstanding example of active co-operation of the church with the state in the interest of political ends was the case of the church in prerevolutionary Russia, where it was committed to the maintenance of the political and economic *status quo*. There, the popular doctrines of the church were Christian humility, patient long-suffering, and submission to the dictates of the czarist state. This was not very unlike the role of the church in England today with regard to British colonial policy and the exploitation of subject peoples. Nor is the Christian church in the United States, as separate and individual congregations scattered across the land, very vocal about economic exploitation, political corruption, discrimination and ill treatment of human beings based upon race, creed, color, or national origin. Too often political forces are directed toward the accomplishment of ends which are not worthy of Christian sanction, and the methods used by political forces are often out of line with Christian practices.

The Christian way of life is based upon the assumption of the Fatherhood of God and the brotherhood of man, with love and the sacredness of human personality as its guiding principles. Rarely do political forces embrace and apply these Christian tenets in the pursuit of political ends. Only when these forces provide governmental machinery and social programs which serve the basic needs and best interests of the people in the largest possible way are they in line with Christian idealism. Not only do political forces often fall short of this standard, but even the Christian church and many of our Christian organizations are woefully lacking in this respect. Thus, protestations from laymen and clergy against political interference from the church may be merely a reflection of uneasy consciences.

No organization or institution can rise above or go beyond the individuals who compose it. Political forces, therefore, like the Christian church, need the support and guidance of men who are committed to the principles and teachings of Jesus, whose inter-est was not in himself, or in any organization, as such, but in the people and their welfare alone.

The theory of the separation of church and state, as it operates in the United States, gives an easy excuse for religious leaders not to become active in politics, even to the point of neglecting their Christian duty to the people. Not only so, but their inactivity and silence have often strengthened the politicians whose interests are rarely based upon the needs of the people. Unmolested, these politicians have been able to pursue their own selfish interests at the expense of social improvement and the vital interest of the people.

Such a sharp demand for the rigid separation of religious from secular life is an abrupt departure from the religious orien-tation of American national life. Roger Williams, for example, in his social outlook assumed that the religious influence in the af-fairs of government would be active but not productive of vio-lence and intolerance. The Christian religion imposes upon every one of its disciples, laymen as well as clergy, the responsi-bility to give Christian direction to those forces for service to the people upon which our governmental, economic, and social struc-tures are established. It is not enough to indict these instrumen-talities by saying that politics is corrupt, that our social system is inadequate and unjust, and that our social structure is un-Chris-tian. These conditions represent the kind of world implied in the emphasis of Jesus on honesty, justice, unselfishness, respect for human personality, and brotherly love.

The Christian church, instead of allowing itself to be used by politicians to accomplish their own temporal ends, has a legiti-mate right and a moral obligation to employ machinery in order that our political system may be brought to reflect more fully and to guarantee more adequately the effectiveness of Christianity in its objectives and methods. The political order, like the chuch, is but a reflection of the individuals and groups who compose it. In proportion as its constituents embrace the Christian way of life, therefore, and apply these principles in their political activities, our political order will most surely exemplify Christian ideals and standards. The place of the Christian way in the political aspect of life would thus seem to be imperative. The church, further, as a basic social institution, not only is a part of the democratic process but has a definite responsibility to help make democracy work.

Despite the validity of the church's place in politics, there still is a widespread feeling that the church and church leadership should not concern themselves with this phase of life. There is nevertheless a growing awarness, on the part of some progressive churchmen, that this is an area in which the church must not only declare itself but actively work to establish a high standard of performance in all branches of public service. E. C. Lindeman, writing in *Social Action,* asserts:

I wish the Churches would begin to emphasize their teaching function and to de-emphasize preaching. The world is hungering for moral guidance. Earnest persons who are aware that all our public issues are, at bottom, moral in character want to know how to deal with these moral elements, but they want advice which is actually usable. The sermonic tendency is to place morals as a point in the equation which the average citizen cannot reach. Ultimately, he [the listener] assumes that these sermons were never intended to be taken seriously, that is, translated into personal and social action. As one of our American pragmatic philosophers once said: "You can tell people in sermons from now until doomsday that they ought to love one another and it will not do the least amount of good; they'll go on hating each other. What is needed is an experiment in which they can learn through trial and error whether it's possible to love persons with whom you are engaged in useful tasks."
Does this mean to bring politics, economics and social problems into the Church and by the same token to drive religion and ritual out? I do not think so. To me only that religion is true which aids people to face realities, and the highest ritual is the good man doing good.[3]

[6] E. C. Lindeman in *Social Action,* XII (1946), 28.

The immediate problem of the church in bringing the influence of the Christian way of life to bear on the political forces of the country is to determine an effective approach. Those who are most critical of the apathy of church leadership do not anticipate a partisan participation. As we view the political scene and take account of inefficiency in high place, the need of a strong educational program emphasizing citizenship responsibility is clearly indicated. At this point of education the church might enter into the political life of the nation. It would be justified because it has pioneered in this field. Our colleges and educational systems have their roots in the early efforts of the church to bring enlightenment to its membership. It has a further responsibility because as a social institution it has developed methods and disciplines that have affected the lives of men, and was the first institution to lay emphasis on social justice as a fundamental human need. The breakdown of democracy is a moral question, involving the character of the individual citizen. The church is the great moral guide and is so accepted. Finally, no other institution can reach a larger number of the people who need moral instruction and guidance in politics than can the Christian church.

Lest we be accused of dogmatism in defining the responsibility of the church in this area, we hasten to admit that there are a number of difficult obstacles that confront such a program as has been outlined. Primarily we must recognize here the inadequacy of the average minister in this field. Very few pastors possess the skills and the understanding of what is involved in initiating an effective program of citizenship. Also, the indifference of the masses, content merely to mouth overworked clichés concerning citizenship, makes doubly difficult the task of creating a stimulating program of action. Another important factor, and one that is generally overlooked, is the fact that political bosses and machine politicians do not want an intelligent citizenry. They thus minimize the importance of issues involved in a campaign and magnify the personal attributes of a candidate.

These are but a few of the many obstacles, but they serve to emphasize the need for guiding influence. The church is the one organization that could do this service in a broad, nonpartisan manner commanding the respect of the nation as a whole. It has been said that if the church should address itself to any human problem for a period of six months, and if a majority of ministers would co-operate, significant change could be effected in any existing attitude. This statement may be overdrawn, but certainly none can deny that the church does influence men's thoughts and acts.

What the church can do specifically to bring the Christian way of life into the political arena is suggested in the following projects.

The first thing would be to create a climate of opinion in church and community that would accept the church's interpretation in matters of public interest. After this was accomplished, the church might develop a long-range, comprehensive program of citizenship—its meaning, its responsibilities, and its rewards. Methods of doing this might take several forms. First, it might be done by bringing pressure on the board of education to develop adequate citizenship training in the public schools. Second, the board of education could establish adult education courses for the older citizens. The participation in these courses might come from the church membership that originally developed the idea. Finally, if there are sufficient resources in the church, it might develop through its own religious education program a citizen training project. Thus, methods could be as varied and as many as the leaders of the churches in a given community.

Another point at which the Christian way may be injected into the political scene is in bringing public service to the level of a profession and in establishing machinery to train and prepare men for all branches of elective and appointive positions in government. This is a most important need in the United States today. One has only to read the papers to recognize the ineptness of many of our public administrators. At no time in the history of this country as a nation has there been such a lack of confidence on the part of the people in their government. Special interests and the resources of selfish groups and individuals seem to have more weight with some members of Congress than do the wishes of the people whom they are supposed to represent. Since, therefore, no institution is stronger than the units that compose it, if we are to have better government we have to create it. Schools should be established throughout the nation, comparable to Annapolis and West Point, in order that young men interested in public service as a career may be educated at the government's expense. The same standard of excellence should be maintained that is required of graduates of the military and naval academies, and the same prestige should accrue to these young men fitted for various types of government service. One of the glaring weaknesses of the American system of public service is that so many elderly people enter it after having achieved some prominence in other fields of service. Harry Moore thus comments on this situation:

> Politics needs young men and young women also. The civil service surely needs both. If one waits till middle age, after service in other fields has brought one into prominence, it is too late for one's best work in government. The idealism of youth is too likely to have faded. Many young people are now interested academically in political problems, but when discussion suggests a possible course of action, the student feels it is outside his area of concern.[4]

One of the contributions of the New Deal has been the use of a large number of young people in federal agencies. Although this use grew out of economic necessity, it has opened up the possibilities of government service as a career for many capable young men and women. This stimulation needs to be infused into an educational program that will exercise a selective influence in developing the best talent for continuing public service in states and municipalities as well as the federal government.

This is an expensive process and would cost many millions of dollars. But wasteful and inefficient government is more costly. In addition to the expenditure of billions of dollars for corrupt public officials, the cost in human dignity and in the sense of the

[4] Harry H. Moore, editor, *We Are the Builders of a New World* (New York, 1934).

sacredness of life is incalculable. The voice and activity of the church must be positive in the direction of insuring the quality and integrity of government. It can thus make it possible for young men of ability to look forward to an honorable career. Surely this is a reasonable price to pay in a country as rich and powerful as America.

The development of higher standards and regard for public welfare suggests another project that could be handled with effectiveness by the church. Christian leadership could demand that men in public service be adequately paid and that all branches be provided with sound social security. These conditions obtain in most branches of service, but should be extended to cover elective officers, particularly congressmen. Under our present system, public office, particularly Congress, is more attractive to men of means than it is to capable men in varied professions and callings who do not have a separate income. A man who spends twenty years or more in Congress, as far as his personal security is concerned, is usually in poor circumstances unless he has private resources. This should not be; congressmen should be relieved of questions of personal security, which is the usual source used by special interests to bend them to their will as opposed to the interest of the nation.

We are now being acquainted with the new war scandals. Congressmen and others in high posts have been involved. The personalities are not important. What is important is that conditions exist which expose a lawmaker, or an official, to the pressures of selfish men and groups. Current salaries are so inadequate that men can be tempted to use their great trust to further some selfish interest. This is a moral issue, and the institution best fitted to exercise a corrective influence at this point is the church.

Such processes and projects are in keeping with the dignity of the church. This is an area close to the everyday life and living of people where the church, if it is to render its greatest service, must enter and bear witness. With the United States proposing to be the moral guide for the rest of the world, it is highly desirable that we investigate and clean up our democratic processes here at home. Although as a social institution it is clearly within the function of the church to participate as the exigencies of circumstance demand, yet any participation must necessarily be in the spirit of its devotion to the principle of justice. It must stand as an impartial critic, concerned only with preserving the principles of morality and justice and correcting abuse through the representative influence of its members.

Ministers who take an active part in politics to the displeasure of those whose private business or political interests they oppose are often derisively referred to as political parsons, unfit to give spiritual leadership to the church. Whenever religious leaders or Christian organizations become aggressively active in trying to get Christian principles applied in business, or politics, or social relations, the vested interests are certain to offer stiff opposition. All sorts of pressure will be used to stop this so-called meddling in secular affairs by the Christian forces.

Whereas the participation of church members in politics may be taken for granted as their rightful exercise of citizenship, objection is often raised against the participation of the minister or Christian leader in political affairs. It is argued that the minister must avoid controversial issues and partisan interests lest the fellowship and unity of the church be broken. To this argument Liston Pope, writing in *Social Action,* has the following to say:

There is indisputable merit in the aspiration of the Church toward universality, and in its profession or concern for all men regardless of their stations or affiliations. And paradoxically, the minister is often sought after by interest groups because it is assumed that he is disinterested. But his alleged transcendence of the power struggle is largely a fiction; his concern for maintaining "the fellowship of the church" may rest largely on the fear that some of the more affluent members of his congregation will withdraw their support. It is probable that more people have withdrawn from the Church because it did not take sides, that is, because it refused to deal honestly with questions of brotherhood and justice, than have withdrawn because ministers or other church leaders took some positive stand. In any event, the function of leadership is to lead, not to pacify, and a minister might profitably brood over one of the principles which the Editor of the *New Yorker* laid down for himself in the first issue of the magazine, to the effect that his policies were not going to be tested in every instance by the effect they would have on his maiden aunt in Dubuque. The effort to be all things to all men may eventuate in being little to anybody.

Whatever his argument may be, the minister is inextricably engaged in the power struggles of his society. He may declare his intentions to abstain from them, or to be neutral as between contending forces, but even that declaration is of some influence in the outcome of the struggles. To do nothing (if it were possible) is to align oneself in effect with the stronger, or with the side which will profit most from inertia. In a fairly stable society, refusal to take sides supports the preservation of the *status quo*. In short, the minister cannot escape responsibility no matter what he does, or does not do. Attempts at neutrality are immoral in principle and abortive in practice, whether in the sphere of international relations or in the arena where domestic factions contend with each other.

It is necessary, then, that the minister find positive principles by which his choices may be guided wisely. . . . Uncritical and unqualified allegiance to any partisan program is as indefensible as a pretense of Jovian indifference and transcendence.[5]

The Christian layman or minister will find very few political organizations or pressure groups based upon Christian idealism or employing genuinely Christian principles and methods in the accomplishment of their ends. But this is his opportunity to make a contribution to Christian social reconstruction. He has a moral obligation to seize every opportunity to align himself with the forces seeking a better society.

Disregard in the United States of many principles of justice, democracy, and decency cannot be taken with the usual American indifference. There is a sharp realization that the testing ground of Christianity and democracy is precisely here, in the United States. Until the Christian way of life has become a reality in all sections of the continental United States, Christianity is to that extent a failure, though every Hottentot in Africa be converted. Until life and liberty of the humblest person is safe and he receives full justice and hearing before the proper authorities, democracy is a failure. This is a challenge that Christian

---

[5] Liston Pope, "The Minister Seeks Guiding Principles," *Social Action*, XI (1945), 35–36.

democratic America cannot ignore. In this whole picture of the Christian way in politics, the moral element is so tied in with the democratic process that it cannot be separated. The principles of social justice, therefore, and the sacredness of the person of the individual, which is important in the teachings of Christianity, cannot be ignored as the conduct of public officials is evaluated; for, indeed, the symbols of religion permeate all phases of life in the United States.

Nascent fascism in American life has taken firm root, derived from lawlessness. Nowhere in American life is the church more recreant to its profession of faith in the Fatherhood of God and the brotherhood of man than in race relations. The problem of the twentieth century is the problem of the color line. It is of vital moment in our profession of Christian faith, in our continuing missionary enterprise, in labor relations, in public service. Here the church has been first to proclaim the precept and most reluctant to put it into practice. Many states are openly defying the government of the United States as they seek to circumvent the recent decisions of the Supreme Court which outlawed the denial of the ballot to anyone because of race and religion. Corruption, greed, and betrayal of trust have become almost misdemeanors in comparison with the expressions of violence that have taken hold of people. Contrary to the principle of the sacredness of personality, human life is somewhat cheap in this country, too, if the daily accounts of murder and rape in newspapers and on the radio are to be believed.

There are indications that special interests, represented by professional lobbyists, exercise such power with the governing forces of the country that the best interests of the people, as a whole, are secondary. Because of traditional procedures in Congress, a small minority has a power out of proportion to its numbers.

This ignoring of the moral implications of the law is also found in the attitude of the individual citizen. He has little compunction in trying to circumvent the legal consequences of an act. In fact, it can be said with some degree of truthfulness that laws are made in the United States to be broken. The power of the bosses, the political machine, and the spoils system is part of the American political picture. All play their part in complicating a Christian approach to the problem of democratic administration in public office. Many men who have entered public service after having developed a successful business or professional career would certainly not approve in private life of some of the things they vote for as public servants. Along with the bosses, machines, and spoils, another subversive factor is party loyalty. This is a compelling pressure, and many men have been disciplined and in some instances excluded from office because they did not support their party, even though the only principle involved was political aggrandizement.

The complications that enter into the life of a professing Christian nation such as the United States are so varied that it is difficult to identify any one source as their cause. On the political scene today, however, the dominating ills appear at the point of moral issues. Lack of personal integrity, greed, selfishness, and similar conditions indicate the responsibility of the church in correcting, or at least confronting, the Christian community with its shortcomings.

There is the unfortunate belief among the rank and file of people, particularly the majority who are not members of the church, that the church not only is reactionary in its outlook but is actually an agent for maintaining the *status quo*. H. R. Niebuhr says, in this connection: "So the church becomes a victim as well as the source of national civilizations. Instead of representing a common Christian ideal and fostering mutual understanding of each other it supports them in their mutual suspicions and fears."[6]

In modern Christianity, however, we find some effort to return to the study of the spirit and ideals of the early Christian church. A few brave souls are turning to these ideals for the solution of many of the ills of our social and political life. The inequalities that have developed in the economic order, largely through the agency of political privilege, appear to the church as a denial of

[6] H. Richard Niebuhr, *The Social Sources of Denominationalism* (New York, 1929), p. 132.

the Christian principle of brotherhood. The development of the various denominations and numerous sects, however, is the real problem faced in this country of integrating the Christian way of life, not only in the political situation but in any other situation. On this point Niebuhr has this to say: "For denominations, churches and sects are sociological groups whose principle of differentiation is to be sought in their conformity to the order of social classes and castes. . . . The division of the churches closely follows the division of men into castes of national, racial and economic groups."

These observations serve to point up the difficulty of a united program to direct the Christian way of life into the streams of secular affairs. The very religious freedom which is part of the framework of the fundamental law of the nation brings not a small measure of support to the spirit of compromise that has drawn the church from its original loyalties.

A careful scrutiny of the points raised in this chapter, involving the influence of religion on the secular institutions, the authority of the church to enter into the various aspects of life, the suggested means by which it might meet the crises in different situations, compels the view that the church cannot promise to solve the economic, social, and political problems. It can only bring its influence to bear in shaping the lives of the Christian community so that the desirable personality traits and character will be implicit in the life of the individual, who in turn will express these ideals in his individual relations with his fellow men and in his responsibilities.

Although the need for a socially effective gospel in the life of the nation is obvious, the Christian church cannot hope to develop a program that will compete with the modern idealism of different political parties, which guarantee ideal solutions for social, economic, and political problems. It can, however, render great service by testing these programs and procedures against its fundamental principle of social justice and uncompromisingly challenging them where they do not measure up.

This, it seems, is the area in which the church is weak. It has not met these forces on a basis of the moral and spiritual issues involved, and by its silence has apparently given consent or approval to programs and procedures that have not been for the best interests of the majority of people. A few ministers have sought to bring religious practice into harmony with the current needs of the day, but the church as an institution has been backward. It not only has sanctioned practices contrary to the fundamental principles of Christianity, but has actually aided in thwarting the desires and needs of human beings. It has failed to deal boldly with the ills of the social system. It has been noticeably silent when its constituents have participated in gross forms of human greed. Christianity has not failed, but the church as the organized symbol of the Christian way of life has failed to live up to its great opportunity.

The necessity for the Christian church to instill the Christian way of life into the everyday affairs of men is as great as is the need for men and women with vision and ability in the governments of the world. No other means is so effective in bolstering public confidence in democracy as wise and sane political measures in time of crisis. We must have men of faith and foresight to propose and carry through measures that will guarantee the peace and insure mutually helpful relations among the nations of the world. Unless from the ranks of modern youth there develops abler men than those who are carrying the responsibility today, the outlook for future civilization will become increasingly gloomy. The present-day situation in the world requires much greater understanding than the situation that faced the older generation of leaders. It will not be easy for young men of ability to break into politics, particularly if they stand for high moral principle and have an interest in social justice. It can be done, however, if they will fortify their souls with a definite commitment sustained by faith in Jesus Christ, whom they wholeheartedly accept as their Lord and Savior. Kirby Page and Sherwood Eddy emphasize this point in the book, *Creative Pioneers*.[7] Politics as an avocation is not only the privilege but the heavy responsibility

[7] New York, 1937, p. 50.

of every American citizen. The essence of democracy is found in the right and duty of citizens to participate in the political control of the nation. Of primary importance is the shaping of basic policies of parties and candidates.

The unquestioned integrity that is required in financial organizations must be developed in the administration of social and political life if the individual and the nation are to receive the benefits to which they are entitled.

The Christian way of life can function most effectively in politics by acting as a catalytic agent. It remains unchanged in its concern for the individual, for the creation of moral fiber, and for justice, at the same time using its great influence to create in individuals the intelligence and desire to participate in a constructive Christian citizenship. This is one of the sure ways in which the government of the people will actually become the government for and by the people. This is one of the ways to guarantee the raising up of men and women who will never permit the government to rest as long as it fails in the discharge of its duty to its Negro citizens. The government, federal or state, can prove the greatest source of oppression of Negroes or the greatest work of justice. In proportion as Christians are able to exercise a decisive influence upon the government, in the same proportion are they in a position to render the Negro minority a service of greatest significance. The difficulty in this situation is precisely the difficulty which has always faced Christians when they have confronted political power. It is a difficulty in which Negroes can find no comfort. It is a difficulty, on the other hand, before which Christian forces dare not be resigned, for to yield here is for them to yield the genius they profess and thus their very life.

5

Social Practices and the Christian Way

JAMES H. ROBINSON

F ROM preceding chapters we have seen that although there seems to be a great deal of confusion about a definitive description of Christian principles which may be applied to specific conflict situations, we are never left without a clue as to the will of God in respect to any phase of the social order. However they may try to escape, Christians may be always quite certain that God does not approve of cruel discrimination based upon racial prejudice. They may be sure that the fatherhood of God and the brotherhood of man is neither an empty phrase nor an exclusive property right. Anti-Semitism is, therefore, an "abomination" unto God. He likewise abhors the way in which any other group is mistreated in our world today or the way in which Negroes occasionally mistreat others. The central teaching of Jesus is that men may have life abundant. Consequently, the God of the Christian way desires and seeks to eliminate any social condition which prevents or impedes personal development. This Jesus taught and this was his all-consuming passion. He turned aside from his world-wide mission of building the Kingdom of God to take account of a little child, a widow, a blind man, a demented young man, and a prostitute as though the whole of his message depended upon any one of these. Jesus

97

himself was unmistakably sure that all men were fundamentally more similar than dissimilar. Jesus' actions were always consonant with the belief that all men are the potential sons of God. If anything at all in his teaching was uniquely different from that of any other religious leader, it was the idea that all men are of supreme worth in the sight of God. The Negro slave gave voice to this insight when he wrote, in the spiritual, "All God's Children Got Wings." Thus, there is a very clear frame of reference in which Christians may work out their social practices as regards race relations.

It is, indeed, a fundamental religious assumption that the will of God is relevant to all aspects of any social situation in which people may find themselves. It is not uncommon, however, to find Christians who are at variance, believing that God's will is particularly relevant to their point of view, but not to that of their opponent, unless, of course, it is related to the opposition in some condemnatory fashion. This is the frequent dilemma in race relations which makes it so easy for many Christians to justify all kinds of patterns therein and thus to make more difficult the finding of a wholesome solution. It is hard to believe that a Christian who leaves a camp meeting or a church and takes part in a lynching, in discrimination, in retreat from idealism in the face of subversive social pressure, and a Christian who courageously acts and lives with all people without prejudice and takes up the defense of minorities both draw their inspiration from the same Gospel. And yet, persons on either side are sincerely convinced that they are right and that God not only understands but also sanctions their actions. Thus we have the contrast of Christian idealism and Christian social practice.

The problem of reconciling the divergencies of social practice and the Christian ideal is not easy, as the centuries of effort and failures clearly indicate.[1] The difficulties arising out of the social patterns of life are numerous and profound. They are a part of the process of America's growth and development, and certainly they

[1] Hortense Powdermaker, *Probing Our Prejudices* (New York, 1944), pp. 7–9.

will be a part of her future.[2] Our present social practices in group relations are inextricably woven into the fabric of our American society. They stand almost like sentinels, barring the path to the application of the Christian way. One important factor often overlooked in attempts to resolve race conflict is the fact that the problems of social mores must be completely understood before they can be dealt with. Caste and class, paternalism, inferior status, segregation, laws and customs, economic exploitation, unfair publicity, unequal educational opportunities, sex prestige, the whole gamut of fears and suspicions and the various methods of controlling minority groups—these are the real culprits which make for difficulty in the realization of the Christian ideal. Christians do not live in a vacuum, but in a world of struggle and strife. The church of which they are a part is in the midst of life, not over, above, or outside it.

Since most, if not all, Christians draw the dynamic for their practices from the church, it is necessary to give some thought to the social function of the church. Again, it must be assumed that the church is an instrument for social change, inasmuch as one of its avowed purposes is the promotion of specific social causes, on the one hand, and a general criticism of all our social practices, on the other.

To begin with, the church is an institution in most practical ways like every other which has evolved.[3] We have of necessity, therefore, to define it in its sociological as well as its theological context. It is the spiritual witness to the reality of God, while being at the same time the human creation of all races, sorts, and conditions of men. The inspiration and guardian of justice, decency, righteousness, it is also an instrument controlled to a large extent by its membership. This point is very important to grasp, because when people suggest that those who do not live up to its highest ideals ought to be excluded from its fellowship, they definitely reveal their lack of real understanding of the nature of the church. Without losing sight of rigorous ideals, the church

[2] Ina C. Brown, *Story of the American Negro* (New York, 1936), p. 45.
[3] Ernest F. Johnson, *The Church and Society* (New York, 1935).

early made room within itself for different grades of members, including even those who could not sustain the full rigor of its ethic. There are two reasons why the early Christian church adopted this policy. First, all its converts were of different stations in life, different backgrounds, and different cultural patterns. None of them, as apparently is the case even now, had achieved sainthood. Second, to have excluded any would have definitely limited the possibility of having even a slight opportunity to work with many of its converts who were eventually led into a fuller acceptance of its message. Such is both the genius and the limitation of the church. This, of course, means that the church as a whole lends itself very slowly to social crusading. Nevertheless, it possesses a powerful dynamic which releases a drive in individuals who gradually, but surely, influence others. Granted that this method is necessarily painful and slow, it is nevertheless one which bears results in the long run.

The question arises, then, as to the problem of the methods the Christian society must use to influence social practices—to change bad ones and to enhance good ones. It is held by some that the function of the church in this regard is to limit itself to general principles and moral mandates. In no sense must it be concerned with particulars. Those who hold this view believe that the Christian society must not be held responsible for methods, but must supply the moral imperative. This, however, is true only in part; for the Christian society does not live and function in a vacuum. It moves amid the practical day-to-day experiences of men and women. There are times when it no doubt has no other recourse, but to say that its function must of necessity be so limited is far from the truth. Perhaps its first attack upon a given social evil will be by the application of its general principles, but it accomplishes very little until it applies these principles to particular situations. No wonder, then, that "radicals" are sometimes so impatient of the Christian way. They rightly feel, even though they are not a part of the Christian community, that the church and its adherents ought to have time for more than mere prophecy. To be sure, Christian citizenship comes only through knowledge and experimental practice. In fact, many Christians who cannot bring themselves to the point of coming to grips with the vexing problem of race confine themselves to platitudes. Their preachments have a place in the care of social practices, but these Christians must themselves be the means of producing conviction which leads to action. What they need is a true understanding of the Christian ethic and the courage to do what the art of spiritual living has shown men can do.[4] Pronouncements condemning discrimination, physical violence to minorities, indifference to the plight of the disinherited, etc., which have been passed by church councils, general assemblies, and religious associations, although they fill many volumes never accomplish their aim unless they are implemented by carefully planned action which reaches ever outward. Such is the sad story of the church in history. It is in this framework that we must work to bring social practices in line with our Christian teachings, since the church possesses only the power of persuasion. With this as a background, we may now proceed to examine the difficult and complex problems of social practices and their relationship to the Christian way.

The most characteristic feature of contemporary American life is its emphasis on caste and class. Although religious leaders, statesmen, and politicians loudly and continually disavow that caste and class play a predominant role in the American way of life, the facts indicate otherwise.[5] Cultural fragmentation and division of class cut across everything in our society. The control of the national resources in every area of endeavor is largely in the hands of the upper classes while the lower classes are forced more and more to take a subordinate place and are relatively powerless and inarticulate. Upper-class people are more homogeneous. They consult together frequently. They pool their power and their resources. They feel responsible for the whole nation, inasmuch as their vested interests are tied up in it. On the other hand,

[4] Robert E. Speer, *Of One Blood* (New York, 1924), p. 162.
[5] E. Franklin Frazier, *Negro Youth at the Crossways* (Washington, D.C., 1940), p. 12.

lower-class folk are harassed by the competition by which they attempt to rise into the upper class. They easily become the un-suspecting tool of the upper classes. The fact that good fortune smiles now and again on some immigrant or some native-born lower-class person and that he is able to rise into a higher bracket gives a false hope to the masses and keeps down social discontent. Their longing for basic security makes them unwilling to run great risks. They become distrustful of their own leaders and more trustful of friendly or sympathetic upper-class leaders. To a large degree, they do not frequently co-operate with one another and are relatively inert. Fortunately, there is a trend away from the rigidity of caste and class with the spread of education, the labor movement, the co-operative idea, and an awakened con-sciousness of the power of the masses. For the time being, how-ever, and for a long time to come, caste and class divisions are and will be one of the dominant factors in our society.

The Negro world conforms to this pattern in two ways. In the first place, it imitates every aspect of the American pattern of class. Within the Negro environment are found all the evils and the good of American life. Lines of difference are tightly drawn despite the fact that Negroes are discriminated against as a group. It must not be overlooked, nevertheless, that the white world has found it convenient to help impose its pattern on the Negro world as a means of control. To be sure, leaders of the white side of American life are most apprehensive when Negroes do not conform to this pattern and show signs of breaking away from it with the rise of the radical or people's organizations.[6] In the second place, being a minority, despised, segregated, disinherited of almost every claim and right to full citizenship, Negroes in general, despite individual achievement, are always forced to as-sume a lower-class status than their capabilities warrant. Thus, their whole existence is determined by the general pattern of caste and class in America. This is true, in varying degrees, not only of Negroes but also of other minority groups in a similar social and economic position.

[6] Brown, *op. cit.*, p. 141.

Our churches, communities, social clubs, some of our schools and colleges, our fraternities, our State Department, to some extent our Army, and to a larger degree our Navy, all reflect the caste and class inherent in our social structure. Minority groups, no less than majority groups, reflect the evil of the divisions in our culture based on origin, family, wealth, schooling, vocation, color, etc.[7] Class is divisive, not only within ethnic groups but also between groups as well. Through the centuries the structure of class and caste has been most unyielding. In fact, it is often hard to tell whether caste or Christianity has had the greater effect the one upon the other. On the whole, Christianity has had little leveling effect on caste and class. More often than not it has accommodated itself to class isolation and stratification. Caste and class have group conflict inherent within their very nature. Obviously, the Negro, the Jewish, the Oriental, and other minority worlds conform closely to the general American pattern. Usually, however, the minority group in general is forced to assume a lower-class status than that of the majority group, thereby doubly affecting the application of the Christian ethic. The caste situation, by holding down any participation and integration of minority groups, has the effect of exaggerating the whole situation and making more difficult the problem of intergroup relations. It is obvious that if the church is often divided along class lines in practice, if not in theory, it will be wholly ineffective in eradicating racial barriers, which in themselves reflect the influence of caste and class. The individual is too prone, as it is, to separate religion and life. It is relatively easy for Christians to justify, to their own satisfaction, all kinds of nefarious social practices in their lives, while at the same time vehemently expressing their espousal of religious ideals to which their practices are absolutely contrary. No one can quote the New Testament so accurately as can the average southern clergyman. Yet very few Christians feel comfortable living in such a parodoxical frame of reference. It would appear that in a good many situations there is little practical relationship between social practice and the Christian way.

[7] Gunnar Myrdal, *An American Dilemma* (New York, 1945), p. 720.

The general pattern of segregation is based, to a large extent, on caste and class. At least it can be said without doubt that caste and class lend every influence and support to the system of racial segregation and discrimination. Class and caste systems always set up rigid control and utilize all agencies of social communication and contact. This control reaches to all individuals through the medium of political, religious, economic, and educational channels. Although the problem of segregation runs counter to all Christian idealism, nevertheless the church itself not only submits to segregation but is itself a segregated institution. In fact, perhaps no segregation or prejudice is so vicious and so thoroughgoing as that sanctioned by religion and religious institutions. Under these circumstances, the larger fact is understandable, that the Christian institution is unable to criticize the state, the school, the community, the labor union, when it is guilty of the same practices. Consequently it loses one of its essential weapons; for the church should always be in the position of the judge and guide. Church bodies and boards are sometimes strong links in the perpetuation of both the general pattern and particular situations of segregation. Religious institutions could and should be among the most effective forces of integration; but, as a matter of fact, they are among the most backward in this regard. They are very definitely a part of the barriers.

Moreover, segregation creates an ever widening gulf between groups and races. This chasm breeds mistrust, suspicion, and erroneous ideas. When special barriers are erected, the soil is made fertile, and in it the sin of hasty generalization takes deep root. The lumping fallacy is encouraged. One minority person commits a crime and all members of the group bear the stigma.[8] Sooner or later, members of the majority come to feel that the minority is satisfied with a segregated society. Unfortunately, and who can blame them, many members of the minority group accommodate themselves to the situation outwardly as the most realistic adjustment possible under the circumstance, and thus the gulf becomes fixed.

[8] Libly Benedict, "The Right to Have Scoundrels," *Saturday Review of Literature,* XXVIII (1945).

If cross-fertilization of ideas is best for intergroup relations, adjustment, and happiness, then segregation prevents one of the best processes of intergroup and interracial good will, understanding, and justice. At the very outset it places an unnatural and unfair limit on the hopes and aspirations of the people who are segregated. It tends to push back the ever upward and onward thrust of life, as Bergson described it when he developed his idea of emergent evolution. Its aim is to dry up the stream of life at its very source. Contempt, unfounded in fact, is bred in the segregator and hate is inculcated in the segregated. Thus, an eternal conflict is created. It may lie dormant for a long time, but its smoldering embers often burst into violent flame, as the history of riots bears hideous testimony. In times of group conflict or crisis there is so little intergroup contact on a level of understanding that emotional tensions, biases, and brutality become rampant before even a few leaders who trust one another can be brought together to focus a common attack on the conflict.[9] Patterns of segregation and social fears are as real, if not more real, between leaders of racial and religious groups as they are on any other level of community life. There are usually few, if any, channels for normal communication among respected leaders in most communities of America. Consequently, not only is it difficult to bring tensions under control, but once they are unleashed they are not easily headed off, since the approach from both sides is hostile and suspicious.

Paternalism always follows in the train of a stratified class structure and segregation. Seldom, if ever, does it encourage the realization of full status for the group or individual toward whom it is directed. Paternalism has always been a part of American race relations. It was no doubt the Christian zeal to achieve true brotherhood which sent the missionary into the South; but in his wake rode a paternalism which never quite permitted the realization of the ideal. It is significant that schools and colleges founded by churches to bring the light of education to Negroes in darkness were with difficulty persuaded to accept Negroes on their boards and faculties long after they had demonstrated their abil-

[9] Editorial, *The Christian Science Monitor*, July 6, 1946.

ity. Paternalism seldom allows the child it nurtures to grow into full manhood. It smiles down in benevolent condescension. It does not even trust its own handiwork. Such attitudes have often led well-meaning persons to believe that the Negro has a child's mind and that therefore he needs continued guidance by someone of superior natural ability.

The climax of social and cultural division is reached when laws are enacted and enforced to buttress a class society or to establish barriers to interracial communication and social intercourse. Such laws seldom stop at the primary objects at which they are aimed. Sooner or later, they begin to expand until they circumscribe the whole of group and community life. They provided a convenient excuse for even those who would really like to see things better. Moreover, the most damnable aspect of social custom sanctioned by law is the fact that it further reduces persons and groups almost to the level of chattel. For example, in those states where there are laws against interracial marriage, the woman in the minority group is reduced to the level of a wench. She has no status whatever.

While such laws work a double hardship on a group already handicapped, they allow the so-called dominant group to perpetrate every abuse against minority persons and property with impunity.[10] Consequently, a disrespect for law is unconsciously created in the minds of the majority. It is often felt that such practices against the minority can be indulged in without having a boomerang effect on the so-called dominant group. This, however, is not the case.[11] The influence of prejudice, discrimination, and injustice on the white race has been clearly proved. Whole regions are riddled by hysteria; the church is almost helpless before every abuse of its teachings of brotherhood, tolerance, understanding, and love; there is a lowered respect for all law, order, and decency; people learn to hate with a hate so venomous that they will destroy their only library or school to send their lynch victim to a hideous death; children learn violence and perversion

[10] Edwin R. Embree, *Thirteen Against the Odds* (New York, 1944), p. 84.
[11] *Ibid.*, p. 87.

by watching and listening to their elders who thwart the law of the land by evasion and subterfuge.[12]

Justice for minorities is seldom equal and evenhanded. In cases of crime by the majority against the minority, law is often accommodated to the advantage of the majority. In cases of crime on the part of the minority against persons or property of the majority the law is frequently too harsh. Nor is decision equitable when crime is committed by minorities against members of the same group; it is usually too lenient. Obviously, this widespread practice in all parts of the nation, though it varies in degree from section to section, is a great obstacle blocking the path of equal opportunity and responsibility of individuals and groups. Unfortunately, few Christian churches do more than pass resolutions condemning these wicked practices.

Communities of a restricted nature which are largely limited to occupation by minorities are in effect ghettos, although we do not like to apply that term to such areas here in America. Nevertheless, to all intents and purposes the effect on the mind of the majority and the soul of the minority is the same as that imposed by any ghetto anywhere in the world. Circumstances are perhaps different only in that the penalty levied on members of either group for crossing the boundaries is not quite so severe.

So long as it is the practice to divide our cities by racial lines, excluding a whole group of persons irrespective of their cultural achievement, social growth, and the economic status which some of its members attain, just so long, then, do we maintain a part of the unjust foundation of the large body of social practices which make difficult the application of the Christian way. The evils which flow from restrictive communities are too obvious for enumeration,[13] but two factors are outstanding and must not be allowed to escape our attention because they are so subtle as to lie innocently beneath the surface. First, there is the hypocrisy and sophistry of those who defend residential segregation by

[12] Tom O'Connor, "Lynch Town," *PM*, August 5, 1946.
[13] R. I. Brigham, "The Price of Segregation," *Survey Graphic*, XXXV (1946), 156–188.

appealing to their rights to maintain proper standards of morals, cleanliness, or beauty surrounding their homes. This is made manifest by the undoubted fact that these same people would prefer a white or gentile neighbor who violated all their standards to a Negro or Jewish neighbor who more than measured up to their most stringent demands. There is little chance of applying Christian idealism in such a bankrupt spiritual attitude, which is characteristic of so large a section of the American scene. Second, and no less important, is the fact that segregated communities usually get a bad reputation. This rises out of the antisocial conditions under which the community lives, on the one hand, and out of unfair and unfavorable publicity, on the other hand. All ghettos and segregated communities are written and rumored about unfairly in the press, magazine stories, and other vehicles of public communication and information. People who are forced to live in such neighborhoods become ashamed of them and, quite frequently, over-apologetic for them. Moreover, members of the majority not only harbor certain fears of these localities but also find it impossible to find a decent working relationship with individuals and churches of the segregated communities.

Because of the nature of the problem, there has grown up an accompanying body of unwritten, though well understood, rules and practices for the type and methods of leadership in the field of race relations and adjustment. It is necessary to deal with these factors not only because they are a basic part of the problem but also because it will be the leadership which ultimately guides the church and the nation to a fuller realization of the Christian ideal. Such leadership practices as are now in effect are of an accommodating nature. They seldom are dynamic or aggressive in their attack upon the vicious problems of race prejudice. They constitute just one additional example of the social practices which make it so difficult for the Christian way to find full realization in the field of race relations.

IV

RESOURCES—INSTITUTIONAL

6

What Can the Church Do?

HARRY V. RICHARDSON

THE foregoing chapters have pointed out the crucial difficulty
which the race problem in America creates for Christianity.
The Christian religion predicates a universal order in which men
shall live together as sons of a common Father without distinctions or discriminations based on color or culture. To achieve this
order is the church's chief aim. Yet, despite the church's aim
and effort, race hatred, or, more accurately, group hatred has
invaded every aspect of our national living and has imbedded
itself even in the church of God. It has split our religion into the
unnatural segments of black and white. It violates our sense of
Christian brotherhood and vitiates the power of the Gospel that
we preach. By warping our judgment and blinding our vision, it
makes clear thought difficult and honest action dangerous. It
raises the severest challenge to the church, and it weakens the
capacity of the church to fight back. Group hatred stands today
as the Christian's vicious dilemma.

The preceding chapters have shown, too, the imperative need
of meeting the challenge now. To conquer race hatred is a *must*
from which there is no evasion, no escape. We must conquer it
first for the salvation of our own souls. We know now that we
cannot simultaneously love God and hate a brother. Early in its
origin Christianity affirmed that the chief expression of love for
God is in the love that we show to a neighbor. Jesus stated it
vividly in the two cardinal commandments of the Christian faith:

"Thou shalt love the Lord thy God . . . and thy neighbor as thyself." It was stated again by another early leader in different words but just as vigorously: "If a man say, I love God, and hateth his brother, he is a liar; for he that loveth not his brother whom he hath seen, how can he love God whom he hath not seen?" This is strong language, but it is clear.

Christianity from the very beginning has refused to validate itself in mystical, magical, otherworldly rites. It persistently grounds its validity in the achievement of a world brotherhood in which all men shall live as sons of God. The conquest of hateful tendencies, then, is at once the sign of the true Christian and our surest hope of salvation.

There is a second imperative reason for conquering the race problem quickly which is pressing upon us with tremendous urgency just now. The race problem in America threatens the well-being of Christianity both as a world religion and as a constructive influence in world affairs. America is today the leading Protestant power in the world. The large number of Protestants and our leading position among the nations of the world combine to make us the very center of world Protestantism. When we add to this our growing influence in Catholic affairs, we see that we shall soon be the center of world Christianity. Because of our international leadership, and because we embrace religion, our country is now the world's leading religious nation.

Because we are at the center of world Christianity, the propagation of the Christian religion will depend in large measure upon us. The funds and the strength of the missionary enterprise will come increasingly from us. Yet most of the non-Christian peoples to whom we shall go will differ in color and culture from ourselves. Until, then, we attain the capacity to live in harmony and equality with varied types of men, we shall hardly be able to carry the Gospel to those so greatly in need. We certainly will not have the moral right. And it should be added, until we master our race-hating tendencies, we shall not be missionaries of Jesus. We shall rather be what so many Americans became in the war years—spreaders of hate around the world.

A third and no less urgent reason for immediately meeting the race problem is the necessity for establishing a Christian order in the world. We have seen clearly that one of two things is going to happen to our globe. Either it will be dominated by selfish, warring power politics, with nothing but death and suffering as our common lot, or it will be governed by some kind of world order with men living in mutual respect for one another and in mutual helpfulness in every phase of national and international relations. In other words, unless the human brotherhood that Christianity envisions is made a guide for life in our time, we have little to look for save a perpetual round of exploitation, destruction, death.

To say that the Christian way needs to be established in the world is no mere platitude. There are other "isms," other ways of life which are fighting to dominate the globe. Although godless and often cruel, these other ways are open competitors of the Christian mission. As bearers of the Christian tradition, we have the inescapable duty of establishing our way in the world. We know that the Gospel is the world's one hope. We know, too, that unless it achieves a decisive victory, our competitors will drive us from the field. It is hopeless to expect a Christian order in the world unless we first can attain it at home.

In a very real sense the race problem is American Christianity's test case. The church is forced to face the challenge of "race" and as quickly as possible bring it to victorious conquest. In our pointing this out, there is no implication of shame or reproach. The conquest of evil is the high vocation to which the Christian has been set apart. It is our opportunity to lead our nation into a better way, and through our nation to lead the world. The Christian holds the vision glorious. Ours is the high, hard mission of setting this vision before the world.

But all this we know. The question before us now is *how* the problem can be met and mastered. What is the part that the church must play? It is the position of this chapter that the church as an institution and as a group of individual Christians can do as much as and probably more than any single agency in the nation to meet the problem of "race" on Christian grounds and to root it out of our national order.

For accuracy in thinking: when we speak of the church we mean not only the two great divisions of Protestants and Catholics but also the many separate bodies taken together, the denominations, which among Protestants number some two hundred fifty and more, to say nothing of the numerous smaller sects. Although differing from one another on points of faith and polity, all are committed to the one God, the one Christ, the one Gospel. All are bound to make the Gospel a living reality in God's great world. By "church" we mean further the local congregation, that working unit of the Christian faith, whose presence in a community is a sign that the Spirit of God is at work in the affairs of men. And lastly, we mean by "church" each individual Christian, whose personal action or failure to act determines the greatness or the weakness of the church.

Any thought of what the church can do must begin by considering what the church has done and what it is doing. The problem of race is not new to the church, and in various ways the church is busy.

As far as Negroes are concerned, the American race problem began with the introduction of slaves into the colonies in the year 1619. Yet very early certain elements in the church recognized slavery's un-Christian character and refused to be silenced in the face of it. They opposed slavery as an economic system and they fought especially against its cruel and inhuman aspects.

Many Quakers, for example, completely repudiated slavery and made the possession of slaves a cause for expulsion from the Societies. Many early Methodists fought the system, requiring their preachers to give up slaves or to pledge themselves not to become slaveholders. Freeborn Garretson said in 1776: "It was God, not man that taught me the impropriety of holding slaves: and I shall never be able to praise Him enough for it. My very heart has bled, since that, for slaveholders, especially those who make a profession of religion; for I believe it to be a crying sin."

Bishop Asbury records in his *Journal* in 1780: "This I know. God will plead the cause of the oppressed though it gives offense to say so here. . . . I am grieved for slavery and the manner of keeping these poor people."

A Baptist convention declared in 1789: "Slavery is a violent depredation of the rights of nature and inconsistent with a republican government, and therefore, [we] recommend it to our brethren, to make use of their local missions to extirpate this horrid evil from the land; and pray Almighty God that our honorable legislature may have it in their power to proclaim the great jubilee consistent with the principles of good policy."

We know now that the antislavery impulse which finally drove human slavery from our national economy had its genesis in the vigorous religious movements of the 1820's and 30's. Many another instance could be cited to show that whenever the earnest Christian decides to stand on his feet and make simple Christian principles a guide in his human relations, he is not a lonely pioneer. He has about him a great cloud of witnesses, strong men and women, who often through severe sacrifice have succeeded in making the Christian way a living fact.

When we turn to present efforts, we see at once that there are two main ways in which the church is attempting to get at the race problem. The first way is through ideological direction, or guidance in right thinking; the second and more limited way is through leadership in social action. We see, too, that the efforts are very varied in their scope. Some are of national, even ecumenical, proportions. Others are independent efforts by local groups.

In the effort to achieve sound racial thinking, the church has made tremendous strides in the past few years, especially since the beginning of the recent war. Particularly progressive are the recent formal statements issued by Christian groups, statements which set forth the church's own racial attitude and which also appeal to the conscience of the nation. In 1942 the First Delaware Conference at Ohio Wesleyan University declared:

We acknowledge with profound contrition the sin of racial discrimination in American life and our own share, though we are Christians, in the common guilt. So long as our attitudes and policies deny peoples of other races in our own and other lands the essential position of brothers in the common family of mankind we cannot safely be trusted with the making of a just and durable peace.

In our own country millions of people, especially American Negroes, are subjected to discrimination and unequal treatment in educational opportunities, in employment, wages and conditions of work, in access to professional and business opportunities, in housing, in transportation, in the administration of justice and even in the right to vote. We condemn all such inequalities and call upon our fellow-Christians and fellow-citizens to initiate and support measures to establish equality of status and treatment of members of minority racial and cultural groups.

We call our fellow-Christians to witness that it is in the nature of the Church that Negro men and women and those belonging to other racial and national minorities should be welcomed into the membership, administrative personnel, and fellowship of our churches, local and national. We urge individual Christians and the corporate body of the Church of Christ to take up the cross of courageous service in action which deals with the problems of race and color in our land.

In this same vein, the Friends Conference on Peace and Reconstruction at Wilmington, Ohio, in 1942, declared:

It is abundantly clear that Friends should be zealous in removing discrimination and prejudice within our own Meetings, schools, businesses and other organizations. It is our belief that in a Christian Society there is no place for prejudice or discrimination because of race or other minority status. We recommend, therefore, working with all minority groups for the fullest realization of civil liberties, for the enlargement of opportunities for education and employment, for the betterment of conditions under which we all must live. We must not slacken our efforts until the full fruits of democracy are placed within the reach of every group in this country.

The General Convention of the Protestant Episcopal church in October, 1943, issued this statement:

In loyalty to the principle, which stems from the Jewish-Christian tradition, that all mankind is one Family in God, we also advocate:

The recognition of the intrinsic worth of every person, and the right of every person without distinction because of race or color to equality of opportunity according to his capacities, insofar as this is within human control;

The application of this principle should begin at home in our dealings with other nations and races and in the treatment of our minority groups. Our own Negroes, to mention one flagrant example, are in many respects denied equality of opportunity. The Negro is not asking for charity or special privilege, but he is asking for an equal opportunity in training and work and culture to prove his worth as a man and as a citizen. It is difficult to see how Christian democracy can offer less than this. The essence of the problem is that the Negro must be treated as a man and citizen, and not as a Negro. "We are members one of another; if one member suffers all the members suffer, together."

We believe that "It is a first responsibility of the Church to demonstrate within its own fellowship the reality of Community as God intends it. It is commissioned to call all men into the Church, into a divine society and transcends all national and racial limitations and divisions."

At the Hood College Conference held in June, 1943, under the auspices of the Council of Churches and Christian Education of Maryland-Delaware and the Washington Federation of Churches, the members suggested the following statement:

That the Church give increased attention not merely to general aspects of the race problem but especially to particular phases of it discovered in individual communities.

That the privileges of membership and full participation in every Christian church be freely extended to all who profess the Christian faith, regardless of race or color.

That churches support legislation which removes arbitrary discrimination against Orientals, Negroes, or other racial groups.

Recognizing that no just and lasting peace will be possible if within national bodies inequalities based on race continue . . .

We urge that our churches exercise their maximum influence to guarantee the racial minorities in America equal and unsegregated opportunity in the economic, political, educational, and social areas of life, and that the churches, in the spirit of the action of the Delaware Conference, set the example in this matter in their own communions.

Most climactic and certainly most extensive in the number of subscribing church bodies is the statement adopted in 1946 by the Federal Council of the Churches of Christ in America, representing all but one of the major Protestant churches in the country:

The Federal Council of the Churches of Christ in America hereby renounces the pattern of segregation in race relations as unnecessary and undesirable and a violation of the Gospel of love and human brotherhood. Having taken this action, the Federal Council requests its constituent communions to do likewise. As proof of their sincerity in this renunciation they will work for a non-segregated Church and a non-segregated society.

The statement then urges the constituent bodies to eliminate segregation in church membership, fellowship, worship, service, and employment.

Statements such as these are most significant. As has already been said, they are strong appeals to the national conscience, but more than this they clarify and declare the church's own attitude on race. In a very real sense they set a psychological atmosphere in which smaller divisions of the church can think and act more freely. When a general body in an overhead declaration commits itself to a definite policy, it is much easier for a local church to undertake progressive measures. It saves an active pastor or church member from being a rebel or a traitor. To be sure, the statements are only statements. They are not yet changes in our social ways. But they do show the way we are thinking, and they point out roadways along which the sincere Christian may move.

In addition to the statements from ecumenical or overhead bodies, there have also been courageous, effective pronouncements from smaller, more local groups. An excellent example is to be seen in the action of the Methodist ministers of the Atlanta, Georgia, area. In a recent political campaign when one candidate deliberately appealed to race hatred as a method of getting votes, the Methodist ministers issued a joint resolution denouncing his method and reaffirming their allegiance to the brotherhood Christ proclaimed.

The statements from ministerial groups in many southern towns condemning the revival of the Ku Klux Klan along with vigorous sermons in the same vein all serve to make the church a vital factor in molding the national mind. In addition to those from ministers, there have also been statements from local Christian groups. Recently, in a multiple lynching in a southern town, two churches of the town in a formal protest denounced the deed and called for the apprehension of the criminals.

There are ways in which the church tries more directly to get at the ideational roots of race hate. All race prejudice is based upon suspicion, fears, misunderstandings, and little antagonisms, most of which are groundless but which persist just the same. The popular mind in America urgently needs direction here. Not only is our mind confused by the frictions that arise in the ordinary contact of diverse human groups, but we are afflicted by the professional hatemongers, the leaders of racist movements, who gain prominence and power through the dissemination of distorted ideas—men who deliberately appeal to every hating capacity within the human mind. These two forces—ordinary antagonisms and abnormally aroused fears and antipathies—keep the popular mind in a constant state of confusion and excitement giving rise to acts of meanness and oppression of which we normally should be ashamed.

The church can show the unreasonableness of these popular beliefs. It can show that the Negro is no worse and no better than any other element in the national population. It can show that he has played as vital a part in the nation's economic and cultural development as any other element. It can show that when given opportunities, Negroes do as well as anyone else. It can show that giving a colored man a decent job does not injure the social structure, neither does it presage Negro domination. It means merely the higher living of one citizen and thus a contribution to the total economic advancement. As each citizen advances, the whole society does, too.

The church can help by showing that Negroes do not want to dominate the nation. They want only to be good citizens, with all the rights and responsibilities that good citizenship entails. Many churchmen today recognize this, but the truth is so widely distorted by professional haters and by a heritage of distorted beliefs that it needs constant reiteration.

We recognize the effort which the church now makes to clarify our thinking along these lines. Many denominational publications devote issues or articles to the problem. Youth literature, Sunday school materials make earnest attempts to disseminate sound ideas. Several of the major bodies have interracial commissions or staffs of paid workers whose duties are to promote clearer understanding in matters of race. The Federal Council of Churches maintains a Race Relations Department; a "Brotherhood Sunday" is observed once a year. Interracial meetings among young people, exchanges of choirs and pulpits are attempts on the part of the church to tear down the structure of race prejudice.

The second way in which the church attacks the race problem is through leadership in Christian social action. That is, the church not only strives to direct our thinking, but also seeks to lead men in doing the things that will achieve a social order in keeping with the will of God. Perhaps it should be said that the efforts in social action are not so uniform or effective as in the realm of ideas.

Quite properly, the church's first act should be to purge its own body of prejudiced, discriminatory ways. Until this is achieved the church is limited in its attack on outside evils. Most of the major denominations practice segregation in local churches, in church hospitals, church schools, and even in theological seminaries. But we have already seen that the church is now conscious of these social sins. Here and there throughout the Christian body attacks are being made against these practices. In most cases the attacks are local and independent. In all cases they are brave. For example, one of the nation's leading denominations has elected a Negro president of its national conference on Christian education. The Federal Council of the Churches of Christ elected a Negro to a vice presidency. A few openly interracial churches have been organized across the country. One old, established church in a large city, upon finding its neighborhood invaded by an influx of Negroes, did not move away or close its doors but opened them to the newcomers and invited them into full membership.

A church in a southern city faced the challenge of welcoming Negro Christians into its services. It first moved to take them in. Later on, it changed the rule to let them sit anywhere in the church, although the state has a segregation law for all public assemblies. Finally, the pastor, officers, and members—not without pain and trouble—wrote into the rules of the church that Negroes could join the church on the same basis as all its white communicants.

A group of Christians from two suburban towns in New Jersey established a scholarship for worthy Negro boys and girls. They widened the circle to include all the groups in each church. They went farther to invite other Negro churches, and finally brought other white churches into the plan. This plan was undertaken first of all because it met a real need; second, because it offered an opportunity for study and education on the race problem; third, it made people conscious of their social responsibility; and fourth, it brought both groups face to face for conversation, corporate planning, and mutual action on a common problem.

There is increasing co-operation between white and colored ministerial associations all over the country. Progress is particularly noteworthy in the South, where segregation and separation have been practiced most vigorously. In one southern state a white denominational ministerial association has invited colored ministers of the same faith to join in full membership.

In social action outside itself, the church is becoming increasingly active. The writer recently attended a joint meeting of the white and colored ministerial alliances in a small South Carolina town. He found that the two alliances met together once each month to talk over common community problems. Following the meetings a united approach was made to the town's governing officials. As a result, much had been done to get fair and effective law enforcement, to clean up vice, and to promote the welfare of all elements in the city's population.

In three cases, according to the writer's knowledge, white and colored ministers have joined in organizing local interracial committees. The local bodies have done much in their towns to improve conditions, to ease tensions, to secure better living conditions for disadvantaged groups.

There are cases, too, in which laymen of the church have been active. Some laymen in a border city went to their pastor just to say they would support him if he would lead out against a group of property owners who were blocking a low-cost housing project in a borderline community. The housing was sorely needed by both whites and Negroes, but was opposed because Negroes were to be included in some of the units. He was reluctant. They came back again with more members, but the minister still hesitated. They formed their own committee and two ministers from two other denominations came forward. The project, which has been held up for three years, after a long and almost agonizing struggle went through.

The operator of a large hotel steadfastly refused to discharge his colored workers simply because they were colored and replace them with white, although considerable pressure was brought upon him. He was a sincere Christian, and he refused to be beaten into an un-Christian act.

These are all noble instances of Christian social action. They testify that at least some elements in the church are at work on the stubborn problem of race. But it is readily seen that they are local and often lonely. They are not yet the work of the church as a whole. And they leave one with a disturbing sense of insufficiency. There are so many points in our national life where the influence and leadership of the church are sorely needed, and yet at these points one sees little if any church activity at all.

Take, for example, the matter of the administration of justice, either in the courts of a city or in the county courts of a small southern town. It is regrettable but true that in almost any session of these bodies one can see all of the injustices which the prophet Amos so bitterly decried and which he predicted would mean the ruin of the civilization. Here the poor, and particularly the colored poor, are robbed openly with little hope of redress. They are fined and jailed often in defiance of law. Right or wrong, a Negro's word has little weight against a white opponent's. And if the Negro insists on the right of his cause, as opposed to a white man's, he is often violently treated. On the other hand, cases in which only Negroes are involved are handled frivolously, without regard to justice or proper correction. Sheriffs, lawyers, citizens often lie unashamedly to "rob the poor for a mess of pottage."

As guardian of the morals of a community, the church cannot look with indifference upon these centers of injustice and wickedness. Yet at the present time the influence of the church in this area of race is very slight. If a victimized Negro appeals to a local white minister for aid, he usually finds the minister evasive, timid, unwilling to interfere in an area which he says is not "religious." Recently in an interracial ministers' meeting a colored pastor complained about the unjust handling of Negro cases in the local court. A white minister stated in reply that, although he was ashamed of it, he had to admit that the white ministry had little influence around the county courts.

It has been said before that evil knows no bounds. It starts with the exploitation of Negroes, but it grows in the immorality of public officers. Thus many a small town finds itself under the tyranny of a handful of corrupt officials, who know no standard save their own satisfaction and respect no right save that of some power more selfish and brutal than themselves. This is the most serious threat to sound democracy; it is the most open challenge to Christian ethics and the Christian church. In the interest of local and national morals, in the interest of Christianity in our land, the church needs to be aware and alive.

Recently in southern politics two men campaigned for high political offices on racist, white-supremacy platforms. One ran for governor of his state, the other for United States senator. Both won. Both will give to southern politics a measure of cheap, demagogic political leadership. Both espouse a social order which is antagonistic in every essential to the Christian way. Christians as individuals and as a church cannot escape either responsibility for or the effects of the character of their government. Politics is not an interest apart from all religious concern. It is either moral or unmoral, fair or dirty. It affects both the welfare and the souls of citizens. Our children, for example, grow up under the influence of the government. Their ideas of political honesty, statesmanship, and democracy are formed as much from what they see as from what they may read in a textbook on civics. To any matter of morals or social welfare can the church be indifferent or blind?

Another area in which the influence of the church is much needed but little felt is that of our economic order. Other parts of this book have pointed out the terrible disadvantages suffered by Negroes and other minority groups. In many fields they cannot get jobs at all; in others they are employed only at low and unfair rates of pay. To deny any group honest work and fair pay is not only immoral, it is almost murderous. It is deliberate strangulation of the physical and cultural development of the victims. It is a direct cause of poverty, ignorance, and disease and all the social evils that go with them. Few practices are more detrimental to our national welfare than the discriminations with which the economic order is rife. Few practices are more thoroughly sinful. Yet in the economic area of the American race problem, the church has hardly begun to speak.

This hurried review of the church and the race problem finds that the church is awake and at work. It is particularly active in an ideological direction, that is, in helping us to think straight in matters of race. It is declaring its own position with increasing courage and it speaks to the national conscience with increasing strength. In social action the church is purging its own body of racial discrimination and, in scattered, independent attempts, it is beginning to offer leadership in Christian social action.

Our review finds on the other hand that the church's attack on the race problem is confronted with certain immediate needs. Chief among these is to recognize the crucial, the terrible potentialities of the struggle in which the church is engaged. Christianity is at war. It is at war against selfish, vicious, exploitative tendencies which are determined to have their way and which, if they get their way will destroy every single value that the Christian religion stands for. If the un-Christian tendencies dominate our national life, the human brotherhood that Christianity envisions will become a ridiculous memory, and an act of simple Christian kindness may become a cause for death. This is no scarehead prophecy. It has happened in other nations. It can happen here.

It is imperative that the Christian recognize the strategic importance of race hate in the struggle. Race hatred or group hatred is the chief weapon in the arsenal of antichrist. Through manipulation of this weapon, the professional haters are able not only to win the non-Christians who represent half our nation but to split and weaken the church itself. To break down hatred is no easy task for the church. It is the first step in the church's strategy.

For, indeed, hatred invades every aspect of our living. It must be fought on every field. The church needs, then, a program of social action suited to the many areas of life—social, political, cultural, economic.

One Christian leader has recently recommended that there be organized

in every local church, every denominational and every interdenominational body a social study and social action group by whatever name it might be called. . . . A striking instance of this idea on the denominational level is the recent Department of Race Relations established by the American Missionary Association of the Congregational Christian Church, with Dr. Charles S. Johnson as director. The Society of Friends has long included among its agencies a Race Relations Committee. . . . State and local interdenominational bodies should have their special social action committees, at least a part of whose functions would be to concern themselves with problems of race relations.

A second need in the church's approach to the race problem is a vigorous crusading outreach. At the present time the church's efforts are directed largely to its own membership. This is quite proper, but we must not forget that only half of America's population are church members. It is the nonchurch half that constitutes the fertile ground for un-Christian practices and ideas. The church's program, therefore, must be directed to that non-Christian, nonchurch half.

It has also been pointed out recently that the role of the individual Christian is important. Resolutions by bodies are significant, but strong, active individuals are important, too. This is a third great need. To quote again:

> The individual Christian in his daily walks and talks can wield a revolutionary influence upon our pattern of life. If tomorrow millions of church members should begin to act personally toward colored men and women as if they were men and women, not colored men and women, the face of Negroes and of our country would light up as if a new sun had appeared in the heavens. If to any one the great changes of which we speak do not now seem possible, then let him set about practising the humbler virtues of courtesy and righteousness in personal relations. That is part of the miracle-making power we seek. Whoever follows such a course can do so with the satisfaction that if it does not bring immediately the National salvation he seeks, it will have the virtue of helping to save his own soul.

Throughout this chapter we have spoken repeatedly of the need for action in the problem of race. The words are not spoken lightly. We are mindful of the price that those must pay who act. It will be high in inconvenience, in unpopularity, sometimes in sheer physical danger. Recently a prominent church leader upon his return from a tour of Russia gave a public address in which he commended certain phases of Russian life. As he was speaking inside two men outside were bearing placards reading: "We are against Communism. We are for 100% white Democracy!" Here was open defiance, not only of opinion, but of a Christian leader as he worked for international good will.

This little event symbolizes the struggle that is now descending upon the Christian church. We are no longer able to preach the milder elements of the Christian Gospel to a world that is quietly neutral. We are at war with flagrant, vicious un-Christian forces. And there can be for us no retreat. If antichrist wins, the church dies. We cannot be a sheltered, retired group, chanting and singing on sequestered corners in a world that the devil runs. Our way of life must be the dominant way here in America as elsewhere, or our way will go. But given intensification of the present church activity, we know that the way of Christ will win.

7

The Role of the Christian College

WILLIAM LLOYD IMES

W E ARE assuming that the Christian college is the church-related college, or its equivalent. The tradition of such a college is that of the higher learning in the arts and sciences, presented together with the ideals of a humane Christian culture, without any prejudice against the applied arts and sciences or against technical and vocational education. The function of a Christian college is not to pose as superior because of its church-relatedness, but rather to act as a leavening power in the mass of the educational life of the day, so that Christ's ideals and conduct and character may become normative.

With these presuppositions, let us go at once into the problem of such a college as it faces the exceedingly vexing problem of the American color line. This complex is not the only maladjustment the Christian college must face, nor is it the only racial difficulty facing the college. It is rather merely one among many social wrongs that cry for redress. It is symbolic of the terrible and extravagant lengths to which the tyranny of prejudice may and does go, whether based upon race, complexion, culture, occupation, religion, or any other distinction. It is the irony of history—not to say of Western civilization—that the very places and people who have shouted loudest for freedom and brotherhood have exhibited the most appalling reaction against those very desirable ideals in human progress by setting up new despotisms in place of the old ones.

What, then, is this role of the Christian college? Or, at the outset, should a college ever be termed Christian? One commentator raises the question: "Does the Christian college have a role that may not be filled by any college?" Our definition we hope is inclusive in this matter, but it is just as well to face the possibility of ambiguity at once. It ought to be true that any college could provide the moral and spiritual leadership that we expect of a "Christian" college, but the fact is that neither secular nor Christian colleges measure up to what is expected by way of moral and vitally religious results. This is not to introduce a pessimistic note before all the facts are presented, but to make a sober and realistic approach to any appraisal of college influence and achievement. That the college has been a very real instrument in the transmission of culture is scarcely open to question, but that this culture has been always moral and religious in aim, even when the college was church-related and church-controlled, may be seriously questioned. It is not our aim to take a partisan view here, but to describe what is actually happening and to let the clear picture stand forth. Nor is this primarily a critique of the church-related college, as such. Our effort is to show that the Christian college has a mission and, without assumption of superiority or apology for its spiritual and religious purposes, to show that it is endeavoring to fulfill a needed task within the field of education. Its real function is to help in the education of the whole personality, so that moral and religious purposes may not be divorced from the total culture.

The Christian college has a tradition and a historical development which will be sketched briefly later, but now we shall take a somewhat careful view of the possibilities and desirabilities related to the above-mentioned function of such a college.[1]

The suggestion should be carried out of teaching the demo-

[1] See the article by President Ralph W. Lloyd in *Christian Education*, XXIX (1946).

cratic way of life both by indoctrination and by college organization to exemplify the virtues and social excellences of democracy.
This, it is true, does not equate democracy with Christianity, but
it must never be forgotten that our best convictions and practices
of democracy sprang out of the Christian tradition and the Christian way of life. Then, further, tactics of social procedure would
follow naturally, so that the planning would be in accordance
with a sound experience in the religious and moral nature of
man. Projects would be undertaken to promote both human welfare and the gathering of new knowledge. Tests and comparisons
naturally would be constantly carried out, in line with the foregoing principles, and when applied to specific and urgent social
problems, such as race relations, the results would be invariably
richer, more vital, and lasting. This kind of experimentation is
constantly being carried on in many colleges, not only in those
recognized here as Christian. The Christian institutions, however, are proving exceptionally fruitful areas for such investigation. The intensely social nature of the inquiry leads us to believe that church-relatedness is not a handicap to the recognition
of the true nature of a college, but is actually a help to the impartial and purposeful study of the life and work of the college.

   The Journal of Educational Sociology, in its issue of April,
1946, publishes a symposium entitled "The Negro College—Its
Place in Democracy."[2] One of the finest emphases in this com-
pendium is a statement in its foreword by Dan W. Dodson, the
managing editor. It is worth quoting: "In the long range, we all,
no doubt, look forward to the day when there will be no more
Negro colleges; that will be only after the evil of segregation has
been removed from our society."[3] Here is one great moral problem, the so-called race problem, handled as it ought to be—
frankly, decently. The type of man who does and says such things
is very likely to be the man produced by our Christian institutions. The moral and religious responsibility that rests upon the
Christian college is therefore clear. Surely we of the Christian

----

[2] *The Journal of Educational Sociology,* XIX (1946).
[3] *Ibid.,* p. 461.

tradition not only should produce such leaders for secular positions, but should make our Christian organs of opinion and instruments of social action thoroughly Christian in word and deed.

The foundations of our great colleges and universities, the Oxfords and Cambridges, the Harvards and Yales of the Western world, have all been laid in the church. These institutions were literally founded for the purpose of supplying a godly and learned leadership for the perpetuation of the Christian faith. They became more and more independent and secular with the growth of modern ideas and particularly with the material counterpart in mechanical inventions and the consequent industrial revolution.

These factors had been bred of the church, yet some became a part of the attempt to destroy the very source and substance of their life and growth. The strangest reversals in history have been these: (1) the denial of Christian contributions to our modern secular culture; (2) the change of the afore-mentioned crusade for freedom and brotherhood, which were distinctly Christian ideals, made possible by the genius of our faith, into a reaction of privilege. Such a crusade should have remained the primary struggle of all significant spiritual forces everywhere.

The church, then, must grapple with these paradoxes of history. The life of the church is both temporal and spiritual; and, being "in the world yet not of the world," the church is required to deal with these reversals and confusions because of its vantage point in time and history. It has a message and purpose that transcend both. If the church college is born of the Christian church and is a part of its very life, it should have the beginning of the answer to the antagonism between an honest religious basis of education and the theories of secularism that have all but swept the educational field. Here the definition of religious basis is important. It means, as opposed to secularism, the frank avowal of and dependence upon a higher and holier Power than nature or than human nature offers. There are many ways of approach to the Power, but all lead to the same end: " 'Tis God Himself may be had for the asking."

A spiritual approach through education becomes a blessing in that it gives the motivation and the power for the pursuit of a worthy end. Further, if any argument were seriously needed for a religious basis of education, it would be found completely in the aims of true education, for the word "education" implies the "drawing out" of the hidden stores of ability, character, and the whole of the inner life of a human being. Indeed, secular education does not really exist, since man himself is not secular. He is secular plus. He is something more than all the world of his physical environment. He feels his dignity when he aspires to know both that world and the world beyond the visible, where purpose and meaning, rather than the minutiae of the daily round of sense impressions and expressions, become a quest. The truism that man is incurably religious is profoundly experienced in this inevitable swing toward a higher-than-mechanical, higher-than-animal life. Here we are on solid ground for a religious basis of education.

Now, what is the bearing of this upon the problems of races? At the very start we see the shallowness of the creed of the racists in our world history. The protagonist of racism is at heart a most arrogant secularist, although he may piously wrap the cloak of sanctity about himself. It is, indeed, one of the surest marks of the baseness of any way of life that it seeks to mask its real purpose in the garb of holiness. The racist pretends to believe that one race, usually his own, is better than all others. In fact, he often goes so far in his system of racial purity as to question whether other groups are quite human. The more we learn of races, the more we discover that the likenesses in all races are far more striking and constant than all their differences. We learn, further, that their differences only complement one another, suggesting that all the existent types reflect the intention of nature, not to speak of the Divine Nature, that there should be a variety in the body of witnesses to the worthfulness and dignity of the human spirit. A religious philosophy would use some such term as brotherhood to describe this. It is not a matter of ethnology or sociology, purely; it is rather a matter of conviction of the invio-

late character of all of human life. The college that has its
grounding in genuine religion can never remind itself too often
that to keep that religion true and vital it must recognize and exalt
both knowledge and love.

Granted that the college has such a religious basis, what is it
able to do regarding our selfish and competitive world order?
Surely the college is not so obtuse that it does not see that much
of its support in money, influence, power has come from those
who are pretty well in the forefront of the system of competitive
strife. The older scientific theories, following the lead of the idea
of the survival of the fittest, superficially appeared to justify the
world of competitive struggle. Such findings, however, as those in
the monumental work of Prince Kropotkin, *Mutual Aid,* place
the emphasis upon the survival of the best, that is, of those who
serve their purpose in mutual helpfulness wisely and well.

The best education that we know today, like the best of prophetic high religion, is quite sure that the old way of competitive
strife is finished. It is outmoded and outdated. Competition is
quite honorable, but what has lately been masquerading as competition is only a modern wolf in sheep's clothing. It is a sign of
intellectual or moral ignorance to advocate "free competition" unless it is known to be really free and really competitive.

The racists always look for moral allies and find them with un-
erring instinct. "The man who hates others because of their poverty is also capable of hating because of color," said an acquaint-
ance of mine years ago when we were crusading against racism
in one of America's great cities. It is quite the logic of things to
begin by hating a man for one thing and to end up by finding
many other things make us dislike both that man and others, too.
Hatreds never run singly; they go in devilish and deadly packs.
And racism is easily pulled in to the pack of human enemies
which are created by an evil and selfishly competitive order.

The college can lend itself to no better task than to help prepare young people to live as human beings, to love as brothers
and sisters should, and to fear nothing save deceit in their own
hearts. If, as the climax of its disciplines in the arts, sciences, and

languages, the college can and will exalt such a task, though infinitely difficult, it will prove the most enduring and ennobling
experience of all educational life. Without it, the future of education is dark; with it, at least we can go forward with hope.

Every place which attempts to impart knowledge at all undertakes the relating of means to ends. If we feel it is not worth
while to work for ends that are beyond the present selfish struggle, then we begin to lose the very near and petty gains that we
think we have. The college that thinks it can go secular is only
deceiving itself. Its truest life is in that area in which high and
holy ends replace the smug and selfish ambitions continually
clamoring for recognition but somehow never getting us anywhere.

The editor of the recently published symposium, *The Christian Answer,* suggests a number of questions that ought to sober
the Christian college and its proponents. They also should sober
many others who may not be willing to label themselves as Christians but who want a better life if they can find it. The questions
are: (1) Why take Christianity seriously? (2) Is Christian belief
intellectually credible? (3) What does Christianity propose?
These questions bear the stamp of their own importance to our
heritage and practice of faith. I shall not discuss them from the
standpoint of theological definition or development, but only in
the light of their unified impact upon the very stubborn reversals
and paradoxes described earlier in this chapter. If, in the Christian way of love in race relations, we have had so many experiences of the lag between belief and practice, is there not something almost inevitably suspect with such a faith? The reply is
not easy, and one cannot laugh the cynic out of court because he
gags at a religion that professes the most creeds, loyally performs
the most elaborate rituals, and yet would not admit a Negro
or Chinese or Mexican to the same Lord's table on equal terms
with the white Christians.

Here it is not the stubbornness of an intellectual process with
which we deal. The devotee does take his Christianity seriously,
but he has never probed deeply enough to find the reason for his

allegiance. He believes also that Christianity is intellectually credible, but he has seldom understood how that mental process is shot through and through with the richness and coloring of human values that transcend material gain or prejudices, or pride based upon such gain. He avers, too, that Christianity has a new kind of world order to offer, the Kingdom of God, but somehow it, too, is a rather narrow and patrician Kingdom, and the plebeians and rabble and outcasts are not there. He does not explain why they are not there, and where they are if not there. He calmly assumes that this order is intended to be white, gentile, and Protestant. One thing above all others Christianity does propose—and if we really believe it, we must take it wholeheartedly or we cannot take Christianity at all. This is its twofold proposition, which is also a paradox, namely, that he who would save his life must lose it, but he who dares to lose it will abundantly find it. I have chosen this deliberate antithesis of Jesus because of its startling and relevant significance for us in a world so bent on gain.

If I make myself secure with power, goods, and prestige, I lose my life. Is not that kind of drama inevitably unfolding itself before us in our world? And the world of education is not hidden from such a spectacle. Indeed, education of the right sort brings out the contrast in bolder relief. The college must not turn away from the spectacle, but must sharply focus upon it. If life is an adventure of no small moment, then the college has no higher function than to prepare personalities to take that adventure in high spirit, with undaunted courage and faith to discern the wisdom of the way that dares defy the laws of self-seeking. Here is the justification of the college's contribution—a far greater one than the development of intellect. It is the business of the Christian college to avoid the errors of cultural institutions which tend to think of their existence and perpetuation as more important than the social function they perform in the world. The best college is within the hearts of those who carry out its purposes and ideals. Buildings, land, endowments, personnel, and product are not enough to make for the outward or apparent permanence that human vanity seems to demand. When the graduates of any institution come back for reunion, they are strongly tempted to feel that old buildings and landmarks are slowly being superseded by newer arrangements and facilities, and that the old, which is sentimentally dear to them, is doomed to destruction. On the other hand, new plans should be regarded as necessary in revealing progress and in helping toward higher ratings by the educational agencies. But a candid view of both the sentimental and the modern progressives' judgments concerning the college will reveal that neither the one nor the other can save it. If the college would save its life, it must lose it deliberately in this self-education of all that it has to a higher and holier end.

It is also the business of the Christian racial college to see that it works itself out of a job.[4] There is a certain vanity about even the best racial college that betrays and cheapens real education. After the fires of the Civil War had died down, the home missionaries from nothern churches and colleges who came South and began their educational task had, of course, a dilemma to face. Should they attempt to build of the freedmen and free men of color a separate world of things, or should they integrate them into the total pattern, letting these folk of African background and of more recent American folkways render their gifts to the whole of American culture? The results of their choice are illuminating and far-reaching. In most instances, their choice largely was the former of the two strategies. They strove to help the black man build up a separate black world, and through the combination of many factors the outcome has been a tragic and confused century of race relations. It followed upon, and in turn strengthened, the arrogance of reconstruction and reaction in the seventies and eighties and thereafter. On the other hand, it contributed to the black man's sense of suspicion and despair. All of this contains a lesson for the contemporary Christian college.

The Christian segregated college has no more excuse for existence than a racial nation. The excesses of nationalism and false

[4] *Ibid.*

patriotism are quite of a stripe with the spurious doctrines that races thrive best where they can maintain racial purity. Recent anthropology has knocked the pet theories of the racists quite askew. It now remains for Christian educators to proceed to the realization of a democratic world order with the religious sanctions that undergird the principles of that order. Here is one of the greatest tasks of both college and church.

There have been beginnings, both in America and in the world at large, of experiments in collegiate racial contacts. They are not many in number, nor do they go into the matters of race or class adjustments as far as we might wish, but, on the whole, they are prophetic of a better world. Antioch College, Oberlin College, Bates College are among the institutions which have a wholesome interracial record and may be mentioned with some pride. Berea College of Kentucky, before the obnoxious laws in education in that state, did a remarkable job of interracial and intercultural training.

In the world at large, such experiments as the College of Beirut, Robert College, of Constantinople, the University of Cairo point in the direction of interracial and interclass education, with abundant examples of crossing of all caste and class barriers. A member of the faculty of Beirut College was active, not many years ago, in helping student and faculty groups plan a scholarship for a student from the far interior of Africa, which is testimony to the desire for racial fellowship and understanding. These are but beginnings and we are aware of their infant proportions, compared with the need for broad and complete integration of human relationships on the high levels of strong education and prophetic religion. One rather bold educational experiment is under way right in the South through the Fellowship of Southern Churchmen. One of the very finest ventures in interracial comradeship was the project, supported by this Fellowship, to assemble an interracial personnel of students to go on the cattle boats to Europe during the summer of 1946. Even in these difficult and tragic times for our European neighbors, we of

America must not fail in our witness that we can and will live like brothers. This is essential if we are to preach the gospel of peace to other nations in a troubled time.

Shall the Christian college frankly make it one of its cardinal points of policy to have its personnel, both student and faculty, interracial? It does not seem possible to have any other ideal, for what can we say if the colleges that profess Christian creeds, stressing the brotherhood of man, do not dare to live up to those creeds? In the face of hostile public opinion, and particularly where this opinion is crystallized into law, it is imperative that all who have any voice in the administration of colleges make themselves heard on this and all related questions which affect brotherhood and democracy. The college has a most serious responsibility and there is no turning back. Either we go forward with those who have before our generation paid the price of progress in sacrifice of reputation and even life or we plunge into a chaos of doubt, despair, and destruction. For instance, the newspaper and radio are telling of the rebirth of Klan activities in many communities.

What shall we say concerning that most necessary part of the college's responsibility—preventive work in the community in which it has its location? The college has such an opportunity. Just now the most outspoken witness in college communities may be found in centers like Atlanta, with its Atlanta University System; Nashville, with its Student Center at Fisk University and the tie-up with near-by socially-minded colleges like Scarritt College; and the University of North Carolina, with its noteworthy efforts by professors and students to make studies of the Negro an integral part of its social studies and services. These centers are not by any means adequately developed, but they are the beginning of a social experimentation fostered by college people and there is genuine concern on the part of the more thoughtful of both races that such effort shall be continuous, and not abortive. Hand in hand with the studies we somewhat loosely call the humanities, there are applications of the findings and convictions regarding brotherhood, justice, mutual appreciation, and co-operation. It is true that if colleges do not find expression, even in small beginnings, for the ideals they hold in classroom theory and discussion, our Christian ethic will remain feeble and fruitless. It is now accepted by many colleges that continuation of our American way of life is dependent upon our willingness to take seriously the duty and privilege of educated folk to lead in wise and bold action, not in the spirit of bitterness toward those who may not agree with our social ethic or who may distort the Christian ethic to their own prejudices. The college has a tremendous advantage here, for it is predicated upon the search for truth and cannot lightly dismiss its responsibility for living and witnessing to that truth, cost what it may.

Something else is happening. There are several centers of learning in the northern states, notably the University of Wisconsin, Antioch College, and Harvard University, that include competent Negro instructors and professors on their faculties. The pattern at first was on the use of such teachers as specialists in Negro life or on matters strictly pertaining to racial and interracial subjects. Now the three colleges mentioned happen to have these Negro teachers in the fields of philosophy, library science, and medicine. A Negro teacher who is not competent to teach in any college is not fit to teach in a Negro college. It will require far more interpenetration of this principle than now is apparent to win a decisive victory over the wrong folkways that have grown up in this land as a result of human slavery and its doctrines of racial inferiority and superiority. But certain colleges have been ready to acknowledge ability in many cases, even when the outside world, always affected by a moral lag, has been slow and hesitant in both its thinking and its doing. The opinion is hardly debatable that of all instruments in our human society fitted to undertake this moral and social reform, the college, next to the church and as a child of the church, is most appropriate.

There is the function of guidance in the cases of recurring tensions that affect all communities, especially when such tensions arise as a result of antisocial practices. People do listen with respect to what educators have to say, even if they are slow in understanding or in being willing to do the difficult things that are prescribed. Here guidance by the college becomes a prime responsibility, for the community will not feel that an educational institution is purely partisan in its stand. The guidance might take several directions. One possibility in most communities is the public forum, in which difficult and controversial subjects can be aired by public assembly, press, radio. Here is where the religiously motivated and controlled school can do its best work. Its plan of guidance can and should be set strongly in the nature of a twofold emphasis, so that the moral life is shown to be related to the search for truth.

There should be greater provision for exchange of students and teachers of differing ethnic and cultural groups. Here we point with hope and expectancy to the work of a few forward-looking agencies like the Bureau of Intercultural Education and also to governmental interest in the sending of such exchange scholars on both undergraduate and professional levels to other lands. One such group was selected by the Department of State in 1946, and it is expected that all institutions of learning will in time be able to provide for their constituents these broadening contacts.

One of the vital and pressing problems of our immediate present and future is that of preventing war. Here is a method that is guaranteed success in furthering the prevention of misunderstanding and prejudice. If the students of our modern world can know one another and if their teachers can know their colleagues in other lands, it will be worth the cost. It is good politics; it is also good education and good morals. And while we are forming committees in our various welfare organizations to prevent such social outrages in the economic structure as the infamous restrictive covenants in housing areas and residential arrangements that foster separation of races and classes, we might well pay attention in our educational foundations and boards of control to the restrictions that often creep into our acceptance of bequests or grants and gifts for such work. It is not too long ago, in Philadelphia, that an educational foundation perpetrated the scandal of providing in its charter for the prohibition of clergymen or Negroes from entering the institution sponsored by the foundation.

What is needed, of course, is both immediate and long-range action with respect to such matters. The very life blood of a college is its freedom in the search for truth. Learning that does not provide for growth in intercultural matters will inevitably become sterile and vicious. Far better to have no formal education at all than to have an education prostituted to prejudice and one in which the very teaching process warps the souls of its students. Benefactors should take pride in the widest possible use of the benefits they offer, since they cannot know when a great leader may emerge out of any race or class. One of the surest ways of securing a strong and wise use of resources is by the education of givers and prospective donors so that they will know the social objectives of real education and be guided against the perpetuation of any private notions that hinder fullest brotherhood. And here, as in other areas, the Christian college has a definite and peculiar responsibility. It can, if it will, influence those who have the means to give so that they will give wisely, democratically, and with full knowledge of the highest social objectives to be gained.

It is important, not in a perfunctory but in a very serious manner, to become acquainted with the rich variety of gifts that all classes of humanity may bring to the sum total of educational life. Some beginnings in this have been mentioned, but here it is necessary to add that the college must be aware of the opportunities for growth and knowledge in this field. A movement is now on foot in the South to study regional resources and relate the colleges of learning to them. These are no longer thought of as merely material, but as spiritual too. Until the college relates its life to all available opportunities for variety and abundance of cultural gifts, its education will remain poor and powerless. The study of chemistry is good, but its relation to human needs is even better, and the fact that a black chemist in a southern college could astound the world with his synthetic products from clay, sweet potato, and peanut makes one wonder what might not have happened if he had done his work with utmost co-operation from all other chemists, regardless of race or class. By their interpenetration of ideas and ideals they might well have made "the desert blossom as the rose." It is for such a cause as this that the true college exists, and it will never find its true life until it loses itself in co-operative endeavor. This is Christian idealism and is the heart of our Christian Gospel put into the body of humanity.

8

The Role of the Young Men's Christian Association

FRANK T. WILSON

W E ARE in the midst of a search for tools suitable for the task of far-reaching social reconstruction. Immediately at our disposal are traditional institutions and agencies upon which we have relied to soften many of our social conflicts and to resolve many of our social dilemmas. The search becomes more desperate and the prospect of discovering adequately fashioned instruments seems less promising as we view our present institutional resources in the light of the dimensions and difficulty of the racial factor in the current social situation.

In dealing with the more delicate problems of human relationships in American society we have the tendency to assume that certain organizations, public and private, lay justifiable claim to the confidence and loyalty of the people in spite of the unconvincing character of institutional behavior. The degree of hesitation to trust these agencies to lead us forward into the future is measured by the discrepancy between profession and practice in the espousal of freedom, equality of opportunity, and the right of democratic participation in every aspect of the programs, activities, and services of these agencies. Beyond the expected consistency between "actual" and "ideal" within a specific organization there is the further requirement for harmony between the pattern of its activity within a community and its verbalized social message to that community.

Although there is going on at the present time much critical appraisal of the philosophies and practices of many social and religious bodies, one is warranted in the belief that the future of such bodies will not be greatly unlike their past unless alterations in basic outlook and modifications in historic methods are far more drastic than institutional self-interest is likely to permit. In this connection the chief problem lies in the choice between maintaining mere structure or effecting such changes as would result in appropriate services to society at this crucial period in our national history. The rigidity of old and familiar forms is a serious impediment to creative confrontation of the conditions that challenge our resourcefulness and courage in the present period of our existence. Outworn forms and antiquated ways of thinking have a way of persisting far beyond the day of their utility as means of individual development or social growth. As we look toward the future in matters involving group relations in the United States, we must struggle against the tendency to believe, or to fear, that the crust of custom is more powerful than man's determination to make the forms of life serve the ends that are revealed in a careful consideration of the meaning and purpose of life.

The career of an organization is determined as much by the decisions of those persons to whom the destiny of the organization is entrusted as by the external forces which provide channels for the expression of its interests. The real desires of men set the goals and give direction to the methods and techniques by which commonly held ends are to be achieved. The surrounding culture provides a medium for purposeful activity and furnishes resources for the fulfillment of specific human needs. The values and ideals held in common by a voluntary association of mature individuals constitute the fundamental bases of judgment by which the quality of practical performance may be tested. Yet beyond this internal measuring rod there is an overarching body of enlightened opinion and pressure of historic events which pronounce doom upon any structure that refuses to yield to the expanding energies of the life impulse. Old encrustments are ripped asunder by the dynamic power of new demands. The frozen logic by which obsolete structures were defended is shattered by vibrant life currents emanating from newly emerging bodies struggling for the chance to exist and contending for the right to serve the new age of mankind.

The days ahead cannot be disjoined from the years through which we have lived nor from the times in which we now stand. That part of our heritage which constitutes the ground of our present hope is rooted in certain conceptions about the dignity of man and certain beliefs about the organization of human effort toward the realization of the highest of man's possibilities. The first of these ideas comes to us in the Christian view of human personality; the second is embodied in our faith in the principle of democracy. Elsewhere in this volume has been set forth both the justification and necessity of rekindling confidence in and commitment to these elements as essential in any view of society which has the prospect of long-term survival. The effectual denial of the worth and dignity of every human being and the refusal to extend to all persons, on the basis of merit, interest, and need, the opportunity to participate in all the affairs and functions of our society have resulted in the impoverishment of our culture and the willful frustration of the aspirations of men who seek nothing less than the exercise of their inalienable right to fullness of life.

The consequent tensions and conflicts by which we are beset are due in part only to the fact that in the world of the present the folly of the past comes to flower. In our own generation the privilege of choice is before us. In most of the things that we really want to do we affirm our autonomy: we assert our ability to judge, to decide, to create. Yet in larger matters where the things at stake involve wide segments of the population or the whole of humanity, we are inclined to seek refuge in hastily invoked theories of external determinism. This protestation of helplessness is a fine cloak for irresponsibility, and it contains all the ingredients of a stultifying hypocrisy. The subtlety with which this escape from responsibility operates in narrowly personal matters is exceeded in both volume and significance as one identifies himself with the aims and activities of special interest groups. If a group is charac· terized by any form of exclusiveness, then conscience and a sense of broad social obligation operate at a minimum level. If such a group assumes the right to extend or withhold benefits or advantages that are needed or desired by a considerable portion of the populace, then its power for large-scale good or ill becomes incalculable.

In the area defined by the title of this book it is impossible to ignore the powerful influence of long-standing social habits, deeply ingrained beliefs, and warmly defended attitudes. No detailed description of our present predicament is necessary in order to convince us that we are more or less torn between the allurements to a new and finer way of life for all people and attachment to a system in which special privilege is reserved for those who have the power to take it and the shrewdness to keep it. The defects and injustices of the total system are reflected most clearly in the operations of those units within the social structure which attempt to redeem its virtues by various kinds of protests against its vices. On occasion the protest is weak and carefully timed. Not infrequently there is persistent witnessing in terms of a center of loyalty infinitely higher than that found in human institutions. There have been and are movements whose chief function has been and is to reclaim and make freshly articulate the submerged idealism of an originally pioneering organization. In the American scene and in the sphere of racial relations the Young Men's Christian Association has a history and a future which compel the attention of those who are seeking tools suitable for building a social structure here in America that is Christian in motivation and spirit and democratic in form and function.

AN APPEAL TO THE RECORD

For nearly a century the Young Men's Christian Association has operated on the American scene. It has been one of the major socio-religious agencies cross-cutting lines of race, denomination, and economic status. Its lines of influence have so extended beyond the borders of the continental United States that today the educational, religious, recreational, and social services of this agency are located in sixty-seven countries in all parts of the world. As early as 1853 the Association included a Negro unit, and by the turn of the century the formula of Negro branches was well established. From the very beginning there has been emphasis upon the interdenominational, interracial, and international character of the movement. The program has covered a wide variety of interests among men and boys of varied backgrounds, and its specialized services have appealed to youth and adults in all of the larger urban communities throughout the nation. In one phase of its activities the Association has tended to be a prophetic and pioneering movement; in another phase it has crystallized into a conservative institution. Certain rather rigid patterns have emerged over the years; and the present structure conforms, in the main, to the general features of segregation characteristic of churches, fraternal orders, business establishments, and social clubs in all parts of the country. The "Negro branch" is the undeniable illustration of this racially determined arrangement.

Locally there has been general accommodation to prevailing public sentiment and close adherence to the existing scheme of adjustments in matters involving the white majority and the Negro minority. Social distance persists and the implications of caste affect the details of institutional management and the opportunities for individual participation. The principle of "separate but equal" was enunciated as the originally advisable approach in the construction of buildings, in accepting members, and in providing services and privileges for the Negro and white constituencies respectively. In the area of ownership and control joint responsibility and authority are reflected through organic connection between committees of management and boards of directors. In matters that are formal, legal, and strictly institutional, the lines converge. In the more informal, personal, and intimate phases of operation the lines move in parallel planes.

A description of programs and activities in urban centers is unnecessary for documentation of the foregoing statements. The story is sufficiently well known to most Americans who are aware of the existence of the Y.M.C.A. The actual and potential clientele of this organization does not speak in a single voice, nor does it affirm a uniform social philosophy. Yet from city to city and from state to state across the country deviations in practice are few and infrequent. Local mores and the attitudes of the financially powerful segment of the population give direction to the formulation of institutional policy. Major difficulties arise in connection with use of swimming pools, eating in cafeterias and lunchrooms, living in dormitories, and participating in the social and recreational program of the Association. In such affairs as public lectures, forums, staff meetings, conferences, group games, tournaments, and financial campaigns there is considerable flexibility. The professional leadership and enlightened laymen in one community after another have attempted to stand against the tide of prejudice and bigotry in the espousal of the principle of integration and thoroughgoing fellowship. Many and varied experiments have been made to break the shackles of conformity to a basically un-Christian and undemocratic system within the Y.M.C.A. Pioneers are still appearing who insist that an agency which has as its objective "the building of Christian personality and a Christian society" must move out beyond the limits of popularly conceived schemes of exclusiveness and restriction of opportunities for full use of community resources by members of minority groups.

Under the stimulation of such leadership ways are being opened for mutually helpful contacts and experiences across racial lines. Significant examples of this daring to live in advance of dominant community sentiment may be cited in nonsegregated summer camps for boys, young people's conferences, interracial club activities in Y.M.C.A. buildings, and in the revision of discriminatory practices in reference to membership in some local branches.

It is obvious that these instances of altering discriminatory practices in the direction of democratic participation would have taken place in those cities where the ferment of awakened social conscience had been at work in areas other than the Y.M.C.A. Even now, however, the process is exceedingly slow and there is slight evidence of any fundamental change of such widespread nature as to mark a specific trend. The maintenance of the Association is dependent upon the good will and support of those citizens who contribute to its budget and those who purchase its services. The supporting constituency is composed of the same substantial persons in the community who tolerate restricted residential areas and who countenance segregation in theaters and discrimination in the use of public facilities. The boards of directors are, in most cases, men who pay allegiance to segregated churches. Both rank-and-file members and official framers of Association policy are custodians of a system of community organization which resists significant positive innovations in the sphere of racial relations.

Against this stubborn wall of opinion and practice some of the professional leadership and many influential laymen are insisting that the Y.M.C.A. has a mission which goes beyond the mere acceptance of community prejudices and which transcends the historic formula of "separate but equal." Such persons are challenging the Association to pioneer along new frontiers in the interest of demonstrating the feasibility of serving the needs and interests of an entire community without distinction as to race or national origin. Thus, an agency that determines to be Christian and democratic faces the alternative of bringing its machinery in line with its basic philosophy or revising its announced philosophy to conform to its practice. At the present moment there is no local Association that is willing to deny its acceptance of the Christian ethic as the basis of its institutional existence. In the statement of purpose and in formulating aims every local unit affirms that "the Young Men's Christian Association we regard as being, in its essential genius, a world-wide fellowship of men and boys united by a common loyalty to Jesus Christ for the purpose of building Christian personality and a Christian society." The language of the foregoing declaration is sufficiently clear and its implications are sufficiently pointed to prevent any confusion about the direction of social emphasis in formal declarations of purpose.

The extent to which local branches disregard or fall below the imperatives embodied in their statement of purpose indicates the degree to which the insights of a prophetic movement can be accommodated to the desire for institutional survival. This is another example of the decline of an ideal in face of what are considered practical necessities. Any agency that operates within the limits of local prejudices must of necessity disavow deliberately or by sheer default its commitment to the demands of the Christian ethic. If the upkeep of buildings, the rental of dormitory rooms, and the sale of various goods and services are threatened by opposition to a policy of nonsegregation and nondiscrimination, then property values are usually elevated above human values. No amount of rationalization can justify such abandonment of a clear-cut Christian principle. And no reference to the constitutional right of "local autonomy" can erase the fact that both democracy and Christianity are betrayed whenever service or membership is restricted or denied on the basis of race.

In every city across the country the Y.M.C.A. is in a strategic position to take the lead in a broad program of social reconstruction. More and more the membership of the several branches is drawn from all segments of the population. There is a decided advantage in its nonsectarian character. The appeal to men and boys brings together in one agency the energy and potentialities of all age groups in the community. As a religious movement the Association can provide a platform and a laboratory for dealing with every human problem that besets its membership. As a social agency it can be driven by the dynamic of its heritage in the Christian tradition. Although the Y.M.C.A. is not the church, nor a church, it shares with the church the present demand for saving its life by becoming increasingly an instrument of justice and a means for unrestricted fellowship among men or losing its life by damming up the channels of real communion between all the men and boys of the nation and of the world.

THE CHALLENGE OF THESE TIMES

One of the chief points of strength in the Y.M.C.A. as an instrument for improving race relations is its national and international outreach. The network of Associations spreading over all the states of the Union and extending into every continent on the globe provides a readily accessible medium for intercultural cross-fertilization and interracial co-operation. On the national scale this organic connection between local branches represents real unity in diversity, in terms both of different types of Associations and of differing amounts of zeal for unconventional experiments in removing barriers which have separated white and Negro groups in American society.

There is wide difference in behavior between desk clerks and physical education directors in New Orleans, Atlanta, and Vicksburg as compared with those in New York, Chicago, and Los Angeles; yet the variation in racial attitudes manifested in reactions to Negroes, Italians, Mexicans, and Orientals comes under the judgment of a central declaration of purpose by which all of these local units are morally bound.

The awareness of membership in a national movement has spurred to courageous action many laymen and professional workers who might have lacked the necessary prod if left to the isolation of a local town or city organization. The consciousness of a fellowship of aspiration and effort stretching across geographical boundaries tends to awaken a sense of the national, if not global, import of any decisive action taken locally in the furtherance of social justice and fundamental human rights. Any triumph over bigotry gives impetus to the whole cause of decency and enhances respect between persons and groups of diverse cultural backgrounds. Every time a Chinese, a Negro, and a Caucasian have the opportunity of engaging in sports, using a swimming pool, learning a skilled trade, living in a dormitory, or discussing an important economic problem without being tucked away behind partitions labeled "yellow," "black," or "white," there is evidence that concerns shared in common reveal to all involved in such sharing the essential unity of mankind's mind and spirit. As the experience deepens, fears are displaced by a growing mutual confidence. Misgivings are superseded by an increased forthrightness in one's approach to his fellow man.

In all of its recent pronouncements the Y.M.C.A. has spoken with vigor and clarity regarding the question of race. The enunciation of national policy not only sets the tone for action on an inclusive national scale but also gives to weak and fearful local groups a compelling objective toward which to strive and a definitive principle by which to criticize their failures. In spite of prevailing local attitudes there is usually a feeling of real achievement when an Association can report that some feature of racial discrimination has been eliminated from its operations or that some form of segregation in its activities has been abandoned. There are occasions on which the Christian Association serves as the conscience of the community as it attempts to give effect to national policy. Left to itself, without the encouragement and moral support of more than a thousand similar groups throughout the United States, a lone local unit might resist much less stubbornly the antidemocratic pressures of its immediate environment. The reassurance that a small band of citizens dedicated to the principle of freedom, equality, and fraternity are not working alone furnishes a tremendous incentive to such a unit to continue the struggle, even against considerable odds. The undergirding of a national policy, the inspiration of a universal statement of purpose, and the encouragement of world-wide aims and objectives are sufficient to give zest to groups of individuals who might be working in remote places of the earth for the development of Christian personality and a Christian society.

The Forty-fifth International Convention of the Y.M.C.A. of North America, representing the National Councils of Canada and the United States, gave expression to the conviction of its constituent bodies in the following terms: "We affirm our conviction that a brotherhood of men throughout the world, cemented by ties of common values and friendship across national, racial, and religious barriers can and must become a reality. This is our Father's world and the Fatherhood of God compels a familyhood of men." This places the issue squarely before a great body of men and boys in every geographical area of both countries (Canada and the United States). The language is not unlike that contained in affirmations of churches and earlier declarations of the Association movement itself. Yet the crucial nature of these times adds to these words a note of urgency. The statement calls for the recognition of a simple fact—"the familyhood of men"—and it makes mandatory the lifting of this fact into functional reality by cementing our brotherhood through "ties of common values and friendship" across all the barriers that disrupt the unity of the human family in our own country and in other parts of the world.

This great convention did not adjourn without going beyond affirmation of convictions. Recommendations were made to local Associations in the effort to set before these constituent groups a vivid reminder of their high calling and in order to indicate lines along which bold resolve requires translation into courageous and consistent action. The following recommendations strike at the heart of the problem about which the Christian Association movement has suffered a greatly disturbed conscience. The very desire to become an effectual agent in world rehabilitation and reconciliation made imperative the cleansing of its own hands and the searching of its own heart in preparation for ministering to the spiritual and moral sickness of a sorely distraught world. Turning to local Associations, the Convention recommended "that they work steadfastly toward the goal of eliminating all racial discriminations and of having all men, without regard to racial or national origin, share justly and equally, according to merit, in our rich social, economic, cultural and political heritage." In addressing such a challenge to the entire local constituency, the Y.M.C.A. movement was drawing upon one of the noblest features in its century-old history. In recalling its own previous expressions on the issue of race, the convention made brief reference to recent developments within the Christian Associations as argument in favor of going forward even more daringly in the years ahead. In these words the past becomes alive in the demands of the present:

> In making this recommendation we note with satisfaction that substantial progress has been made in interracial relations within the Y.M.C.A. since the adoption of the following resolution by the forty-third International Convention of the Y.M.C.A. in 1931:
>
> That we go on record as urging all associations to take definite steps toward the goal of making possible full participation in the association program without discrimination as to race, color or nationality.
>
> The Convention now affirms this resolution and calls upon local Associations further to implement this essential goal.

The role of the Young Men's Christian Association in renewing the spirit and reshaping the structure of our social order will be discovered largely in terms of what it has done most helpfully during the years of its own internal growth. In estimating the probable contribution of this agency to the solution of a problem which increases in complexity and deepens in severity month after month, one must avoid being purely historical or idly hopeful. Present expectations must be informed by irrefutable past achievements. Any great new advance will have been nurtured in the soil of earlier strivings and will spring out of the fertile grounds that have been prepared by long and careful cultivation. What comes forth now as fruits will disclose the markings and contain the substance made inevitable by the unvarying logic of the roots. Because the Christian Association movement has been at work in the expansive field of race relations there may yet be a goodly harvest, if they who early put their hands to the plow turn not back, and if the tillers of the soil faint not as they bear the burden in the heat of the day.

SOME IMPRESSIVE MILESTONES

A close examination of the structure and functioning of the Young Men's Christian Association reveals four organizational phases which provide four clearly distinguishable levels of participation by Negroes and persons from some other minority groups. First is the local phase. Here the ideal of democracy and Christianity stands in sharpest contrast to institutional practice. In all but a few places segregation in buildings and activities is the characteristic arrangement. Goings and comings across the line of race are measured by the necessities of institutional management and timed by the pressure of professional responsibilities on either side of the racial line. Areas of communication are kept open by occasional "exchange visits" and intergroup competition of a not too intimate sort. Even at these local points the Y.M.C.A. is likely to be ahead of other agencies in discussing community problems involving racial tensions and in working for improvements in such matters as health, housing, employment, and police protection for the entire population.

As a result of contacts between responsible adults, whether meeting formally as officials of the Association or coming together as citizens to plan some city-wide undertaking such as a community chest or bond drive, additional spheres of mutual interest are developed and the foundation may be laid for a progressively rewarding human fellowship. When the staffs of the branch and the central Association meet together and when the chairman of the committee of management sits with full responsibility as a member of the board of directors, something happens which has significance beyond the confines of the Association. At the local level the Y.M.C.A. serves as clearing house on public affairs and frequently as rallying center for defenders of the rights and obligations of all American citizens. Under the auspices of an organization which lays claim to the resources of the religion of Jesus it is not uncommon that an influential citizen finds ways of working for human justice and social righteousness which may be denied him in his business establishment or in his social club. Here also may be the beginning of a youthful comradeship which will increase in depth and vigor until by the force of the liberated spirit all the barriers to an abiding friendship are torn away. As this happens to persons through an organization that is being weighed in the balance to determine its adequacy as a liberating force in the local community, the agency itself becomes transformed and the life of the community moves to a slightly higher level.

There has been no more interesting demonstration of united effort on a city-wide basis than resulted from the benefactions of the late Julius Rosenwald for the construction of Y.M.C.A. buildings for service to Negro men and boys. However unfortunate was the crystallization of the formula of "separate but equal," there was, nonetheless, in the response of citizens to the challenge of the Rosenwald gifts a remarkable example of solidarity among socially responsible people in twenty-five cities as they closed ranks to raise money for extending the benefits of the Y.M.C.A. to a disadvantaged group through well-equipped and efficiently staffed buildings. Campaigns for raising funds within a particular city brought together in committees, on solicitation teams, and at reporting sessions leaders, both white and Negro, from every section. The experiences gained and the contacts made in "Rosenwald building" campaigns have laid the foundation for a different kind of expansion in Y.M.C.A. services and in community relationships. Segregated buildings and segregated programs cease to be defensible as the awareness of common interests, common needs, and common location dawns more and more fully upon the local leadership and supporters of the Christian Association. When the Y.M.C.A. breaks the pattern and the moral sensibilities of enough people are stirred, the church and other community establishments will find it impossible to be at ease with less than a serious gesture in the direction of integration and broadly inclusive participation.

The second structural phase in the life and work of the Association is regional. Within recent years the plan of areas with area councils has emerged. Through this medium local units derive the benefits which accompany any sharing of ideas and pooling of resources in the pursuit of socially useful objectives. Since, geographically and psychologically, the area is somewhat removed from the actualities of the local situation, there is greater readiness among members of the councils to agree to advances in this wider sphere than there would be if they were making decisions and taking action in a given locality. Not only do conferences, retreats, and staff meetings sponsored by area councils include Negro staff and committee members and delegates, but also there is a policy to hold such gatherings only at such places and under such conditions as will guarantee full and equal accommodations to all participants, without segregation or discrimination in any form. In the carrying out of this policy it happens frequently that hotels, camps, city Association buildings, and restaurants are induced to modify their practice of racial discrimination (albeit temporarily) in order to serve an interracial group.

Nationally, the Y.M.C.A. has made its boldest strokes in the cause of democracy and a Christian social order. A sustained campaign of legislation, pronouncement, education, and persuasion has been waged through the national board and the national council and implemented by the national staff in working with area councils and local Associations. The national policy with reference to race stands firmly against segregation and discrimination. The principle of integration is embodied in all recommended procedures regarding general membership in the Association and specific services on national committees, commissions, council, and staff. As currently interpreted, the function of Negroes in these national legislative and administrative bodies is not confined to representation of a particular constituency or limited to professional services to a special segment of the membership; rather, such individuals operate as fully accredited persons, whose judgments and counsel and skills are brought to bear upon every aspect of the life, thought, and activity of the movement.

When it is recalled that the national council of the Y.M.C.A. is influencing the ideas and opinion of more than a million members in well over a thousand centers throughout the United States, one can begin to reckon with the tremendous power that might be exerted in the interest of public enlightenment, progressive legislation, and desirable social reform. One of the bright chapters in the history of the Association as a national organization is the record of the Public Affairs Committee authorized by the national council in 1934. This committee, through its publications, study guides, reports on contemporary events, and bibliographies, has "brought forward at frequent intervals matters of public concern and has proposed lines of action." The period during which Y.M.C.A.'s have been called upon to face these public issues covers the very years in which any matter vital to the public welfare has been hotly controversial. Whether the question was focused on military service, employment and wages, education, transportation, or civil liberties, no comprehensive dealing with the issue could avoid coming to grips with the racial factor.

In leadership training the entire nation has profited from the skills that have been developed and the broad social outlook that has evolved when Negroes have joined with other laymen and other professional staff members in formulating policies, in planning and raising budgets, and in rendering important program services without regard to racial identification. Out of this kind of background, and largely because of unrestricted opportunities for cultivating leadership abilities, scores of men have gone into other lines of nationally significant work with the social philosophy and technical equipment engendered and refined in the Y.M.C.A. secretaryship or on one or another of the official bodies of this organization. The fields of work that have benefited most substantially through this transfer of personnel are college and university administration, public administration, college teaching, social work, the ministry, and missions. This sifting into diverse occupations has been the occasion for the transmission of a philosophy which is on the side of exalting human values above any of the mechanisms of a complex industrialized social system.

The origin of the Southern Interracial Commission in the years immediately following World War I is an instance illustrative of a quickened sense of obligation on the part of a national agency to move unhesitatingly into a difficult area of tension and conflict. Whatever one may think of the devices utilized by the Interracial Commission in connection with racial prejudice and mob violence, there was undeniable gain in having the National War Work Council of the Y.M.C.A. direct some of its funds and expend some of its energies in a field so fraught with danger for the whole nation. These blundering and awkward beginnings opened a new realm for social engineering. The present outreach and influence of the Southern Regional Council and the Southern Conference on Human Welfare are enlargements and improvements upon an idea and a plan initiated by the Y.M.C.A. over two decades ago.

The National Council of Student Christian Associations represents the most advanced outpost of decisive action in the Y.M.C.A. as a whole. In its policy the principle of equality is set forth unequivocally. The composition of all conferences sponsored by the national movement (except in one of its nine regions) is interracial. Membership in regional and national councils, participation in the deliberations of regional and national assemblies, and service on committees and commissions are open to all persons who desire to share in the fulfillment of the purpose of the movement. Negro staff members are not restricted to working with branches in Negro colleges. Interest and competence are the major requirements.

Student Associations are at work on the raw edge of racial injustice. Local units engage in study and action designed to eliminate practices of segregation and discrimination on college campuses as well as in nonacademic communities. College administrators find in many of these Associations a constant embarrassment to institutional smugness. At its best the Student Christian Association movement incarnates the ideal of essential human brotherhood. Through the activity of these groups the admissions policies of educational institutions have been challenged and discriminatory procedures altered.

Through serious study, discussion, and an open platform, support has been developed for proposed legislation against the poll tax, for a permanent Fair Employment Practices Commission, for equal educational opportunity, and against lynching. Student Associations, both in official capacity and through individual action, are demonstrating a technique of wider social change by taking the lead in living in advance of public sentiment and working in practical ways for the things in which they believe. With the National Student Council of Young Women's Christian Associations, the National Student Y.M.C.A. affirms that "all people are children of God, and we are concerned that they grow and develop as he intended they should." Furthermore, its intention is expressed in words that prove to be strongly compelling: "Believing that God the creator made man in his own image, we cannot rest while one person is enslaved and degraded . . . we must study the nature of the political, social and economic forces of our world, and work for racial equality, economic justice and political effectiveness." This is the Y.M.C.A. in its highest moments and at the peak of its idealism. To live under the discipline of such affirmations is good for the Y.M.C.A. and will enable it to develop into a redemptive force in the realm of race relations throughout the United States.

Among its assets as an agency working for the establishment of "the Christian way in race relations" the Christian Association movement may look to its history, to its philosophy, and in some degree to its structure. Because of its capital investment and its dependence upon a predominantly middle-class clientele, however, its anchorage in the *status quo* is a severe handicap.

In facing the demands of the future, the Association must do these things in order to give effect to its Christian affirmations:

1. Push with increased vigor and with greater consistency the policy of full and unrestricted participation in committees, commissions, boards, councils, and professional service without distinctions based on race.
2. Give leadership to commercial enterprises by extending services in dormitories, swimming pools, and cafeterias without racial discrimination or segregation.
3. Work for the abolishment of the racial "branch" and for the extension of membership privileges on the basis of inclusive community service.
4. Maintain an open platform for the discussion of controversial social issues and provide educational leadership in the eradication of racial prejudice.
5. Recruit qualified young Negro men for professional placement in strategic Association centers throughout the United States and for full-time professional service in the world-wide program of the Y.M.C.A.
6. Encourage the entire constituency to support legislation and court

action in defense of civil liberties and a single standard of American citizenship.

To do all these things the Y.M.C.A. will move against itself in some areas of its own life. It will move across new frontiers of bitter prejudice and hostility. Yet the dynamic of its Christian commitment will require that voice and effectual power be given to the prophetic fringe in its life and thought.

9

The Role of the Young
Women's Christian Association

MARION CUTHBERT

THE Seventeenth Convention of the Young Women's Christian Associations, meeting in Atlantic City in March of
1946, made organizational and social history when by a large
majority it adopted a series of resolutions calling for the integration of Negro women and girls into the main stream of Association life as a conscious goal of the organization. For those who
had known of the deep concern, the long history—as social-work
movements go—and the processes by which this organization
works upon any part of the problem of furthering the good life,
this culminating declaration of practices as well as intent with
regard to Negro people in its constituency could come as no
surprise.

As part of its way of work the Y.W.C.A. began in 1934 a long
period of self-study which resulted in *The Standard Studies of
1936–38 and 1938–40*. Here were gathered up concepts and
ways of work operative throughout the Association and here were
projected those ideals and those bases of operation with which
the Y.W.C.A. proposed to carry forward its work.

The Y.W.C.A. has been mindful for a considerable period
now that it has no alternative to the course of action with regard
to the inclusion of Negro women and girls as expressed in its

most recent statements. No other course is consistent with its past history, with the viewpoint of by far the larger part of its professional and lay leadership, and with its declared purpose. This purpose, which has been accepted by the vast majority of the community Associations and written into the constitution of the national movement, declares that the Y.W.C.A. intends: "To build a fellowship of women and girls devoted to the task of realizing in our common life those ideals of personal and social living to which we are committed by our faith as Christians. In this endeavor we seek to understand Jesus, to share His love for all people, and to grow in the knowledge and love of God."

Realistically, the Y.W.C.A. says in *The Standards Study, 1936–38*:

The difficulty of reaching, or of approaching these standards is not minimized. The task with which the movement is faced, if it is to be true to itself, will be arduous and often a painful one. It demands faith and sacrifice. No other organization, so far as we are aware, attempts to do what the Y.W.C.A. professes to do in uniting within one fellowship women and girls from every walk of life, each with a potential contribution to make to the others. Perhaps we have set ourselves too high an ideal. If so, it is better to recognize that fact and confine ourselves to more attainable goals. That would be the realistic and honest course. And yet, we have occasional glimpses of the creative power of such a fellowship, an occasional deeply satisfying experience in our association with our "fellows" that forbid us to admit defeat.[1]

Continuing, the study goes on to state that second to this first assumption of purpose for a "standard" Association is that of a democratic administration as an essential condition. In a democratic society, "personality can best develop because the individual meets with respect and encouragement: . . . he *counts* as a responsible member of the society. He has *status*—a recognized relation to the whole. He *belongs,* and is recognized as belonging."[2]

The Y.W.C.A., moving steadily toward the goal which prac-

[1] *A Study of Administrative Practices and Relationships,* part of a report of the National Board of the Y.W.C.A. to the Fifteenth National Convention, p. 11.
[2] *Ibid.,* p. 13.

tice, to date, and enlightenment had envisioned for it a decade ago, recommended in 1946:

> Since the purpose, adopted by the national convention and tested in Association experience through the years, stands as the one statement of faith and resolve to which all Associations are committed.
>
> a. That the purpose be used as a measuring rod for all policies and practices to the end that only those may be adopted or maintained which contribute to the Christian and democratic inclusiveness of the Association.
>
> b. That the implications of the purpose be recognized as involving the inclusion of Negro women and girls in the main stream of Association life, and that such inclusion be adopted as a conscious goal.[3]

There are several major reasons why inclusiveness has been and continues to be of such importance to the Y.W.C.A. The Association has been aware of, and believes there is no escape from, (1) the essential concepts which it states are the heart of its reason for being and the core of any valid program, (2) historic sequences, and (3) the influence of great personalities.

It is well known that the Christian Associations operate as religiously motivated programs of social work. The religion from which these organizations have sprung, and which still today is dominant in their programs, is that aspect of the Protestant expression of the Christian faith which is concerned with the search for truth and with the love of all men. It is a program of behavior as well as of faith and belief.

In the hands of women, this concern has expressed itself in ways consistent with woman's approach to life in our society. Whether there is, in this *approach*, something basically "feminine," or whether this approach is only one of those unavoidable developments among women, considering the whole of our culture, need not be debated at this point. For the emphases here noted are admitted as characterizing a large part of the activities of women, and as giving them a stamp which differentiates them in fair degree from ways of work observable largely among men.

Women are concerned with the way in which life grows. The

---

[3] *Interracial Practices in Community Y.W.C.A.'s* (New York, 1944), p. 118.

bearing of children and their subsequent care during the first formative years undoubtedly are the bases from which this concern stems. Division of labor, in the home and in ways of earning a living, all contribute to the development of this interest in the *how* of growth, an interest in much minute experience, introspection about such experience, the concern for the nature of relationships in it, the recognition of the increases in growth through individual and group experience, and verbalizations about the achievement of such growth and the projection of new and desired goals to be attained in the whole area of personal and social living.

This reality of the woman's concern for the *how* of life is well reflected in the purpose of the Y.W.C.A. in those phrases "build a fellowship," "ideals of personal and social living," and "in our common life."

Women, again, have something of a special awareness of particular periods of life, for concern with the growth process must have a special interest in unique periods. Every age of life is important, but that time which marks the crest in sensibilities and the first flush of productive power, the years of youth, is particularly momentous, not only for the person, but for society as well.

That the Y.W.C.A. is aware, in this woman-approach, of this period of uniqueness is evident not only because it is a "young women's" Christian Association—many organizations are devoted to the needs and interests of youth—but because it focuses upon one of the most important needs of this period: to keep youth rightly related to maturity. The phrase, "to build a fellowship of women and girls," is not casual; it is the expression in woman-lore that the best growth is balanced, graduated, and always related.

And women also know, from the ways in which they must deal with life in our society, that to bring forth children and engage in their rearing is done in relation to two modifiable but never disappearing actualities: human beings will undoubtedly continue to want children; and the children must be born into this kind of world. For though there are modifications about the bearing of children, a number of realities remain constant about it; and while the world is modifiable—with a great hope everywhere among people that, more and more, change for the better may be encompassed as time goes on, especially in human relationships—it is still clear that there are a number of realities about the world which remain constant also.

A chief one among these realities is the kinds of people. Quite aside from any religious or spiritual considerations, it is impractical to fume against the kinds of human beings who are now on earth and hold back the bringing on of new life until it can be brought forth in the "right" conditions. Women learn, in the most intimate ways, to live with what they must; and from this constraint has evolved some perception and understanding of the possibilities in the diversities of human beings which are overlooked in immature living, with its manifold rejections. This wisdom of acceptance of the people of earth is caught up in the phrase, "to share His love for all people," and in this phrase is that anchor aspect of the purpose of the Young Women's Christian Associations which holds a whole program steady, while the insights of love, as revealed through the teachings of Jesus, light the goal.

In indicating some aspects about the approach of women to life, as expressed in discernible ways in the Y.W.C.A., it should be noted that such development is not exclusive to women any more than the broad-scale operations of masculinity are exclusive to men. For as women develop greatly in human stature they display, as additions to womanly behavior, characteristics of aggressiveness, daring, inventiveness, and profound creativity. And as men attain to fine flowering they display, as additions to manly characteristics, women's traits of tending and tenderness; the understanding of the small, and the possibilities for its glorification; the grace which can accept life, even as it modifies it for living.

The Y.W.C.A., the woman's branch of one of the great social movements of the last and the present centuries, because it has been in the hands of women has developed, from the logic of its constituent elements and the evolving needs of a society undergoing great social change, a program characterized by a concern for the totality of life—the inner and the outer life and all aspects of both: the religious life, an ethic and worship; the secular life, ethical living in the earning of one's living and in personal group contacts.

It should not be overlooked that women have had some assets on their side as they developed this woman's movement. With limitations of outlet in other kinds of related work—professional work in the church and administrative posts in education, for example—there has probably been a somewhat greater potential of superior leadership, relatively speaking, for this socio-religious work. Women also, handicapped in amassing funds and equipment to the same extent that a similar group of men would have done, have found themselves happily free, at points, from the weight of possession. And many women leaders in the work have been championed by the men of their immediate families who themselves have played a less observably forward role. All this is to say that in the development of this lay religious work the whole social situation should be examined if true and useful interpretations of behavior are to be obtained.

The evolving needs of a society undergoing great social change are too numerous and too profound to be analyzed within this interpretation. But the changes in the later stage of the industrial revolution are well known to all; it is sufficient only to note that the changes brought about are precisely those which demand attention to the way in which life grows, is growing now in one of the great periods of the-end-and-beginning of things, in an always evolving world.

Within the Y.W.C.A. itself the historical development with regard to the Negro minority among its constituency throws light upon the Association's position on the matter today.

When the present national board of the Young Women's Christian Associations of the U.S.A. was formed in 1906, all of the work among Negro women and girls, whether operating in-

dependently or affiliated with the then existing American committee or international board, became an immediate concern of
the new national movement, and in 1907 Miss Grace Dodge, the
first president of the board, called a conference of southern white
women in Asheville, North Carolina, to discuss the matter. These
women expressed a real interest in helping colored girls in the
southern states but felt that on account of the prejudice this
could best be done if organized and supervised from head-
quarters.

But social consciousness grew with the years, and in 1915
another conference was called in Louisville, Kentucky, to which
were invited both Negro and white women, and also three men.
This group moved far ahead in its thinking and its recommendations, which included (1) the appointing of a committee composed of white and colored women from or of the South; (2) the
recognition of the need of trained leadership among young colored women; (3) the proposal of the branch relationship as the
best method of co-operating in city Associations.

Of the utmost significance were the following principles for
developing the work: (1) there can be but one Young Women's
Christian Association in any community; all other work must be
a branch of the central Association; (2) the central body may ap-
point a member of its board of directors to be chairman of the
colored work. A third principle, developed somewhat later as the
War Work Council got under way, states: (3) no work of any
kind should be attempted (that is, with colored people) until the
board of directors develops a consciousness of all that is involved
and is ready to assume responsibility for the acute situations
which may arise later and which are likely to occur in the process
of learning together.

Stress was put, at this time, in developing a movement among
colored girls and women and not for them. The work among
younger girls followed uncritically the pattern of separate Negro
Girl Reserve clubs even in the communities where there was not
compulsory segregation. On the other hand, in the case of work
with industrial women the interracial rather than the biracial

philosophy was suggested. In general, the advice given to local Associations in their approach to work among Negro people stressed: (1) the use of natural groupings; (2) the acceptance of mixed groups asking for consideration; (3) the consideration of individual applications for specific activity based on personal qualifications.

All of this work was developed during the war period and, until 1931, under the Council on Colored Work. Miss Elizabeth Ross (now Mrs. George E. Haynes) had been the first Negro member of the national board staff, appointed in 1908, to be the special worker among colored students. In 1913, Miss Eva D. Bowles was appointed to the national board to have special supervision of city work, and it was under Miss Bowles that work was co-ordinated in the Council on Colored Work.

The picture today presents a striking development from these beginnings: (1) There is no Council on Colored Work; work is across race lines, serving the entire constituency. (2) Work across race lines holds for both the Negro and the white staff members of the national board and for board members, and is developing in this fashion in local Associations. (3) Committees on colored work have given place to interracial committees, and these work toward the wholeness of all racial groups within the Association. (4) The Conference of Negro Leadership (formerly the Negro Branch Conference) voted itself out of existence in 1942 with the recommendation: "In calling another national conference we look forward to calling a national human relationships conference, interracial in character, with common problems to be emphasized rather than differences." (5) A subcommittee of the Public Affairs Committee of the national board has been developed with responsibility for working on the national interests of racial minorities. These interests include (a) measures for effective dealing with lynching and all forms of mob violence; (b) the support of measures for enlarged economic opportunities for Negroes; (c) support of the federal government in policies of interracial co-operation rather than separation.

For the Negro group as a whole the national Y.W.C.A. has

taken the position of "the recognition of all people, of whatever racial background, as having not only equality of status before the law but being entitled to equality of treatment in the life of the nation."

It is clear that in all of this development the Y.W.C.A. has nowhere nearly approximated its goals. It would be strange, indeed, if this organization had been able to accomplish what other organized aspects of society have never been able to do, that is, to reach their set goals. But there are criteria for measuring the growth and the stature of organized groups in our society. Perhaps the most important of these are the following: (1) Are the principles of the organization accepted intellectually and emotionally by significant numbers of both the leadership and the followership of the organization? (2) In actual practice, is the program of the organization moving in the direction indicated by these principles?

Viewed from these posts of observation, the Y.W.C.A. shows up well. For not only is its purpose, already quoted, used again and again in dealing with concrete situations by the rank and file of the membership, as well as by boards and committees in setting up program objectives, but pronouncements on the major social issues, made in convention or issued by the various committees of the national board, have consistently received the support of a majority in most of the local Associations. There are not many Associations which do not stand, for example, with the national movement on the matter of how the Negro members of the Y.W.C.A. should be related to the whole Association, and how the Negro people in our country should live in it, as citizens. In supporting the national movement in principle, a sizable group of Associations are puzzled, and some are baffled outright, as to what to do, conditions in their respective communities being what they are. But it is one thing to feel impotent for action and quite another thing to believe that the actions proposed are fundamentally unsound.

There is dissenting minority opinion in the Association on fundamental positions of the organization, and the existence of this opinion should not be minimized. Occasionally it takes the form of active opposition to the majority opinion and seeks to overthrow the latter. Such action, however, is rare. The most characteristic expression of the minority viewpoint is best described by its own statements that "it is not ready yet to go so far"; "the goals are good but the methods suggested questionable"; "the national movement must give better help in personnel and advisory services if better work is to be done in local communities on major problems in relationships."

As for literal progress being made along the lines of the Association's principles, not only is the shift in position of the whole Negro group within the Y.W.C.A. testimony to a genuine progress, but in those matters more observable to the eye of the general public positive changes are coming about. These can be seen in three major aspects of Association life: in its leadership, in its services, and in its structure.

The position of Negro women leaders, both as members of boards and committees and as professional workers, has already been noted. More and more, in local communities and on the national level, they are to be seen as representative of the whole organization and speaking and working for it in this fashion.

As for services: camps, dormitories, cafeterias are increasingly being opened on a basis of full equality to Negro women and girls. There are not many communities, excluding the places where patterns of segregation are legalized, where some change along these lines has not already occurred or is not under serious consideration.

One of the most important places of profound change is in the structure of the organization itself. In the beginning the Y.W.C.A. accepted, with little or no questioning, the American pattern of segregation in structure as an adequate device for including Negroes, and the Negro branch was promoted. But a very great change in attitude has come about in viewing the Negro branch. From seeing it as a device to keep Negroes out of the central Association, it has been rationalized as a device for helping them eventually to move into it. But lately this latter position has been attacked by a spearhead group within the Association. And action to accompany the new thinking has already taken place, for in several Associations, in the North, the Negro branch has been done away with and the general facilities of the Association have been opened to Negro members. In several others such a move is being studied. It is interesting to note that some of the most sizable and difficult opposition to such a step often comes from the Negro women themselves, for like the majority of human beings they may fear the new; or they may be unwilling, at first, to pay the price in loss in numbers of leadership places in the Association for the gain to be made in being in a more fundamentally right relationship to the whole. These and other problems beset Negro leadership as structural changes are proposed and experimented with, but the expectancy is that the period just ahead will see decided clearance, on the part of both Negro and white leadership groups, in the matter of sound ways to achieve integration at the points of equipment and of organizational structure.

Speaking of the progress of the Association with regard to this whole matter of inclusion, it has been said:

We have groped, and we are groping; we have been imperfect, and we are imperfect. . . . But we have had a firm foundation on which we have built and on which we can continue to build.

That we shall continue so to build seems to be not just a question of possibility but an imperative laid upon us. The National Board's recognition of this imperative is demonstrated by the following statement on Negro-white relationships, which it adopted on March 3, 1943 . . . :

As the National Board of the Young Women's Christian Association entered into the tasks of 1943, we reaffirmed our belief in and respect for the dignity and worth of human personality; we said that "across all boundaries of class and faith, race and nationality, the Young Women's Christian Association seeks to act as a vitalizing, steadying influence."

In the months following this affirmation, there has been clear evidence that the vitalizing and steadying influence of the Young Women's Christian Association is urgently needed in working for the elimination of the heavy injustices experienced by the Negro people. A world-wide struggle for freedom is meaningless, the sacrifice of life in the war will be of little avail, unless democracy is made real for all people.

The times demand that we make an honest examination of all inter-racial practices within the Association. Are they Christian and demo-cratic?

The times demand that we move courageously to correct the practices in our own organization which do not meet such tests.

The times demand that we adventure in new ways of integrating Negroes into all phases of Association and community life.

We believe that along this path will be found new vitality for the Association. Standing firmly upon our faith in God and on commit-ment to the way of life exemplified by Jesus we must all be willing to pay the price for this program.

To this program we dedicate ourselves, pledging mutual helpfulness to each other as we move step by step toward making it real in the Young Women's Christian Association. In the life of our nation we can be a cross-section group in which there will be no racial discrimina-tion, no crippling prejudices. As we strive to achieve this in our organization, we shall be an effective witness to democracy in our communities.

Our history, undoubtedly blundering at spots, undoubtedly exalted at many others, lies behind us. The answer to how well we shall build for the future lies in whether the words of this statement can be left only words, or whether the Young Women's Christian Associations of the United States of America will make them a living reality.[4]

In convention, assembled in the spring of 1946, the Young Women's Christian Associations decided that the words of this statement were not to be left as words only when the delegates by a large majority adopted resolutions calling for the integration of Negro women and girls into the main stream of Association life.

This growth of concepts has marked the turning from a service-centered program to a movement-centered one, in which the concern for a way of life is dominant. This is not to say that the Y.W.C.A. is less concerned to offer those services which in some part meet the needs of girls and women today, but it does emphasize the fact that the very offering of such services shall be

[4] *Ibid.,* p. 10.

in line with the purpose of the Association. A number of factors have contributed to this shift in emphasis.

Foremost among the contributing factors is the presence in the national organization of the student Y.W.C.A.'s. Probably nothing has been of greater importance, for these groups of young women, members of over five hundred college Associations, bring the qualities of high idealism, religious conviction, and invincibility to Y.W.C.A. goals and methods. Their own National Student Council has been basically interracial in its membership since its organization in 1922. It has been foremost among young people's activities all over the country, particularly in the South, in breaking down patterns of segregation. It has time and again pushed the whole national movement to a consideration or a practice which moved it along the lines of inclusiveness. The Association's study of its interracial practices, already referred to and quoted from above, came as the result of student insistence, voiced in three conventions, that the Y.W.C.A. undertake this self-study.

Frankly experimental in its methods, the Y.W.C.A. could face the possibilities in outcome of such a study knowing that, whatever recommendations might be forthcoming, there would always be a philosophy, an experience with method, and a leadership adequate to the proposals.

The quality of leadership which the Young Women's Christian Association has attracted to its cause and its program has been noted often as being of unusually fine caliber. There are good reasons why this should be so: women of high ideals and leadership abilities of several kinds have found a major outlet for their ideas and ministrations in this all-woman-managed organization; their activities have received both lay and professional recognition; their efforts were early rewarded by the sound establishment of one of the most important women's movements in our country, and in the world.

From this leadership one recalls quickly, from a goodly company among both the living and the dead, some of the women who have stood forth clearly and courageously for the complete acceptance of all people into the Association fellowship, as a witness to the rightness of the Christian way of life, as a witness to the organization's integrity, and as a witness for the larger society that such inclusion was not only right, religiously speaking, but actual in fulfillment of much of that happiness on earth which man so diligently pursues.

Mabel Cratty knew that "vision lights any pathway." Eva Bowles gave the motivation for many steps when she declared, "We go forward together." Leslie Blanchard made wise decisions from the sure knowledge that the only justice adequate for human needs is that "justice grown imaginative through love." All around the world friends in and out of the Association are strengthened by the assertion of Anne Wiggin's life that the "strongest cable is understanding among the people"; young and old have found shelter with Winnifred Wygel who knows that "love is a very wide room." And Cordella Winn caught up the faint and the bold with the proclamation that "we accept our share with joy." Juliette Derricotte was testament that "one comes as a person, always." Fern Babcock was testament to the truth that "friendship is a rock upon which to build any house," Mildred Inskeep, to that insight which knows that "trust is the first portal crossed to understanding." Henrietta Roelofs knew there could be "no peace without justice for all," Rhoda McCulloch knows "the way can be found only by the help of the white light of the spirit," Ann Elizabeth Neely knows "we shall not want for pathfinders if we place ability first." Mrs. John French is proof in grace that "faith will overgrow custom," and Mrs. Henry Ingraham stands wide-armed for "this, my Father's world."

Just what are the beliefs and practices of the Young Women's Christian Association which provide it with objectives and give it its own individual character among programs of social work, and a special position even among the programs of religiously motivated social-work organizations? And what bearing do these beliefs and practices have upon the development of the interracial character of the Association?

The inclusive character of the Y.W.C.A. has already been pointed out in the statement of the purpose "to build a fellowship of women and girls," "to share His love for all people." Two kinds of differences are noted readily in this: all races; and youth and age. But an examination of the membership reveals more than this, for there is equal concern that the membership be inclusive of whatever differences in culture still obtain within the larger pattern of our American culture; of whatever class distinctions; and of all occupations and activities in our vivid, fast-moving society. In many programs men, also, share activities with women, even though the Association remains by membership a women's organization.

Probably no organization is more concerned with the harmonious working together of youth and age than the Y.W.C.A. This is not due to a weak sentimentality about young people but rather to the certain knowledge that the freshness, the enthusiasm, and often the sharp insights of youth can have a better practical fulfillment when coupled with the experience of maturity, if that maturity is aware, fully, of such contribution from youth and is minded to make use of it. There is, in addition to the student Y.W.C.A.'s in the colleges, the younger girls' work in groups most often called the Girl Reserves. And in the clubs of industrial and business and professional women are a majority, naturally, of young women. In classes, interest groups, and other kinds of groups, girls and young women are also found. It is not merely their presence in the membership, however, which is of such significance at the point of inclusiveness; it is rather that in working out the Association's objectives and in deciding upon methods of work these girls and young women furnish a leadership considered coequal in importance to that of boards and committees and professional staffs.

Also, among the beliefs and practices of the Y.W.C.A. which give it its own individual character is the recognition of equality as between lay and professional leadership. Volunteers are looked upon not simply as helpers on chores but as leaders, coequal with professionals, in shaping the policies and program. The

Y.W.C.A. believes that the *volunteer*, as a result of her concern for the whole of society, can contribute perspective, objectivity, and freedom of personal opinion to any community organization. The *professional* worker will contribute a knowledge of the materials with which she must work: for the Association, the nature of its constituency and its needs; a knowledge of ways of work with people; and a knowledge of how to find and keep the significance of experiences in order that new programs may be soundly built. This combination of perspective, experience, and training makes a manifold of strength by which to advance the common good.

With such a combination in leadership the usual feeling of organizational self-consciousness is intensified and the resulting self-examination is more deliberate and thorough. It is just possible that some aspect of the continual self-study of the Y.W.C.A. is due to something that has been termed "feminine subjectivity." Be this as it may, the forthright approach to this task, the willingness to face the findings of such study, the courage to drop old ways and devise new ones attest to a high order of sincerity and integrity.

The development of interracial work in the Association can be examined in the light of these characteristics at several levels: the concept of inclusiveness, the concept of leadership, and the willingness to engage in self-study and to rebuild programs in the light of the findings. Beginning with the inclusiveness in membership, Negro women and girls, by their presence in large numbers, give rise to "an American dilemma" within the organizational structure of the Y.W.C.A., and permit it to be worked on there. White girls and women are aware of Negro girls and women both as members of America's largest minority and also as co-members with themselves of the Association. For any question that could be framed in terms of "What would I do about a Negro?" can be restated more pointedly "What will I do about a fellow member?" and conversely, on the part of the Negro girl or woman, the question "Could a white person be trusted?" becomes "Can I trust a fellow member?"

In addition, a good deal of real ability in the Negro group lies, perforce, in those groups of low economic level with much of the activity there at a deadly level of monotony. With the Y.W.C.A. offering an outlet for good minds among any and all of its members, and with the limitations of life operative in other areas, Negro women and girls have found unusual opportunity for self-expression and for leadership, and their contribution to the whole movement has been admittedly notable.

This has been true both in membership group activities, such as programs among younger girls, in the student movement, and among business and industrial women, and also among board and committee groups. It is interesting to note the rapid advancement of Negro women in the Association from a leadership confined exclusively to their own race to positions of prominence in the whole organization, in local Associations and at the national level, which involve responsibility for its total work. It has been pointed out that the five Negro secretaries on the national board staff carry professional responsibility for the total constituency. This also is true of the five Negro members of the national board, who serve on the standing committees not in regard to Negro interests only but for the various aspects of the total work of the board. Of even greater significance, perhaps, is the acceptance of Negro women on local boards and committees in this fashion, for the national work has for some time had an administrative leadership which wanted to and did make use of the freer opportunities for accepting Negro leaders as persons than are usually to be found in local situations. Negro women are on most boards of northern Associations and on many boards of southern Associations, and although the freedom in operations is more developed in the northern groups, the concept is present in most of the southern Associations, which are moving forward in the matter of full participation.

Negro professional leadership has been quick to avail itself of opportunities present in the Y.W.C.A. These opportunities, though representing desirable personal and professional positions, have been, for the most part, far from simple and easy administrative posts, if any professional work that deals with human needs and relationships could be so labeled. For the Negro secretary, more recently better described as a program director, has had to be, in addition to directing a program, administering a budget, supervising volunteers and sometimes other staff members, an interpreter of the Negro group within the whole community Association, a leader among the Negro minority in the community, and an interracial leader for the whole community. More recently, as the understanding has grown that a Negro woman may have, as any other professional worker may have, special skills and abilities within the area of strictly social work and informal education, she has become a contributor of her special skill to the whole program where such professional skill is needed. Negro professional leadership has accepted these opportunities gladly, encouraged by the gains in the whole Association which the Negro woman's double and often treble contributions have helped to bring about.

The role of Negro leadership has been significant, also, in the self-study processes which characterize the Y.W.C.A. For here again, Negro women and girls, feeling confident of the integrity of the Association in listening to their viewpoints and giving them full consideration, have poured out much of the feeling that under less favorable circumstances would be withheld, to the detriment of individuals and the organization. There has often been an excess of outpouring with few sympathetic ears available, but this, too, has been understood, for if the Y.W.C.A. itself is not so culpable as it has at times been declared, it knows that at many more times it has deserved the fullest expression of criticism for un-Christian practices. It knows, further, that even if within itself it manages to right many of the bad practices, it must stand ready to hear outpourings as long as society as a whole is characterized by undemocratic and un-Christian relationships.

On the whole it can be said that the Negro in the Y.W.C.A. reflects much of the new position to which he is attaining in the society as a whole, with more awareness on the part of the Y.W.C.A. of this new position, more general desire to see him make this new position secure and advance to new heights, than is found in society at large.

For democracy is on trial in our organizations as well as in our total national community. Are we to have in our nation, in the world, fair play, the acceptance of man as man, a genuine participation in all tasks by all, not only that the great burden of work of the world may be moved, but that it may be moved along in the best fashion because abilities are allowed natural outlets? This question the Y.W.C.A. has asked of itself. A continuing vitality in the organization demands that a positive answer be given. We have drained our human resources, in many of the old places where we looked for leadership, by the poor employment of these, by sheer waste, and by war, the greatest folly in waste. The total human resources need to be called into play now to recruit human ability adequate to human needs. The Y.W.C.A. knows how profound a truth this is, in the light of the march of human events and the present state of societies. It knows how true this is for its own needs. And in addition it knows that from within groups that hitherto have been quiescent or held down new springs of desire spurt up. There can be no holding back of peoples of color, among whatever groups that have occupied secondary places in the modern world, for there is a bursting vitality in these groups, a determination to find a new place for themselves, that will not be gainsaid. If there were not such desperate need for fresh strength for humanity as a whole, the urgencies within minorities to find and keep for themselves a new status are great enough to get acceptance by those wise in the ways of growth and the laws of movement. The Y.W.C.A., as an international women's organization as well as a national one, is aware of the new desires of people of color all around the world; perhaps it were better said, old desires now finding new expression. It sees these desires as eminently good in themselves; it is hopeful that acceptance of them can come in increasing integrations rather than through the irreparable losses encountered in the useless standing against the avalanche.

Of the Young Women's Christian Association in our society it can be said that it is a true social organism. Its ability to make some part of genuine social situations its program of concern and action; its ability to stay at the green-growing tip of our evolving society; its understanding of the stresses and strains to be undergone if such a relationship to the whole is to be maintained—all of this testifies to its genuine nature as a true and positive organ of the whole. It remains structured upon true life patterns of ordinary relationships—associations for friendships, for work interests, for intellectual and spiritual communication. Those are its patterns upon which all that is surface social-work planning is done. It is partial at the point of being a women's organization, a fact that is due largely to historical accident; but having come down from such a beginning, it has capitalized on what might be termed the woman's approach to society as an approach only, for its concern is with the totality of life as it undertakes, through informal educational ways, to work for the enhancement of human personality as a whole.

What can we look for from the Y.W.C.A. in the years just ahead? There is every reason to expect a continuation of its present thinking with respect to policies and position. Within itself, Negro women and girls may be expected to function increasingly as full members throughout the whole program—in the general clubs, classes, and other groups and as leaders for the whole, making their contribution to the defining of policies and the devising of programs. Within the Association, again, they can be expected more and more to be served through the accommodations provided for all, in housing, food, camping, recreation, and training facilities.

As for the Association as a community agency, it is altogether reasonable to expect that it will continue to champion the rights of Negroes, as a group, in our whole American society.

The Young Women's Christian Association will not become perfect. What it does achieve will not be achieved overnight. It may lose some ground at spots as it goes forward at others. But it is a complex and highly functioning body, equipped to deal with a complex and highly functioning society. With all of this complexity it has managed to keep a singularity of spiritual quality, Christian in essence. Perhaps it is not too much to say that if the basic structures in our society hold, the Young Women's Christian Association will be discerned as one of the strongest tissues in that holding, or that if our society fails, it will probably be one of the last of the interior organisms to perish.

10

The Role of Social and Civic Organizations and Agencies

GEORGE EDMUND HAYNES

THE individual person as an end in himself and as the base of human value is the goal of democratic equality and freedom drawn from our ideals of the brotherhood of man and of natural rights. The state and the self-interest of organized groups, therefore, are to be judged by their effect upon the individual's freedom and welfare. In that light we shall try to analyze the aims of these organizations and agencies, to get an understanding of their activities, and to form some estimate of their value.

For the first time since the founding of this nation Americans now find their basic philosophy of democracy—social, economic, religious, and political—challenged. The Communist (Marxian) theory, in contrast, claims also to draw its inspiration from the idea of the brotherhood of man. The value of the individual, however, is in terms of what he means to the state and the social group. The upsurge of the masses through history is the source of social progress. The Nazi doctrine of the master race has also made a bid for American allegiance. It spins its web out of the super-state, controlled by supermen. The master-race concept is now discredited by the defeat of Germany and Japan, although it still struggles for power in Europe and in America.

Whatever harmony and co-operation the different racial and

cultural groups in America can achieve under our concept of democracy, with or without the help of social and civic organizations and agencies, will be contrasted by other peoples not only with our struggle against the master-race theory but also with interracial achievement under communistic societies, especially Russia.

PUBLIC AGENCIES

On the National Level

The policy of the federal government in dealing with the American Indians, until the law of 1934, was to treat them as wards. From the beginning of the English settlement the attitude toward Indians was largely repressive. Indian policies from 1870 to 1934 were based upon wardship.[1] The main governmental activity was to provide them with subsistence and to help them preserve their tribal life. A new policy is developing in the direction of enabling Indians to become fully integrated citizens, even where they maintain their tribal organization and live on reservations.

There have been several attempts since Negro emancipation, in 1865, to get the federal government to set up agencies to deal with white-Negro relations. Since the failure of the Freedmen's Bureau and of a special congressional investigation of interracial clashes in 1870, only two types of special services have been undertaken by the federal government. Neither of them, however, has assumed wardship, as was the case with the Indians.

During World War I, the United States Secretary of War appointed Emmet J. Scott and the United States Secretary of Labor appointed this writer as special assistants to advise them on policies and plans affecting Negroes in the armed services and in labor, respectively. This action set a pattern and during the depression of the 1930's, advisers were appointed in several branches of the national government, especially in the Department of the Interior and the alphabetical organizations of the

[1] John Collier, "The Indian in a Wartime Nation," *Annals of the American Academy,* CCXXV (1942), 29–35.

relief and rehabilitation administrations. During World War II, similar advisers were appointed in the War and Navy departments, the War Manpower Commission and other agencies. Their main function was to guide administrators in helping to remove or prevent discrimination in governmental policies and procedures.

The second type of national special service was the provision of federal officials with administrative authority to act on matters affecting white-Negro relations. For many years the developing Agricultural Extension Service of the Department of Agriculture had officials who administered work among Negroes, but none dealt with interracial affairs, except indirectly. One Negro was made an administrative official in the Department of Agriculture. Others were appointed in the National Youth Administration and the Farm Security Administration. In 1942 the first Negro was appointed to a federal judgeship in the Virgin Islands, and in 1946 this same person, Judge William H. Hastie, was made governor of the islands. The Registrar of the Treasury and the Recorder of Deeds in the District of Columbia have frequently been Negro appointees.

The Fair Employment Practices Committee, authorized and appointed by President Roosevelt under his war powers by Executive Orders #8802 and #9346, was the first federal agency with administrative authority to act upon phases of interracial relations since the Freedmen's Bureau. The President declared in his order that there should be no discrimination in the employment of workers in the war industries or within the government because of race, creed, color, or national origin, and this committee was given power to investigate cases of discrimination, to receive and investigate complaints of employees, and "to take appropriate steps to redress grievances."

The Committee used four methods: arbitration between the complainant and the employer, directives to employers to "cease and desist" from practices judged discriminatory by the Committee, public hearings to bring public opinion to bear upon recalcitrants, and referral of cases to the President when deemed "necessary or proper to effectuate the provisions" of the executive order. The large majority of cases were settled by the first two methods. During the four years of the Committee's existence only two cases were referred to the President. Bills have been before both houses of the Congress for legislation for a permanent Fair Employment Practices Commission. One caused a long and bitter filibuster in the Senate.

The War Manpower Commission during World War II and the United States Employment Service have had minority group sections which gave attention to policies and activities for full justice to these groups. These sections, however, were largely advisory and derived their powers from the administrator who created them.

On the State Level

Public bodies dealing with race relations in the states had their major beginning during World War I when governors of sixteen states nominated and gave semiofficial status to Negro workers' advisory committees of white and Negro leaders, on the basis of a plan worked out by the author when he was special assistant to the United States Secretary of Labor. In some states, postwar committees or commissions developed as a sequel, notably in Michigan, Missouri, Maryland, New Jersey, and Pennsylvania.

Records of twelve such bodies were available in 1946 in the following states: California, Connecticut, Illinois, Indiana, Kentucky, Massachusetts, Maryland, Minnesota, New Jersey, New York, Pennsylvania, and Wisconsin. Six of these agencies were set up and their personnel appointed by governors under their executive powers and six were started under acts of the legislatures.

The purposes of these state agencies fall into three main classes:

1. To "study," "investigate," "examine and report" upon economic, social, cultural, health, and other conditions; to study areas of social tension.
2. To make recommendations, based upon study or investigation, looking

toward action by the governor, by the legislature, by arms of the state government, or by private citizens and organizations.

3. To act under their own authority to remove or prevent discrimination or other injustices; ". . . to improve race relations; . . . to serve as a guiding and stimulating agency for activities of civic, community, and other bodies concerned with inter-group relations; . . . to stimulate and encourage educational activities and to encourage tolerance; . . . to launch interlocking programs of action"; to provide for fair employment practices.

Until World War II the activities of all such public state bodies, as well as activities of state bodies having wider functions than those dealing with race relations, were largely confined to study, to investigation, and to education. Within the last five years, however, there has been a trend toward the enactment of legislation giving authority to special bodies to deal directly with discrimination by other means. This has been signally evident about employment but has applied also to other rights. The New York and New Jersey laws, enacted in 1945, the Massachusetts law of 1946 and the Connecticut law of 1947 declare that the right to work without discrimination because of race, color, religious creed, national origin, or ancestry is a civil right, and authorize the respective bodies that are to carry out the laws not only to use methods of conference, conciliation, and persuasion but also to investigate, study, and launch educational programs against discrimination. They may create councils and advisory agencies for the investigative and educational purposes of the law. They may also investigate and hear complaints and issue orders to a person, employment agency, labor organization, or employer "to cease and to desist" from acts and practices judged in violation of the legislative provision. They may call upon the courts to review their findings and punish violators. The complainant or respondent may also appeal to court against a decision of the Fair Employment Practices Authority. It is an "alliance of the police power of the State with the educational forces of the State" to remove or prevent discrimination.[2] Similar bills have been pro-

[2] *First Annual Report* of the New York State Commission Against Discrimination, July 1, 1946, pp. 1–8; chaps. 368 and 151B, General Laws, Common-

posed for enactment in the legislature of at least eighteen additional states.

Space does not allow much consideration of the state departments of education. A number of states are giving some attention to intercultural education and at least four states, California, New York, Massachusetts, and Texas, have well-established programs.[3] A study of 123 teacher-training institutions in the United States shows that many of these in metropolitan communities are developing broad and effective programs of intergroup education through courses in social studies, including experiences through the mingling of white and nonwhite students in dormitories, classrooms, dining rooms, etc.[4] These institutions can offer better training because they are in a better position to place graduates of minority racial and cultural groups and so can more easily take them in as students. They are better able also to secure lecturers and speakers from the minority groups.

Many teacher-training institutions are hampered in intercultural education "by their geographical environment," which may be "accentuated by possible population trends of the postwar period." There has been comparatively little selection of candidates for admission to these institutions on other than academic and physical criteria, which have not included evidence of "a deep love for human beings, and a burning desire to promote their welfare."

On the Local Level

Many local interracial committees, councils, or commissions have been appointed by mayors of cities, as in the striking case of the mayor's committees in Chicago, New York, St. Louis, and Los Angeles. The Los Angeles County Committee for Interracial

wealth of Massachusetts; unpublished address, Harold A. Lett, Chief Assistant, Division Against Discrimination, Department of Education of New Jersey, December 18, 1945.

[3] Julius E. Warren, "Inter-group Education through State Departments of Education," *Harvard Educational Review,* XV (1945), 111–116.

[4] Frank E. Baker, "Inter-group Education in Teacher-Educating Institutions," *Harvard Educational Review,* IV (1945), 104–110.

Progress and the Citizens' Committee for Latin-American Youth, organized in 1944 by the county board of supervisors, is one of the few, if not the only, interracial efforts on the county level. Committees in Harrisburg, Hartford, Cleveland, and probably one or two other places have been established by action of city councils. The Detroit Interracial Committee was established by both the mayor and the city council.

The work of these committees has varied widely. Some of them have been merely advisory to the mayors and others have undertaken educational programs to influence the activities both of public and of private agencies. A few of them have undertaken to study the local racial problems and to publish their findings. Some have simply been committees-in-being with intention of doing something if and when the opportunity or need arises. The public committees in New York, Chicago, Cleveland, Los Angeles, and one or two other places have funds' and employ executive staffs. In Chicago, Cleveland, and Los Angeles these funds come from public monies. In New York and probably other cities support comes from private sources. Like local private agencies and organizations treated in a later section, these public ones have a close-up relation to the day-by-day intergroup problems.

Probably the most significant interracial work by public agencies on the local level has been in the public schools. Many cities could be cited for important developments in administrative policies and methods, as well as in content of curricular and extracurricular activities. Des Moines was perhaps the first city school system to give direct attention and planning to interracial education. Courses of study in history, geography, literature, and other fields, from the elementary grades through high school and in public forums for adults, were undertaken as early as 1930. The Springfield (Mass.) Plan, which was applied to selection of teachers, to administration, and to content of all school courses and activities, has probably received the widest attention because of its scope and thoroughness. Many other educational authorities in cities such as Pittsburgh, Chicago, Newark, and Detroit were stimulated or encouraged by the Springfield example.

On the National Level

The private organizations may be classified into five groups, according to the auspices under which they function. These fall under labor, religious, educational, free-lance, and miscellaneous headings. To some extent their auspices affect their aims and policies as well as their activities.

The labor organizations may be mentioned first. They have special committees of the general organization to work for integration of racial and cultural groups, they carry on interracial activities as a part of their general program without a special committee or, as many craft unions do, they compromise or segregate. Some labor organizations undertake to integrate the general purpose of labor in terms of protest against discrimination. For example, the C.I.O.'s Committee to Abolish Racial Discrimination aims "to translate into effective action the stated purpose of the C.I.O. . . . ," namely, "to bring about the effective organization of the working men and women of America regardless of race, creed, or nationality, and to unite them for common action in the labor union for their mutual aid and protection." The United Automobile Workers, C.I.O., admits Negroes into full membership and activities without discrimination. Another labor organization projects its aims in the field of race relations within the framework of the general union, without special committees, "to unite in one organization, regardless of creed, color, sex, nationality or political affiliation. All workers are eligible for membership who are directly or indirectly engaged in the maritime industry."[6] The majority of A.F. of L. unions accept Negroes, many in separate unions, and some exclude by constitution or ritual.

The second group embraces those organizations and agencies

---

[5] Along with material from other sources, seventy agencies were studied, as described in the *Directory of Agencies in Race Relations*, edited by Dr. Charles S. Johnson and published by the Julius Rosenwald Fund, Chicago, 1945.

[6] *Ibid.*, p. 49.

under religious auspices—Protestant, Catholic, and Jewish. This class of organization is given treatment elsewhere in this volume. There is, however, a group of national agencies that draw their support and personnel from religious bodies but operate on a civic or social basis apart from ecclesiastical control. For example, the Commission on Community Relations of the American Jewish Congress aims to develop a program of action in combating anti-Semitism "based on knowledge rather than on speculation." It co-operates with all groups, Jewish and non-Jewish, "interested in learning the facts about minority tensions and acting to relieve them." It is "a research unit with the responsibility on the one hand of evaluating and comparing techniques already receiving wide use and, on the other, of developing more effective techniques where necessary.[7] Similarly the National Conference of Christians and Jews, Inc., "a voluntary association of individuals, aims to promote justice, amity, understanding, and co-operation among Jews, Catholics, and Protestants of the United States, and to analyze, moderate, and finally eliminate group prejudices . . ." but "neither seeks uniformity of religious beliefs nor undertakes to represent official religious bodies."[8] These agencies have worked directly through their own local committees and leaders as well as indirectly through supplying services of social science experts and supporting projects in public schools and other educational institutions.

The third group of organizations operate under educational auspices. These organizations deal mainly with intergroup education. They include, for example, the American Council of Education, a federation of organizations and institutions concerned with education, the Bureau for Intercultural Education, and special departments of the National Education Association. This group of agencies has aimed to study teaching materials in intergroup education, to promote experiments in teacher-training institutions or programs for pre-service education, to promote "sys-

---

[7] *CCI Facts on Friction*, (Commission on Community Interrelations, American Jewish Congress, No. 11, April, 1946.)

[8] *Harvard Educational Review*, XV (1945), 142–143.

tematic development of aspects of inter-group education in the public school systems," to bring to the public "fuller understanding of the necessity of a better education for all people," and to encourage "seeking the essentials for the perpetuation of our democracy."[9] They have sponsored meetings of teachers and others interested in intergroup education and have provided teachers with suggestive information. They have helped schools to develop programs, curricula, and material for intercultural education and have published informational and learning material. In 1945 the American Council on Education enlisted eight state colleges to experiment in training teacher candidates in methods and principles of intergroup education. After a year "exploring prejudices, deepening understandings, activating cooperation," and learning "some things that work to reduce intergroup hostilities and that lead to goodwill and united action," they held their first "workshop" on the problems of intergroup relations in teacher education in the summer of 1946. A significant study of intercultural education in seven typical public school systems in seven cities has recently been sponsored by the Julius Rosenwald Fund and the Bureau of Intercultural Education.[10]

The professional schools of social work, many of them affiliated with large universities, have contributed considerably to advancement in race relations, both through instruction of future leaders, through work these graduate students do in the urban centers, and through scientific studies by both the students and faculties.[11]

The fourth group is composed of free-lance organizations that draw their constituencies from parts of the population particularly sympathetic to the purposes for which each organization stands. Typical of this group are the National Association for the

[9] Charles S. Johnson, *op. cit.*, pp. 12, 43.

[10] Theodore Brameld, *Minority Problems in the Public Schools* (New York, 1946).

[11] Members of the faculty of the Atlanta University School of Social Work have published significant articles and several books in this field over the past ten years.

Advancement of Colored People, the American Civil Liberties Union, the American Council on Race Relations, the Council Against Intolerance in America, the National Urban League, and the Southern Regional Council. A study of the aims of this group discloses three major objectives, with possible combination of two of them in some cases. The stated aims focus either on breaking the existing group patterns, on serving individuals and groups suffering from the ills and handicaps of the existing system, or on proceeding on the theory that the system can be changed by gradual modifications of its features. Those of the first type speak of "full participation by all citizens, equal rights and equal opportunities," the abolition of racial discrimination, of disfranchisement, and equality of rights and distribution of public facilities, funds, etc. The other types aim toward understanding, co-operation, and national unity among the groups or to promote "justice, amity and co-operation," to investigate conditions, to integrate Negroes in existing programs, "to analyze, moderate and finally eliminate group prejudices." And finally one, the Indian Rights Association, aims "to promote the spiritual, moral, and material welfare of and protect the legal rights of American Indians."[12]

There is a fifth group—social organizations with miscellaneous purposes that include race relations in their purview. Several philanthropic foundations, such as the General Education Board, the Julius Rosenwald Fund, the Russell Sage Foundation, and the Phelps Stokes Fund, fall into this group. It also includes such agencies as the American Newspaper Guild, the American Free World Association and the Coöperative League of the United States, that aim to affect race by their programs of economic and social change. These organizations either serve Negroes by their financial largess or include them as integral parts of their membership.

Finally, the aims and activities of political and sporting organizations have so affected race relations that some mention of them should be made in the miscellaneous class. No national and few

[12] Johnson, *op. cit.*, pp. 32, 51–56.

state conventions of the major political parties the past three generations have met without some attention to white-Negro relations. Their strategy and the effects on government and public policy have been largely determined by their interracial action. Negro leaders have been conspicuous in their national, state, and local affairs as well as in those of minor political parties. In sports the A.A.U. in college athletics, the American participation in Olympics, and the decision of the management of the Brooklyn Dodgers to let down the bars against Negroes in baseball are having effect beyond the circles of sports. And in the pugilistic arena, the attitude and practice of equality to all comers of all races and nationalities, including the present heavyweight champion of the world, Joe Louis, has exerted influence wider than is generally recognized.

An analysis of the activities of these national private agencies of all the types described discloses several general kinds.[13] First, mention may be made of appeals to good will or patriotic sentiment through general hortatory propaganda, in speeches and harangues on the platform or over the radio, in mass meetings and popular conventions, and in special publications.

Second, there is a legal appeal for civil rights through cases carried to the courts to assert, protect, or establish the constitutional rights and privileges of Negroes, Indians, Japanese-Americans, and other racial minorities.[14] For example, the case of Lloyd Gaines, who in 1938 was denied admission to the Law School of the University of Missouri because of his race, was appealed to the United States Supreme Court by the National Association for the Advancement of Colored People. The court ruled that all states must provide "equal educational facilities for all qualified students" and that this obligation could not be met by paying

---

[13] Professor Goodwin Watson of Columbia University has made a classification and evaluation of all types of intercultural improvement agencies on the basis of their methods under "Exhortation, Education, Participation, Relation, Negotiation, Contention, Prevention" in *Action for Unity*, Jewish Affairs Pamphlet, I (1946).

[14] Cf. Paul E. Baker, *Negro-white Adjustment* (New York, 1934), p. 259.

tuition in universities and colleges outside of the state. This case caused Missouri and other southern states to spend thousands of dollars for Negro graduate and professional education, and further results are in process of development. Another example is the test case brought by the American Civil Liberties Union about the evacuation of Japanese-Americans from the west coast and their detention in camps under the War Department edict of 1942.

Another type of legal action has provided for legal defense when the accused has been a member of a minority group, particularly in situations where there have been race clashes between Negroes and whites. For example, Dr. Ossian Sweet and his brother, who were shot in Detroit in 1925, and the victims of the so-called "Elaine riots" in Arkansas were defended by the N.A.A.C.P. The famous case of the Scottsboro boys, first defended by the International Labor Defense League but largely overshadowed by the raising of funds for the communist movement, and later taken up by an independent citizens' group, the American Scottsboro Committee and the noted criminal attorney, Samuel S. Liebowitz, are other examples.

A third form of legal action, somewhat different from the above, consists in cases of discrimination against individuals under existing civil rights laws or under federal laws, as in the case of interstate travel and the Selective Service Act. The action in some of these cases has varied with the different states, since some of the laws provide both civil and criminal action. The Civil Liberties Union, the N.A.A.C.P., the Workers' Defense League, and several specially set-up defense committees have brought legal action under such laws in behalf of clients of minority racial groups.

Legal appeal and legal defense are different from a third type of effort carried out by many of these organizations to secure state or national legislation in behalf of the enjoyment of democratic rights and privileges by minority racial groups, particularly Negroes. These efforts have resulted either in the removal of evil practices, as through antilynching laws or anti-Ku Klux Klan laws, or in the removal and prevention of discriminatory practices in public or quasi-public accommodation in hotels and theaters. In addition, nondiscrimination provisions have been sought in general enactments, both state and national, such as education bills, health acts, social security, employment compensation. Last but not least have been the efforts to secure special laws setting up commissions for improving race relations, against discrimination, and for instituting fair employment practices.

Besides the efforts for legal appeal, legal defense, and anti-discrimination legislation, there has been a long and effective line of work to influence the administration of laws and regulation so as to include or benefit American Indians, Negroes, and other racial minorities equally with other elements of the population.

The activities of many of these organizations are of educational, social service, or social action character. The educational methods have included the promotion of group study and discussion, which has taken the form of study groups, lecture-discussion conferences, institutes, seminars, and workshops. Some such study-discussion has been for leadership training' but much of it has been for the orientation of the rank and file.

Preparation and publication of written and printed matter has absorbed a great deal of the attention and resources of these organizations as a part of their educational programs. Reams of mimeographed material and literally tons of printed matter have been prepared and distributed. We make no attempt here to pass upon the quality of such or to differentiate between published material that is largely for the promotion of the organization itself, and the raising of its funds, and what is of a purely educational quality for orienting and teaching the leadership or the rank and file. Nor has sufficient study of this published material been made to indicate how much is confined to factual data and how much to propaganda and publicity of certain ideas, theories, or ideologies through which the particular organization wished to influence public opinion.

Several organizations in the last two or three years have also given special attention to the professional training of leaders with regard to the biological, psychological, sociological, and other scientific facts about races and their relationship, as well as training in the technical skills required for successful leadership in this field. Seminars, conferences, institutes, and interracial clinics for the orienting of leaders—national, state, and local—have been growing in effectiveness. In recent years also there has been a development of technical guidance in public educational institutions, mainly on the high school and college levels, both in the matter of the organization and content of their curricula and with regard to the supervision and direction of their extracurricular activities. In addition, two or three organizations, such as the Bureau for Intercultural Education, have addressed themselves especially to the preparation of teaching and learning materials and the administrative methods and techniques of public school systems. They have taken some key cities, notably Gary, Indiana, and Detroit, Michigan, as laboratories.

Many of the organizations have given considerable attention to investigation, most of which has had to do with specific problems or social conditions and some of it with legal cases through which the organization has aimed toward social action. At times investigation has been solely for the purpose of giving constituents an accurate report on the facts in a given situation. Frequently, as in the procedure of the interracial clinics, sponsored by the Federal Council of Churches' Department of Race Relations, investigation has been preliminary to local community action.[15]

Direct action against segregation has been taken by a few national organizations, mainly religious agencies like the Y.W.C.A. and the Federal Council of Churches, which "renounced the pattern of segregation" and called upon its constituent communions to do likewise. Both the national Y.W.C.A. and the Federal Council of Churches have refused to hold their conventions or meetings in places where hotel accommodation could

[15] Cf. *ibid.*, p. 258.

not be secured for all their constituents without discrimination. In contrast, the National Conference of Social Work has an accommodation policy about hotels.

Public protest and agitation through mass meetings, picketing, newspapers, the radio, and other means have also been a part or all of the activities of many organizations. These types of activity, termed "direct action," have assumed a larger place in organizational programs in recent years, probably stimulated by the examples of the labor unions and the left-wing groups.

Striking examples of such "direct action" have been given by labor unions that have carried their meetings to various hotels in different cities and by the March-on-Washington Movement, which was organized in 1942 for mass pressure by Negroes themselves "for full and unconditional equality of status of Negro and white peoples." The Movement first threatened and planned a mass march from various industrial centers to Washington, D.C., to petition President Roosevelt for action against job discrimination. The President issued Executive Order #8802 against discrimination in industry and government because of race, creed, or national origin, and established the Fair Employment Practices Committee to implement the order. The March-on-Washington Movement then adopted an extended program of nonviolent direct action.

In the last two or three years, there has risen a national free-lance movement, known as the Congress on Racial Equality (C.O.R.E.), developed under the idea that it is a mistake "to assume that only Negroes can effectively act for interracial justice." This movement has attempted to be a national clearing house for local groups that "aim to avoid all violence of action or attitude in carrying out their program," but are developing disciplined, nonviolent action against the color line. Interracial groups from these local committees have visited restaurants, theaters, churches, and other places where color bars have existed, and have insisted on equality of treatment. Their method differs from that of the legal-action agencies because they have not invoked legal measures but insist that those who participate shall maintain an attitude "of goodwill and reconciliation, even in the midst of a non-coöperative campaign."

The giving of awards for meritorious action or achievement, such as the five-year development of the Harmon Awards for Distinguished Achievement Among Negroes and the art exhibitions which grew out of them (donated by the late William E. Harmon and administered by the Department of Race Relations of the Federal Council of Churches), helped to change false ideas about Negro ability and stimulated potential creativity. Experiments in interracial contacts by indirect approach where matters of mutual interest have become the centers of common effort on the part of members of different racial groups is another type of action which has been widely practiced.[16]

Private organizations and agencies on the state level are so related to the national organizations and their aims and methods differ so little in essential respects from those on the national level that any special treatment of them would add little to the picture. There are only a few—mainly the state interracial commissions, in several southern states—that have continued active after being set up by the Southern Interracial Commission following World War I. They have brought white and Negro leaders together for co-operative action, molded public opinion, and carried on many goodwill activities.

In the Local Community[17]

As one approaches race relations in the local community and studies the efforts of both constructive and destructive forces disclosed, his judgment reaches no other conclusion than that here people come to grips directly with their problems of living together. He is also impressed with the fact that organized efforts in the local community to deal with racial and cultural relations are legion. Not only do many of the national organizations have local branches or affiliated bodies, but there are many unaffiliated

[16] Cf. *ibid.*, pp. 228–229.

[17] Description of seventy local organizations, in as many communities, in the *Directory of Agencies in Race Relations*, and records from twenty-one cities where interracial clinics were held—1944–46—were the sources of facts for this section.

intercultural and interracial committees, commissions, and other special organizations having either social, civic, educational, political, or religious roots. There are also similar agencies that function as parts of the local institutions and agencies through which the local community expresses its total life.

The aims of these private local organizations and agencies fall into six types. Those, first, that seek "understanding," "goodwill," or "co-operation" comprise the largest number. Some of them add such terms as "tolerance" or "bettering race relations." Next are those agencies and organizations that "protest grievances," "oppose discrimination," or "dispel rumors" and false statements. Then a number of them propose as their ends "justice" and "equality of opportunity" or "respect for individual equality." Another type, largely paternalistic, aims to "improve living conditions" of Negroes or to secure better health, housing, recreation for them. A larger proportion than one would expect aims to integrate Negroes and other minorities on a democratic basis into the community in situations such as public schools or other community agencies, or to apply democratic principles in employment. A few communities have organizations of the council or clearing-house type for the most effective use of public and private resources to meet the needs of all the people, including those of racial minorities. The special agencies like local councils for fair employment practices or committees on interracial or intercultural public school policies and practices are not covered in the general classes just described.

The activities of the local groups are even more varied than their stated purposes. The large majority carry on some kind of educational publicity by addresses, mass meetings, radio and newspaper publicity, or mimeographed and printed material. Some of this is special propaganda that does not seem calculated to secure overt behavior or action, but a surprising amount of it does. Other groups promote more systematic educational work (1) through lectures, well-planned conferences, institutes or seminars for regular periods of time, study-discussion groups; (2) through the introduction of Negro and other group history into the public schools and of suitable books into public libraries; and (3) through interfaith, interracial, or intercultural festivities. Many local organizations, especially local branches of the N.A.A.C.P. and the Civil Liberties Union, are alert for action on civil rights, especially for Negroes, and local affiliates of the National Urban League carry out effective social-work programs. Some mention getting Negroes on grand juries and into local federal jobs. Fellowship worship services and civic and fraternal group activities are carried on in some communities.

Two important facts about these local developments call for particular mention: the auspices under which they are held and the trend toward co-ordination of agencies and resulting division of labor. The large majority of local groups have rested upon individuals, often citizens of prominence, who, however, did not usually bring to the interracial committee or commission much authority or support from the community groups. All too frequently these individuals did not have the connections with agencies through which action could be effectuated. In recent years, especially in communities that have held "interracial clinics" with community self-surveys and meetings of representatives of many groups to plan co-operatively, the interracial councils or commissions have sought underpinning by means of membership support from the ongoing agencies through which the community functions such as churches, schools, labor unions, and business associations, as well as from influential individuals.

Along with the development toward organizational support has been a trend toward clearance and co-ordination of services so that minority groups might be served as other groups are served by the regular community agencies. The community services to minority groups thus are integrated with those provided for other elements of the population and the sense of "belonging" seems to be growing among them all.

EVALUATION AND CONCLUSION

The evaluation of organizations and agencies included in this study discloses two trends, one of aim and one of method, and an evident need for co-ordination of organizations and efforts of these agencies. The trend in aim is definitely toward attacks upon over-all segregation patterns as a major means of removing the caste system. Undoubtedly this tendency for direct attack upon segregation offers promise for democratic progress. The trend in method is toward scientific and technical training for leaders and toward sounder education through all the avenues of instruction for the rank and file in the scientific facts and ethical and religious principles involved.

Legal action through the courts and through preventive and remedial legislation has an increasing place in organizational programs. This seems a hopeful trend in view of the larger function of government and law in determining human relations. It is also true that changes in the folkways that crystallize into law, either through legislative enactment or through court decisions, have increased chances of improvement, intercultural and interracial.

The far-reaching effects of such legal and legislative action as shown in the civil rights cases successfully handled by several organizations indicate the value of such work for changing caste patterns. The improved citizenship status of the Indian, the increased pay of Negro teachers, the equitable distribution of public school funds, the provision for advanced education for Negroes and their exercise of the franchise in southern states, the change in city zoning ordinances as well as the restrictive covenants are all evidence that appeals to legislatures to enact fair-practice laws and appeals to the courts to enforce them and to guarantee constitutional civil rights spell changes in the patterns of the caste system.

The record of results from the educational work of the public school leaves no doubt of its effectiveness. The major point for improvement is in community outreach, lest pupils become frustrated by opposition from parents and neighbors when they try to practice outside the school what they are taught inside.

General integration and clearance organizations, that include all—minorities as well—have been mainly controlled by the white majority. When interracial improvement organizations have been controlled by Negroes or other minorities, they have been largely special pleading agencies for their particular group. They have undoubtedly advanced the groups they served but to some extent they have tended to continue after the condition which they aimed to eliminate has been changed.

The need for co-ordination of programs and efforts, with the consequent division of labor and reduction of overlapping and duplication, becomes more evident the farther one probes into the structure, aims, and functioning of scores of national bodies. Three attempts have been made toward such a development in past years in two national interracial conferences and in the Joint Committee on National Recovery, fostered by twenty-four organizations and agencies interested in larger service by government to minority racial groups. The first national conference was held at Cincinnati, Ohio, March, 1925, under the auspices of the Federal Council of Churches' Department of Race Relations and the Southern Commission on Interracial Coöperation, which brought together leaders from many social, educational, business, fraternal, and religious organizations.[18] The second conference was held in Washington, D.C., in December, 1928, under the auspices of an executive committee formed by sixteen organizations, with the author as executive secretary. The latter meeting was preceded by extensive research under Dr. Charles S. Johnson as research secretary, including an effort to get participating organizations to analyze their own programs and relationships with a view toward some sort of continuation of an advisory council. Each of these conferences was followed by significant publications that provided "a reasonably faithful contemporary picture of Negro life and relationships with the white race in the United States" and a synthesis of experience and data "as a sound basis for planning programs of improvement," but no

[18] Charles S. Johnson, *The Negro in American Civilization* (New York, 1930).

organized council or committee for common planning and action resulted. A significant experiment in co-ordination on the state level is now being made in California.

The Joint Committee on National Recovery was set up in Washington, D.C., in 1933, through the co-operation and financial support of twenty-six religious, social, and civic agencies, to prevent discrimination in the industrial codes that the federal government set up under the N.R.A., and to integrate Negro workers, farmers, and consumers into the federal administration of the several relief and recovery programs during the period of the depression of 1930's. With an office and an executive secretary in Washington, this committee was active for about two years and paved the way for later interorganizational action.

Many agencies seem to proceed on the assumption that significant social service or social action have been achieved when they have "spoken their mind," passed a resolution, or given wide publicity to a question or a situation. Individual behavior and group patterns are little affected by such verbalization. More and more, leaders and the rank and file should judge organizations by evidence of achieved changes in behavior of individuals and interracial group practices and customs.

Even where action has been taken it is often not clear that the organization acted in the light of well-defined aims or a well-planned program or had the skill to check on its results. Leaders should give emphasis to these phases of proposals for race adjustment. One of the wholesome signs is the increasing application of scientific methods and spirit, as illustrated by the development of the interracial clinics, the institutes, conferences, and workshops.

Again, while the achieving of equality under democracy makes the breaking of the caste patterns imperative, there seems to be need for work by some organizations and agencies that focus on service within the existing patterns. The children who need education and welfare service now will grow up before segregation patterns can be changed. These agencies should take care, however, that their aims and methods do not hinder the needed social change and that they cease as agencies when changes do come.

It is well to remember the work of the organizations here discussed has been promoted in some instances by religious bodies and in other cases have been developed by individuals whose inspiration was religious. The Christian way has available to it, therefore, not only agencies admittedly religious, but many of a social and civic nature.

In conclusion, even this preliminary review shows a decided change in the interracial climate in about thirty years. Our urge toward freedom and equality of all persons of all racial groups shows greater action after World War II. The period just before, during, and following World War II shows contrast with the same period of World War I in the reduction of open interracial conflict, in the more positive participation of our government for the protection and participation of racial minorities, and in the multiplication of movements, organizations, and agencies on the national, state, and local level to cure or prevent the social ills of racial tensions and hatreds. There seems to be a growing realization that the world leadership of America makes the freedom and welfare of racial minorities a national concern.

V

RESOURCES—INDIVIDUAL

11

The Obligations of the
Individual Christian

BENJAMIN E. MAYS

~~

CITIZEN OF TWO WORLDS

THE Christian is a citizen of two worlds: the world that now is and the world that ought to be. He is a part of the existing order with all of its imperfections, shortcomings, and brutality. Yet he can never accept the present order. He is committed to an order that is only partially in existence. He holds a loyalty to something that transcends this earth. He owes allegiance to the way of life as set forth by Jesus in the Four Gospels. He is obligated to believe in the kind of God Jesus portrays in the Gospels—a God who is the author of life and the world and who is the Father of all mankind. The Christian's ultimate allegiance is to the God of Jesus Christ and not to any particular economic, political, national, racial, or denominational order.

The Christian is also committed to a belief in man. This involves a belief in the intrinsic worth of each individual and, since God is the author of life, a belief in the kinship of all humanity, in the fatherhood of God, and in the brotherhood of man. Though living all the time in an imperfect world, the Christian is obligated in all social relations to strive to square his life with the best there is in the Christian tradition.

If a man really believes in God, in Jesus, and in man, there will be, and there must be, tension between him and the world in which he lives. And this tension can never be completely resolved unless he accepts the world as it is—which the true Christian can never do.

THE CHRISTIAN IS NOT A SLAVE

The Christian, by virtue of his twofold citizenship, is not wholly a slave to his environment. There is a tendency to excuse oneself for falling below the Christian requirements on the ground that man is a creature of his environment and that it would prove suicidal, socially, economically, and politically, if one should act independently of what most people believe and do. If there is any one sure conviction of Christian teaching, it is the fact that the Christian not only can rise above his environment but can transform it. The story of every truly converted man in Christian history, from Paul's conversion up to the present moment, proves conclusively that man can break with his environment, can forsake old habits, can cut the chains that bind him to the mores of society, and can set in motion a spirit that will create a new order. When he does rise above his environment or break with old habits and customs out of loyalty to a higher order, the ultimate outcome is good. If the Christian has faith and is willing to trust God, if he gives his allegiance to the world that ought to be, he usually finds himself landing on higher ground here and now. In scores of instances where progress for the benefit of all mankind has been made, it has been made only when someone dared to prove loyal to a greater good than the good currently practised. This can be proved again and again in all areas of life. Transformation may not always be immediate. It may come within a short time and it may be continuous throughout the centuries. Harriet Beecher Stowe, Henry Ward Beecher, Frederick Douglass, and others helped to transform a slave society into a free economy. Men like Roger Bacon and Charles Darwin rose above their immediate environment and contributed mightily toward the creation of a new world through science. The prophets of Israel have transforming influence after twenty-six or more centuries. Jesus is more potent now than he was nineteen centuries ago. If bad men can change the world for evil purposes, certainly good men can transform it for good purposes.

HUMAN BEINGS FIRST

The first obligation of a Christian is to see peoples as human beings. In a prejudiced economy such as ours differences have been played up so long that one is tempted to see peoples first as Gentiles, Jews, Japanese, Chinese, Mexicans, or Negroes. But each individual is first a human being and secondarily, and largely accidentally, a Jew or a Negro. The moment one sees men in terms of race, nationality, social position, or even religion, he is likely to set up differential treatment for them in his mind and in his behavior. The writer has seen Negroes apparently breathe a sigh of relief when they learned that the victims in a great accident were all white people. The death of white people does not seem to affect some Negroes as much as the death of Negroes. He has also seen white people behave in a similar manner when the victims were Negroes.

Recently in Atlanta a Negro, having fallen off a garage, was seriously injured and lay suffering in a pool of blood. Two Jewish girls saw the accident. One of the girls, not knowing that a driver of an ambulance for whites is not supposed to haul a Negro, called a white undertaker to send an ambulance. The ambulance came, but when the driver and the person accompanying him arrived and saw that the victim was a Negro, they refused to take him. The girls pleaded but it was no use. They had to call a Negro undertaker. To the driver, it was just a "nigger." His life was not important.

One sees this differential at its worst in cases of jobs and wages and in some of our courts where Negroes are being tried, or where Negroes are being handled by the police. To many of these officers, lawyers, judges, and jurors, the victims are nothing but "niggers," and that means that they are not to be taken seriously or treated equally. This way of thinking explains why it is almost impossible for Negroes to get justice in the courts in many sections of our country. It explains, in part, why several thousand Negroes have been lynched in this country since emancipation. It also accounts for the fact that practically none of the lynchers have been brought to justice. It is this way of thinking —considering some biologically inferior or superior and some inherently better or worse—that accounts for the basic injustices that exist in our interracial practices. It is the refusal to believe that all men are sons of God and of equal worth in his sight. The Christian is obligated by virtue of his commitments to the Christian principles to look upon every individual as a son or daughter of God.

Jesus enunciated this principle in eloquent language in the story of the Good Samaritan. The neighbor is not necessarily a member of one's particular group, race, or nation, but one who transcends all artificial barriers and responds to human need wherever found. If the Samaritan had seen the robbed, beaten man as nothing but a Jew, he certainly would have acted no better than the priest and the Levite who passed by on the other side.

If the Christian cannot begin here, nothing else matters. If he can begin here, the consequences of his beliefs and actions will find wholesome expression in everything that he does of an interracial character.

INTEGRITY AND CHARACTER

The second obligation of the Christian in an interracial program, whether it involves Gentiles, Jews, Orientals, Mexicans, or Negroes, is to be honest and tell the truth. Although considerable progress has been made, it is still often true that members of interracial groups do not face issues honestly and squarely.

Slavery and the hardships that confronted Negroes during the days of reconstruction made many of them hypocritical and untruthful when dealing with white people. They developed techniques of survival which made them smile when they wanted to fight; techniques of flattery which enabled them to get what they wanted; techniques of saying what they knew white people wanted them to say, which helped them to survive in a hostile environment. Slavery and the conditions under which Negroes have had to live in this country since emancipation have been exceptionally hard on their integrity.

The fundamental danger, therefore, confronting all minority Christians in race relations, especially Negro Christian leadership, is that the desire to please and to be acceptable to the white majority and the desire to be well spoken of by them will be so strong that Negro Christian leaders will be inclined to do and say what they think will prove helpful to them and acceptable to the white majority. This is understandable. It takes considerable courage, more than most people possess, for a member of a subordinate race to speak honestly on certain questions in a manner that he knows to be contrary to the wishes of the race that holds the advantage. And those in power do not always make it easy or comfortable for the disadvantaged to express an honest opinion, however logical or right it may be. This is not wholly a theoretical argument. Many people know from experience that what some Negro Christians say when speaking on the question of race among themselves is not what they say when speaking across race lines. Especially is the Negro Christian likely to be evasive when the subject involves complete equality of the races and that much-feared phrase "social equality." This trait is not peculiar to the Negro. It is a human trait, and parallel situations can be found in history.

If the Negro Christian honestly believed that being hypocritical or evasive were the way to advance the cause of the race, it would still be unfortunate; but one fears that in all too many cases the selfish motive dominates and the individual is concerned with advancing himself to positions of influence and power. If this is the case, it is most deplorable.

The plea here is for Negro Christians to be wholly honest in this area, because truth is better than lying, integrity is better than hypocrisy, and genuine progress in race relations can be made only when all parties concerned are honest. If this is not true, then it must be admitted that injustice is better than justice, lying is better than truth, and hypocrisy is better than honesty. Whether there was a time when this method was useful and necessary is not to be debated here. Our contention is that if that time ever existed it has passed now. New techniques of honesty are pressing themselves upon us and no Christian can evade the obligation to be honest.

Then, too, white Christians of integrity are beginning more and more to look with suspicion upon the Negro leader who seeks by hypocritical means to establish himself in their good graces. Increasingly, today, they seek the Negro leader who will give them a true interpretation of what he believes Negroes think. If the Christian leader cannot be honest at this point, the leadership of Negroes will pass to other hands. A critical Negro public is demanding that Negro leadership be straightforward and sincere.

There is another area in which the lack of sincerity crops out. If many white people believe that the white race is superior to the Negro race, it must be said in all candor that many Negroes have helped to perpetuate the belief. Even now there are churches, owned and operated by Negroes, in which they segregate themselves and thus help to perpetuate a system which they know is un-Christian and undemocratic. Negroes often admit that they do not believe in this system but they want to court the favor of those in positions of influence and power. It is persons like these that white people quote when they say that Negroes want to be segregated and jim-crowed. A lack of honesty at this point retards the growth of Christian interracialism. But the danger is that one usually becomes what he does. If Negroes segregate themselves long enough, they will themselves ultimately accept and believe in segregation.

Negro Christians and Negroes generally need to test their integrity in another area. They have been pushed around so much and have been intimidated so long that they are often tempted to blame any failure on their part to racial discrimination. It is certainly true that many of their failures are directly traceable to segregation and discrimination. No honest mind could deny this fact. But they sometimes excuse themselves for shortcomings when the fault is not in discrimination but in themselves. Human beings tend to blame something else or somebody else for their failures rather than to accept responsibility for their own deficiencies and to seek the means of overcoming them. Negroes need to be careful not to accept inferior standards for themselves just because they are a suppressed people and then complain when the high standard set for other Americans is applied to them. However difficult segregation and discrimination may make the attainment of this ideal, integrity offers no other course of action for the Negro Christian.

The white Christian is often lacking in integrity, too. It happens that some Caucasians tell Negroes untruths without any pang of conscience. Though the situation has greatly improved, lying used to be the main technique exercised by white ticket sellers when they did not want to sell Pullman space to Negroes. Hundreds of persons of color have been refused Pullman reservations by this device. After being denied, Negroes have had white friends go to the window and make inquiry only to find that there was plenty of space available. Negroes have experienced the same treatment at the theater ticket office. Many Negroes seem to think it is all right to lie to white people and many white persons act as if they believe it is quite all right to lie where Negroes are involved.

NO PREFERENTIAL TREATMENT

Many Causasians depend on the fact of their whiteness. Too often they think they have a right to occupy positions superior to those of Negroes on no other ground than that they belong to the white race. If statistics could be obtained, they would probably show an enormous number of white persons who take it for granted that they have a right to the leading positions in all fields and that in no case should Negroes have top places, however competent they are. There are no doubt millions in the white race who would refuse to work under Negroes. In the government, in education, in social work, and in civil life generally, many white persons hold top positions with Negroes working under them who are far more capable than they, both in academic attainment and in administrative ability. Were it not unwise to do so, these statements could be supported with specific documentary evidence.

Some years ago the executive of a welfare agency was assuming responsibility for a study of Negro life in a certain city. The executive of a Negro agency and two persons from the outside were to make the study: two Negroes and one white. When the chief executive, who was white, learned that a Causasian was in the group, she insisted that he should direct the study. When it was pointed out that not one of the three had distinguished himself in research, that one of the Negroes held an A.B. from an outstanding eastern college and an A.M. from a great western university, and that the white person held an A.B. from a respectable southern college and an A.M. from an outstanding southern university, she exclaimed, "But Mr. — is white." It must be said for the white colleague that he made no such demands and the study was made co-operatively. But when it was finished, the chief executive insisted that the white man's name appear first on the study, and it did. A Negro should be neither penalized nor favored because he is dark, black, or brown. A Caucasian should be given neither special privilege nor top position just because he is white. One should earn his way on merit and by the sweat of his brow and the exercise of his brain. This is the simple requirement of justice.

The white Christian is obligated to accept his role as a normal human being, not as a member of a "superior" race. He should not expect to receive what he is not willing to give. He should not expect to perpetuate the master-slave relationship or the paternalistic attitude in his dealing with Negroes. The more enlightened Negroes become and the further they are removed from slavery, the more they are bound to resent paternalistic behavior.

To be specific, Caucasians have no right to expect Negroes to provide "special" segregated seats for them when they attend Negro churches or other affairs sponsored by Negroes. It is difficult to determine which is worse, Negroes who continue to perpetuate such a system or the white people who insist on it and accept the "special privileges." Negro and white Christians are both under obligation to exercise their influence to break down segregation based on color or race. Even where segregation is upheld by law, Christians should not accept it complacently, because it negates the personalities of those segregated. When the law is wrong, Christians must work to change it. A Christian must give no more than he can take. For a member of the white race to call a Negro "uncle," "boy," "George," "nigger," and insist or expect that he, in turn, be called "Mister" is an attempt to uphold white supremacy by force. To expect a Negro Christian to take off his hat in an elevator in the presence of white women and to expect the white Christian to keep his hat on in the elevator in the presence of Negro women is both un-Christian and ungentlemanly. Womanhood and not race is honored when special deference is shown to women.

SELF-RIGHTEOUSNESS

The Bible is right when it implies and states specifically that one of the cardinal sins of mankind is self-righteousness. When one listens to Negroes criticize the shortcomings of white Christians, one is inclined to believe that Negroes are the very essence of righteousness. Negroes are not necessarily virtuous because they are suppressed, and other racial groups are not necessarily depraved or lacking in virtue because they occupy the position of privilege. He who criticizes others should earn the right to do so by purging his own soul of the sins that he condemns in them. Mahatma Gandhi was eminently correct when he insisted that the Hindus must get rid of untouchability and make the relationship between the various castes of India just and humane if they were to be justified in their insistence that England cease oppressing them and give them complete autonomy.

At least three things should be taken into consideration by Negroes:

(1) As far as is known, no one race has a monopoly on virtue and no one race has a monopoly on those things that are evil. Negroes are potentially no worse and potentially no better than Gentiles, Jews, Chinese, or Japanese.

(2) If Negroes develop the spirit of hate and revenge and wish for the time to come when the scales are turned so that they can inflict the blow upon white people, they are as evil as those who suppress and exploit them. In such a case, God will not sustain them any more than he is going to sustain the dominant race in what it is doing to the weak peoples of the earth. Regardless of who the oppressors are or may be, the day of retribution is always inevitable. The Negro is no more a favorite of God than the white man.

(3) Negroes frequently take out upon themselves what they would like to take out upon the members of the dominant group. That means it frequently happens that Negroes are just as brutal and cruel to one another as the members of the dominant group are to them. This is to be explained in part by the fact that pent-up emotions and hurts must have their outlets. Negroes who are afraid to take out their revenge on members of the white race for the discriminations and wrongs inflicted by that race upon them often find themselves doing to one another what white people do to them. The large number of homicides among Negroes can be partly explained on this basis.

This does not mean that Negro Christians are to take a complacent attitude toward the wickedness in society because they are involved in that wickedness. It is an attempt to say that Negro Christians seldom allow an opportunity to pass by without pointing out the un-Christian character of white Christians. Although we are convinced that there is much to criticize in white Christians, the Negro's case would be stronger and much more effective if he recognized the shortcomings in himself and if he were as critical of his own non-Christian behavior as he is that of the white man. A recognition of these facts not only would save him from the sin of self-righteousness, but would drive him to the point of repentance; and when he criticized white Christians, he would do so with cleaner hands. In other words, he should earn the right to criticize.

Negroes are obligated to practice democracy in those areas where they have the last word—in their schools, in their homes, and in their churches—if they are to condemn America for undemocratic practices. Likewise, they must exercise Christian virtues in their interracial endeavors. The fact that many white Christians deny these virtues to Negroes does not justify Negroes in denying them to members of the white race, especially in those areas where Negroes have complete control.

If the Negro Christian can take the attitude described above, he will be able to do two things that are much needed in many interracial programs. First, he will be able to face the problems involved with saner objectivity. Minority groups are sensitive. They are sensitive because society has made them so by the jeers, sneers, and discriminations they have met on every hand. These experiences at times make Negroes and other minority people supersensitive. They sometimes feel that they have been objects of discrimination when no slight or discrimination was meant. But even when discrimination is deliberate, it is usually dealt with more effectively if the problem can be approached objectively and with considered judgment.

Second, with the attitude just described the Negro Christian will be more poised. Negroes often feel the urge to "get white people told," give them a tongue-lashing, or point out to them how mean and unjust they are. It cannot be doubted that there are times when this needs to be done and that too many white people are mean and unjust—just as there are too many Negroes who are mean and unjust. It should never be done, however, in a vindictive spirit or for the mere sake of getting revenge. Criticisms are likely to be more effective and better received when those who give them accept the fact that they themselves are not perfect and that they are part and parcel of the evil they condemn. The objective, sensible position for Negroes to take is to oppose in their own behavior and practices that which is un-Christian or undemocratic, just as they oppose it when found in Gentiles, Jews, or Orientals.

THE NEGRO CHRISTIAN AND HIS PREJUDICES

The temptation confronting all minority racial groups is to think of another minority in ways characteristic of the dominant, ruling majority and to treat it just as the dominant group treats them. Negroes are likely to take over the white Gentiles prejudice against Jews, and Jews are tempted to, and sometimes do, discriminate against Negroes just as white Gentiles do. Likewise, Negroes may be found guilty of prejudice against Japanese Americans, Mexicans, and Chinese just as these are sometimes found to be prejudiced against Negroes and afraid of association with them.

More than once the writer has heard intelligent Negroes generalize about Jews just as he has heard Negroes and white people generalize about one another. He has heard Negroes say prejudicial things about Jews, the same kinds of things which, in his travel in Europe and around the world, he has heard white Gentiles say about Jews. But Jews cannot be catalogued any more than Negroes and Gentiles can. Such expressions as "Jews are dishonest" and "Jews will do anything for the dollar" are just as erroneous and un-Christian and show just as much distortion and prejudice when voiced by Negroes as when uttered by white Gentiles. Anti-Semitism is a deadly disease and the Negro Christian should take no part in it.

The Jew is no better and no worse than the rest of God's children. A few years ago, the writer experienced prejudice in a Jewish store, one of the outstanding stores in the nation's capital. The store refused him a credit account because he was a Negro, although the credit bureau had established the fact that his credit was good. Another Jewish firm in Washington bowed to Gentile prejudice by establishing segregation in its rest rooms. How unscientific and unfair it would be to judge all Jews on the basis of such incidents! Over against these expressions of Jewish weakness, one must see Brandeis, one of the ablest and fairest Americans ever to sit on the bench, and Rosenwald, one of the most generous philanthropists, an outstanding friend of Negroes. And as a historical reminder, one must not forget that the man whom we call Jesus was a Jew. If Negro Christians fight against the discrimination and prejudices which they experience day by day, they should guard against displaying the same prejudice and discrimination in their attitude toward and in their contact with Jews, Chinese, Mexicans, West Indians, Japanese, Indians, and other racial groups.

A SANE AND CRITICAL APPRAISAL

The topic "A Sane and Critical Appraisal of Liberals" might have been placed under "Integrity and Character"; but there is sufficient difference in content and emphasis to justify placing it in a separate category.

It is probably true that no large number in the white race honestly believes, in words and in deeds, in the equality of the Negro—if equality means that Negroes are to be judged wholly on the basis of character, opportunity, and ability, and that they are to have exactly the same chance to get on in the world as white people. If this is true, there are degrees of liberalism. One person may be just one step ahead of the conservative or the traditionalist in his belief about Negroes. Another may be two steps ahead. Still another may be miles in advance of the ultraconservative or reactionary. Here the Negro needs to be exceptionally discerning. It often happens that a member of another race who is barely two steps ahead of his contemporaries in his conception of racial justice is hailed as an outstanding liberal and a great friend of Negroes. Members of the white race are sometimes rushed too fast because they said something in public that sounded right on the race issue or put something in print that made good reading. Such persons should be commended for their courage and definitely appreciated; but they should not be led to believe that they have become true liberals when they have barely "gotten their feet wet" in the area of practicing and living high religion. There are at least three dangers:

1. The man who is just beginning to be liberal may be frightened away from the cause if he is advertised as a great friend of Negroes; in which case, he may return to his conservatism.

2. He may be fooled by the acclaim and come to believe he is farther along than he is. If this should obtain, there will be disillusionment farther down the line and his own growth may be retarded. Then, too, it should be taken for granted that a man is supposed to say and do the right thing and should not expect to receive special reward or praise because he does that which the Christian religion demands.

3. When undue credit is given to a member of another race because he seems liberal and then it is discovered that he has been overrated, the Negro may lose faith in whites and say, "No white person can be trusted to ring true." The fault is not in the other fellow. The appraisal was premature and unrealistic.

Developing the art of flattery in an effort to survive and get along, the Negro has become an expert in it and the white Christian must be sure that he is not being taken in when Negroes praise him too much.

CHRISTIAN FELLOWSHIP

One of the main duties of the Christian is to foster Christian fellowship across racial lines. "In Christ there is neither Jew nor Gentile, bond nor free, male nor female. . . ."

In the area of race relations today, the church is weak. It is so partly because it usually denies Christian fellowship across racial lines. Most of our churches are not churches of God but churches of men, of custom, and of tradition. Until the individual Christian and the clergy are able to set themselves over against the state, against tradition, and against custom and say by words and deeds that when a member of any racial group crosses the threshold of this house, he is no longer in the custody of men but in the custody of God, and that in God's house the state or society has no voice and no jurisdiction, the church will be weak and impotent; it will have no right to speak to the secular order about its behavior. Freedom of worship, if it means anything at all, means freedom to worship God across racial lines and freedom for a man or woman to join the church of his or her choice irrespective of race. Separate churches for the people may not be un-Christian but segregated churches are un-Christian. Denominational churches, for example, are not necessarily un-Christian; but churches organized purely along racial lines can hardly qualify as Christian. If worship and fellowship are denied because of race, it is definitely un-Christian. A white Methodist would not hesitate to worship in a white Methodist church of which he was not a member, and he would be welcomed. The same would hold if a Negro Methodist wanted to worship in a Negro Methodist church of which he was not a member. Since the church belongs to God and not man, why should not a Caucasian be at home in a so-called Negro church and a Negro Methodist be at home in a so-called white Methodist church? Why should a white Baptist be free to worship in a white Methodist church while a Negro Methodist is denied such a right? If there can be fellowship across denominational lines within the race, why should there not be fellowship across racial lines within the same denomination? Why should not a man or woman who confesses Christ and who is willing to accept the faith and regulations of a particular church be permitted to join the church of his choice? Why is it that a Chinese, a Japanese, a Mexican, or a member of any of the other colored races can worship in any white church without embarrassment and the Negro in many instances cannot? Every Negro Christian and every white Christian should ask, What is my responsibility to God in this area? Christians should study their local communities and see what they as individuals can do to further Christian fellowship across racial lines.

INDIVIDUAL RESPONSIBILITY

Fellowship within the church is not enough. People can worship together and go away feeling self-righteous while the evils in the community go unchanged. The master and the slave worshiped together in the early church, but no one challenged the institution of slavery. It must be kept in mind that the Christian is a citizen of two worlds and that his ultimate loyalty and allegiance is to God. In the final analysis, he is accountable only to God; and if accountable to God, he is not a slave to his environment.

A Christian is not bound to believe every lie that is told about Jews. Even though every member in his household may believe it, he does not have to believe it. He can study and find out the truth about Jews. He can seek to know some Jews personally and establish friendship with them. He can in his own way, by action, words, and pen, refute the unfair things that are frequently said about them.

Despite jim crow, segregation, and discrimination, which he meets almost incessantly, the Negro Christian does not have to hate white people. Even when he piles up evidence to prove that efforts are being made to keep him a second-class citizen, it is not foreordained of God that he has to nurture rancor in his heart and hate in his soul. He can rise above hate.

The white Christian does not have to believe the propaganda that in order for the white race to be prosperous, socially respectable, economically secure, and politically free the Negro must be kept down, segregated, lynched, discriminated against in education, in industry, in politics, in government, and in life generally. He can find out the truth about the Negro. He can know what science says about race. He can learn what the Christian religion says about race. He can know what the federal Constitution records with respect to equality of opportunity for all. The white Christian does not have to bow to prejudice of this kind. Once discovering the facts, he can order his life progressively in the light of truth.

A Christian in business does not have to cheat and steal. He does not have to exact unfair profit. He does not have to horde his money when good causes cry out for support. He does not have to discriminate against races in his employment. A politician running for office does not have to run for office on an anti-Negro platform.

In all of these areas the Christian cannot excuse himself by saying, "I cannot go against tradition, I cannot buck the mores; I cannot jeopardize my political, social, or economic future." None of these arguments will suffice. The true Christian is a citizen of two worlds. Not only must he answer to the mores, but he must give an account to God. And with God's help he can be loyal to the highest and to the best that he knows.

VI

THE OUTLOOK

12

Judgment and Hope in the Christian Message

HOWARD THURMAN

I

IMPLICIT in the Christian message is a profoundly revolutionary ethic. This ethic appears as the binding relationship between men, conceived as children of a common Father, God. The ethic is revolutionary because the norms it establishes are in direct conflict with the relationship that obtains between men in the modern world. It is a patent fact that attitudes of fellowship and sympathetic understanding across lines of separateness such as race, class, and creed are not characteristic of our age. Whatever may be the concomitant reasons therefor, we are faced with the naked truth that twice within a quarter of a century our world has been involved in two wars and at the present moment most of the countries that have survived are themselves armed camps. This tragic picture indicates, at least, that we have not found a way by which to implement the insights of the Christian ethic or that the ethic itself has been rejected.

The religious implications of the ethic demand that the individual place at the center of his life a completely unswerving commitment to a God who is conceived in terms of supreme worthfulness. This conception of God finds its manifestation at many different levels of life. The far-reaching significance of this fact becomes at once the guarantor of whatever universal validity there is for the ethic itself. In the final analysis, life must sustain the ethic or it is a snare and a delusion. Practically stated, it raises the question and answers it in the affirmative as to whether or not a man who undertakes to live in the world on the basis of the Christian ethic can expect to be sustained and strengthened in his great endeavor.

The genius of the ethic is found in the great call of Israel, "Hear, O Israel, the Lord thy God is One, and thou shalt love the Lord thy God with all thy mind, heart, soul and strength; and thou shalt love thy neighbor as thyself." In the mind of Jesus this was the creative summation of the Law and the prophets. Here we have the astounding insight that there is no distinction between the God of life on the one hand, and the God of religion on the other. The insight is central and inescapable and may be regarded as an incisive statement of the character of the universe. God is one even as life is one; life is one because God is one. However it is stated, it adds up to the same thing.

God is the source of life. This is a basic assumption, a qualitative premise upon which all of the varied structures of meaning rest. This, of course, means that every creature is grounded in God in a direct and primary manner. It would follow, therefore, that all creature potentials, both positive and negative, are indirectly grounded in the same manner. The relationship of any particular form of life at any specific level, however highly differentiated, to the source of life is ultimately identical with life itself. That which sustains a rattlesnake cradles the turtledove; that which nourishes the strawberry makes the poison oak to thrive.

The kinship that exists between forms of life is not to be found merely in structural similarities or identities, important as these may be. But it is to be found primarily in a common ground of origin and sustenance. The struggle between forms of life, between higher and lower, between strong and weak, even when this struggle is on behalf of sheer physical survival in terms of food, must be regarded as fratricidal. The more highly developed the form, the more clearly discernible should be the facts of kinship both within the species and between the various species. This is the inevitable conclusion to be drawn from the assumption that there is but a single source of life, and that source is dynamic and creative.

The recognition of God as the source of life carries with it the judgment that life is alive. The statement that life is alive may seem utterly redundant and therefore meaningless. It is the insistence that inherent in the conception of life as a category is the same pulsing vitality which is quite apparent when we consider an individual or organism. It is easy for the term to be regarded as a metaphysical abstraction when applied to the ground of being. The character of life is essentially dynamic, carrying a certain seeming autonomy all its own. What is observed in the simplest creeping insect is but a picturesque expression of the activity which is the ground of all being. From this point of view mechanistic or materialistic interpretations of life seem singularly without meaning.

We are so overwhelmed by the dramatic and existential aspects of life, such as growth, orderly functions of organs, total behavior characteristics of various kinds of organisms, etc., that each living thing seems to be in itself quite autonomous and self-contained, having no reference to any sustaining factors beyond the environment in which it finds survival. There is something which seems quite automatic about all living things. One recalls that in the New Testament the reference is made to the earth as being automatic in its relation to life. Every tree, every dog, every man seems to be essentially and uniquely alive without any contact with any deeper level or ground of vitality. And yet it is to be noted that trees die, animals die, men die, but trees remain, animals continue their existence, and men are fruitful and multiply. The gross vitality of all living things is the ground sustaining each particular one; human beings in this sense are but one variety of living things. A vital urgency maintains the process of fructification without regard to the disintegration of any particular expression of life.

The assumption that God is the source of life means that the aliveness of God is infinitely more significant than, and is basic to, the aliveness of life. It means further that the patterns of life manifestations as expressed in the manifold development of potentials are without ceiling terminus. They can be limited only by the aliveness of God. This is equivalent to saying that they are without limitations.

II

It is one of the curious paradoxes of religion that what it demands of man, conceivably the highest manifestation of life, is so overwhelmingly and obviously particularized that it tends to force a specious distinction between the secular and the sacred. This may be due to the evolution of the mind. The moment fine distinctions as over against gross distinctions became articulate for human beings, separate universes of discourse were possible. The technique of rationalization matured. The sacred came to be regarded as that which was, in some unique sense, the divine domain. Religious ceremonies, deeds of a certain kind, categories of particularized behavior, rituals, and the like all were interpreted as being a part of the religious frame of reference. It is to be noted that all experience remained one in essence, but the conditions under which experiences took place and the need which they met in the life of the individual became the clue to their definition. If it be true that structurally all experience is one, then to check one experience as being of God and the other as being of the devil is a question of value judgment rather than of experience itself. The moment a divine quality of uniqueness is given to a particular category of experience, the way is clear to make a false distinction between the God of life and the God of religion. The insistence that all life be lived with high ethical religiousness becomes the only valid basis for living. When men say that religion is not practical, they are really affirming that the God of life and the God of religion are separate and distinct. In other words, they mean that the God of religion is an illusion or a figment of the imagination or merely the cry of anguish in the presence of a world of imponderables.

It follows, then, that in the insistence of religion that God is one, there is precluded the possibility of a distinction between the God of life and the God of religion. God is one and man's relationship to God is automatically one of kinship through origin. This kinship implies an organic relatedness between God and creature. The awareness of this relationship expressed on the lowest level of life is in terms of gross responsiveness to sustenance; on the highest levels of life there is included not only gross responsiveness but a self-consciousness of mind. The unique thing about the awareness of mind is the fact that it is a self-awareness as distinguished from an awareness of something external. In fact, I am conscious of myself as a thinking organism. To the degree which this self-awareness becomes inclusive of other manifestations of life by which it is surrounded and of which it is a part, to that degree does it become mandatory for the individual thus aware to regard others as he regards himself. The higher, therefore, that one's self-estimate becomes, the higher of necessity will be the regard with which one evaluates one's relation to others. If God sustains and is the ground of the organic life of man, then, by the same token, he becomes the ground of those aspects of the life of man that are the distinct results of man's personality achievements. The realm of thought, feeling, desiring, dreaming is sustained by that which sustains man's physical body. It is reasonable then to affirm that he who undertakes to deal kindly with his fellow men or to walk with them in paths of justice and mercy may expect the same support that his environment gives to his physical body.

The question then is, Is it reasonable to assume that the universe is grounded in a limitless vitality that can sustain the revolutionary demands of the Christian ethic? When a man on a quite rational basis can justify his hatred of another man and can then reject this hatred as being unrighteous and therefore life-denying, will the universe leave him unaided and unsustained or may he expect the strength and the vitality needful for such an enterprise? It is my position that the guarantee of the ethical demand is to be found in the underlying vitality of the universe as expressed in the aliveness of life, which in turn is sustained by the God of life.

There is a sense in which the aliveness or the vitality of life may be regarded as being neutral. This would seem to be indicated in what Jesus has to say about God's causing the sun to shine upon the just and the unjust without discrimination. It is true that he who demands an ultimate resource will become the channel through which that resource moves and in his experience will become powerful, apparently omnipotent, whether he be benevolent or demoniacal. The seeds of continuity are the ethical or unethical quality of the goals that are sought. It is reasonable to me to place well within the range of the mind and power and love of God not only the releasing of infinite energies on demand but the screening of the ends to which these energies are directed. If the end be rejected because it is life-denying and destructive, there can be no ultimate sustenance for such an individual or nation. The judgment of God appears again and again in the process of history, dramatized in the rise and fall of peoples who have neglected to build their civilizations toward ends of high ethical responsibility. If a man be selfish, hardened as to sympathies, insensitive to the needs of others, in the end he destroys himself because life denies him at the last its blessing, and the qualities that he manifests he becomes. This does not mean that the wicked do not prosper, but it does mean that the diabolical character of the enterprise itself destroys the vehicle so that finally energies are scattered and dissipated. He who places his life completely at the disposal of the highest ethical end, God, to him will not be denied the wine of creative livingness.

The bearing of all of this upon the intricate relationships between Negroes and white people in the United States is not far to seek. If it be true that the normal relationship between men is activated kinship, grounded in a common dynamic origin, then attitudes of mistrust, of fear, of prejudice, whatever may be the extenuating justification for them, are a repudiation of the ethical meaning of life. He who undertakes to approach his fellow as a brother and will with courage, intelligence, and integrity fashion his life on the basis of such an imperious demand can depend on the God of life to sustain him even in his moment of greatest despair and frustration. The hardest task is to be found not in affirming this kind of conviction but rather in discovering techniques of implementation that will make so great a commitment a common part of the daily round of experience. Our hope is in a devotion to life in this dimension and our judgment is in the barrenness which we sustain in not living this religion.

13

Judgment and Hope in the Nature of Man and Society

RICHARD I. McKINNEY

THE writers of the foregoing chapters have emphasized the areas of persistent conflict and challenge in certain basic and often difficult human relationships of our time. The argument is quite definitely set against the framework of what seems, to this group of writers at least, to be the fundamental imperatives of the Christian faith with respect to man's relation to his fellow man across so-called racial lines. Of the various questions which appear in the issues involved, there remain for further consideration and discussion those having to do with certain aspects of judgment and hope for our present situation as may be in evidence in the nature of man and society.

Someone has remarked that "we learn from history that mankind does not learn from history." One of the greatest questions of our time is whether man has the necessary inner resources to make it possible for him to build a kingdom of brotherhood. Does he have the necessary insight and will to profit by the mistakes of the past and to establish the conditions for building a stable community? In this atomic age as perhaps never before, man is having his supreme test at this point. It is now fairly commonly agreed that we are in a race between civilization and catastrophe, between life and death. There are those who, upon reflecting on the history of man's development, have concluded that it is hardly to be expected that civilization and brotherhood will win. Indeed, some are standing by waiting for the catastrophe. One can understand a pessimism of this sort. The ever manifest pride, selfishness, and greed, the will to power and the repeated personal and social conflicts of history all lead one to question whether man has the capacity to overcome the potential crisis of our age. It may well be asked, therefore, whether we can see any basis in human nature as it is for our hope in the establishment of a society of brothers.

THE CHRISTIAN UNDERSTANDING OF MAN

As far as Christian faith is concerned, the possibilities of human nature are best seen in the light of the Christian doctrine of man. Attention has already been drawn to this by other writers in this book.

The nature of man, as viewed apart from any religious presuppositions, is variously interpreted. According to some schools of thought, human nature is not too greatly removed either in quality or in destiny from other forms of animal life. Here man is simply an advanced form of animal, but still an animal, destined at last to suffer the fate common to all other creatures. Support for this view is derived from, among other things, the mechanistic aspects of human nature. It is said that man is primarily a part of and subject to the immediate environment in which he lives, and therefore is of no more ultimate significance in the universe than the so-called "lower" animals which he dominates.

In any such view of man there is of course little if any hope for his transcending the bonds of self and environment. Moreover, the universe is indifferent if not hostile to the innermost longings in the hearts of men. No one has expressed this view with more beautiful poignancy than Bertrand Russell, when he says that "brief and powerless is Man's life; on him and all his race the slow, sure doom falls pitiless and dark. Blind to good and evil, reckless of destruction, omnipotent matter rolls on its

relentless way."[1] If this is an accurate description of the significance of human nature and its destiny, then one may agree with
Mr. Russell that about the best man can do is to grit his teeth
against "the trampling march of unconscious power" and endeavor to make the frustrations of life as bearable as possible and
accept the inevitable annihilation with stern fortitude.

Between the view of man as a mere animal and the view of
him as a child of God there is a wide gap. Yet man has persistently refused to be content with a low view of himself. Through
the ages he has, in response to deep stirrings within him, sought
his destiny in the stars. A brief analysis of the rise and function
of religion offers some clue to the understanding of his nature.

The rise of religion in man is prompted in part by his wants,
his ambitions, and his felt needs for a more complete adjustment
to his world. Primitive man found himself surrounded by forces
over which he had no control and which often seemed to him
arbitrary and capricious. There was no "sweet" mystery of life
for him, for life was hard and unpredictable. Then as now man
needed adjustment to himself, to his fellows, and most of all to
the forces of nature of which he was so acutely conscious but before which he was so inadequate. In the process of his seeking
security and self-realization religion arose, as a "binding force" in
human relationships, as a factor for inner peace, and as a stimulus
to achievement. Ceremonials, rituals, and magic were all used as
means for expressing his religious emotions, his longings, and his
strivings for a sense of security in the universe. Thus religion
may be defined in terms of man's upreach, his endeavor to find
the best in life, and his quest for the Supreme Being, with the aid
of whose powers he could achieve the sense of security he so
much desired.

A second aspect of our understanding of the rise of religion is
the response which man makes to what he calls divine. This response is along the line of man's personal relations with his God
and with his fellow man. Religion is not merely the values he
finds in his social relations, although these play a large part in his

[1] *Selected Papers of Bertrand Russell* (New York, 1927), p. 14.

life. Nor is it merely "what the individual does with his own soli-
tariness,"[2] even though it often becomes necessary for man to
be alone before he can hear the voice of his God. Somewhere between these two extremes we find the true picture of the nature
of religion. It is man's *total* response, both as an individual and as
a social being, to the universe in which he finds himself. Inherent
in this total response is the feeling that the universe has some
kind of teleological factors which man can recognize and in
which are resolved all the difficult problems of evil and suffering
which finite minds try so feebly to understand. In religion man
finds the basis for harmonizing all the various perplexities and
diversities of his experiences, both individual and social, and
through it he seeks a better world.

If the foregoing discussion is a correct analysis of the rise and
function of religion, it follows that man is a spiritual being. This
assertion is at the heart of the Christian understanding of man.
Fundamental in the Christian doctrine of man is the belief that
man is made in the image of God. As a child of God he is unable
to achieve fullness of life apart from God. God must be the beginning and the end of all his endeavors. There is something in
him which does not let him rest content with the merely visible
factors in his experience. At the limit of his physical powers and
of the demonstrable factors in his experiences, something deep
within him murmurs, "Excelsior!" Man is a creature of faith and
hope, without which there is no meaning or rationality to his life.
Moreover, he is a rational creature, whose mind almost unconsciously seeks for order, unity, and stability. All his values and
ambitions derive their meaning from his conception of God and
his relation to the universe. As a spiritual being he seeks the
validation of himself, his fellows, and of all the values which
have come down through the cultural heritage of the race. No
matter to what heights he attains he always sees positions above
him yet to be achieved. Again, man is endowed with an elemental freedom of action. He is a person, not a puppet pulled on
a string. He is a free agent, not a machine manipulated as a pawn

[2] A. N. Whitehead, *Religion in the Making* (New York, 1926), pp. 16–17.

by some far-off Machinist. It is precisely because of his relation of sonship to God that he assumes the position of the highest creation of God. To the extent that he endeavors to be loyal to the divine within him, to that extent is he living in accordance with his true nature.

SIN AND JUDGMENT

One of the basic assumptions of the Hebrew-Christian tradition is that man is a sinner. The Christian doctrine of sin is predicated upon the idea of man as a free agent, responsible to God for all his conduct. This conception implies a limitation which God voluntarily imposes upon himself, for if he is to allow man freedom, God must refrain from interfering with that freedom. Man possesses the power of choice and his failure to choose the highest possible good for himself in a particular situation is sin. As H. R. McIntosh says, "The origin of sin must lie in the abuse of freedom."[3] There can be no sin where there is no freedom of choice between possible courses of action. Man's unique position in the universe as a child of God implies a unique privilege for him, but at the same time, it places upon him a special obligation to act in accordance with his highest possibilities. Very early in life he learns the elemental meaning of "right" and "wrong" conduct, and also very early he recognizes his ability to elect one or the other. The idea of sin, moreover, involves not merely right or wrong, but also choices between different levels of goodness. We are called upon to choose between the highest possible moral action for us in a given situation and other courses of action which, although they may not be wrong in and of themselves, may nevertheless represent less than our best. In such a situation, to choose consciously the lesser rather than the highest good is sin. For all men the highest good, the highest ideal, is God. Since no one at all times chooses the highest course of action he knows, it follows that all men have the stain of sin upon them. The doctrine of original sin is best understood with refer-

[3] H. R. McIntosh, "Sin," *Hastings Encyclopaedia of Religion and Ethics* (New York, 1928), XI, 543.

ence to the ever manifest tendency on the part of man to discount the will of the Highest and substitute his own judgment for God's will. This is the perennial experience of individual men. We may not be able to find the Garden of Eden on a map, someone has remarked, but we can find it in every man's heart.

The sense of sin and guilt is quite common to the race. Individual men have moments of reflection when they are deeply and painfully aware of the feeling of sin and guilt. The inner judge of every man, his conscience, keeps him constantly reminded of his obligations and moral failures. The sense of obligation, which is basic in human life, is derived in general from the attitudes of the group to which we belong. Its hates, its fears, and its appreciations are handed over to us and become a part of the fiber of our being. The important fact is that man has in him a feeling of obligation to do what is in accord with the highest possibilities expected of him.

In his most sober moments of reflection man becomes aware of his deep personal inadequacies. The Prayer of General Confession puts this mood in classic phraseology. The history of the race is one of man's erring and straying from God. We, "like lost sheep," follow "too much the devices and desires of our own hearts." We do that which should not be done and leave undone that which should be done. In the searching light of spiritual reflection man discovers himself to be ever so imperfect and lacking in moral and spiritual health. Thus does the spiritually sensitive soul come to a consciousness of divine judgment upon his inner nature. One feels that he has disobeyed God and thus violated a fundamental conviction. He feels that he has acted less than his best. The highest level upon which this violation can take place is on the plane on which God is conceived as love. Here one has been disloyal to the highest relationship that he knows, and the feeling of sin and guilt becomes acute.

The predominant emphasis in contemporary interpretations of sin is upon man's egoism and pride. Reinhold Niebuhr, for example, cites pride as basic in the nature of man's life. He distinguishes three types of pride which can be observed in man, namely, the pride of power, the pride of reason, and the pride of virtue.[4] Niebuhr finds that back of the sin of pride, however, is the sense of insecurity, which prompts men to exalt their own ego and will with the consequent deterioration of their inner personal life and their relations with their fellow men. With reference to the pride of power, Niebuhr declares that "the truth is that man is tempted by the basic insecurity of human existence to make himself doubly secure and by the insignificance of his place in the total scheme of life to prove his significance. The will-to-power is in short both a direct form and an indirect instrument of the pride which Christianity regards as sin in its quintessential form."[5]

The pride of reason is interpreted as the failure of man to recognize that his knowledge is only finite rather than ultimate, as he often claims it to be. Thus he becomes ignorant of his own ignorance. The following comment which Dr. Niebuhr makes on this type of pride is particularly apropos to this discussion:

The insecurity which hides behind this pride is not quite as patent as the pride, yet it is also apparent. In the relations of majority and minority racial groups, for instance, for which the Negro-white relation is a convenient example, the majority group justifies the disabilities which it imposes upon the minority group on the ground that the subject group is not capable of enjoying or profiting from the privileges of culture or civilization. Yet it can never completely hide, and it sometimes frankly expresses the fear that the grant of such privileges would eliminate the inequalities of endowment which supposedly justify the inequalities of privilege. The pretension of pride is thus a weapon against a feared competitor. Sometimes it is intended to save the self from the abyss of self-contempt which is always before it.[6]

The third form of pride is essentially self-righteousness, and is recognized in man's tendency to assume that whatever virtue he possesses is absolute and eternal. Not willing to be considered a

[4] Reinhold Niebuhr, *The Nature and Destiny of Man* (New York, 1941), I, 188.
[5] *Ibid.*, p. 192.
[6] *Ibid.*, p. 198.

sinner, he loses sight of his own sin and consequently of his real relation to God. "The sinner who justifies himself does not know God as judge and does not need God as Savior."[7] This sin, according to Niebuhr, "involves us in the greatest guilt. It is responsible for our most serious cruelties, injustices and defamations against our fellowman. The whole history of racial, national, religious and other social struggles is a commentary on the objective wickedness and social miseries which result from self-righteousness."[8]

There is still a fourth form of the sin of pride, stemming from the third, namely, spiritual pride, to be seen whenever we claim that our human ideals and achievements are identical with those of God or sanctioned by him.[9]

The foregoing analysis of the deep-seated roots of sin in human nature throws light upon man's basic limitations in the development of ideal human relations. Man stands in constant judgment before God. Divine judgment upon him individually and collectively has been witnessed in all generations. The whole of the Hebrew-Christian tradition assumes that he has a peculiar relation to God and certain definite responsibilities toward his fellow man. The Hebrew prophets, and Jesus as well, apparently worked on the assumption that human nature had in it elements making for living in terms of divine sonship and human brotherhood. Whenever men have refused to recognize or to practice the principles of human brotherhood there have been inevitable consequences inimical to their total well-being. The sickness of society, as seen in repeated wars, selfishness, and greed, the struggle for status and power, and the various consequences of our frequent blindness to the welfare of our fellow men all reflect aspects of divine judgment upon us. It has been said that we may break the Ten Commandments but we can never destroy them. Again, we break ourselves when we attempt to break the laws of

[7] *Ibid.*, p. 200.
[8] *Ibid.*
[9] *Ibid.*

God. Consequently the basis of divine judgment is inherent in the very nature of mankind and in society as well.

One of the important features of the consequences of sin is the rupture of fellowship, first between the sinner and his God and then between the sinner and his fellow men. Man is so made that he cannot live without fellowship. Without it life loses its essential meaning for him. Whatever he does against his fellow man acts as a divisive influence in society and he reaps a harvest of misunderstanding and broken fellowship which issue in ill will and sometimes violence. We live in a world of moral and spiritual law as well as of physical law. Although the consequences of our breaking the moral law are not as immediately recognized as are those of breaking the physical laws, these former consequences are quite as immediate and quite as real. The attempt to live as though we are not our brother's keeper or to disregard the law of human brotherhood, which all history shows is basic in human relations, is to bring down the judgment of the eternal God upon us.

One of the tragedies of history is that man has persistently hesitated to apply the Christian ethic of love and brotherhood to his social situations. The ancient Hebrew prophets recognized the law of brotherhood, and always pointed out to their people that the judgment of God would most surely be brought down upon them if they failed to rectify their ways. The history of the Hebrew commonwealth demonstrates, among other things, that the insights of the prophets at this point were real and profound. The teachings of Jesus on the oneness of humanity are plain. The early Christian Fathers recognized the necessity of the cultivation of the spirit of brotherhood across racial and national lines. In the ongoing development of civilization, it is clear that man has been at his best when he has acted in terms of his unity with and responsibility to his fellow man. When in the struggle for power men have ignored the law of love, they have tragically deceived themselves and have brought on themselves and their posterity the misery and suffering which are in a real sense the expression of the judgment of God in history.

THE BASES OF HOPE

We come now to a consideration of what possibilities we can find that will give us hope for mankind to build a world based on the principles of human brotherhood. John Bennett has remarked that "Christian theology has never been pessimistic about what God can do with man, although some forms of theology seem to have assumed that the social order is too much even for God"[10] Despite the reality and the persistence of sin which we have endeavored to point out in the preceding section, we must attempt to find some bases in human nature and society for an optimism which is at once realistic and healthy. Pointing out that there is a need for hope in the eradication of caste in American society, Buell Gallagher says that "There are some theologians, currently popular, who deny the possibility of social salvation. For them the gospel ends with the declaration that man is a sinner. They espouse the current heresy of social total depravity."[11] It is the belief of the present writer that there are grounds for hope, and that it is the obligation and the opportunity of Christians to focus attention upon them.

One of the first truths for our consideration is that man has a capacity for good. The problem of sin and evil for some is so acute that it is difficult for them to recognize that there is an inherent goodness in human nature which not only must not be ignored, but must be the touchstone of any movement looking forward to improvement in race relations. It is very easy to assume the goodness in man and to focus attention almost exclusively upon the evil. The fact is that history is full of examples of men, both famous and unknown, who have transcended the narrow limits of selfishness and have sacrificed themselves in the interest of a noble cause. But perhaps it was not sacrifice after all. For the great souls who spend themselves for a truly noble cause have found in that process the fulfillment of their innermost

[10] John Bennett, *Christian Realism* (New York, 1941), p. 53.
[11] Buell Gallagher, "Conscience and Caste: Racism in the Light of the Christian Ethic," *Journal of Religious Thought*, II (1945), 25.

nature. They have found a richness and fullness of life impossible of adequate description. Even the racial demagogues must couch their appeal in terms calculated to stir the basic will to goodness and right among their followers. If we can work on the assumption of the inherent goodness in men, our motivation for improvement in race relations will not be undercut at the outset.

Psychologically, as previously suggested, man is subject to feelings of sin and guilt as well as of obligation. His conscience never lets him rest content with conduct which is not morally right as far as he is able to determine what is morally right. But conscience has to be enlightened, for it is largely the product of the particular environment in which we have grown up. There are those who seem to feel that they cannot conscientiously follow a practice of brotherhood and fellowship across racial lines. It appears that they believe it morally wrong for them to do so. Here conscience has been perversely conditioned by the un-Christian beliefs and practices of the social order. The sense of guilt that our attitude on race is un-Christian is in itself a basis for hope. Increasingly men are becoming aware of their shortcomings in this area. Increasingly church groups are beginning at least to make pronouncements upholding the Christian ideal in race relations. Although something more than pronouncements is needed, of course, it is clear that there is a growing conscience on this subject. Repentance is needed and is increasing. A number of men are beginning to see and realize that our shortcomings on race not only will issue in disturbances locally but also will contribute to throwing the world once more into a catastrophic struggle. Buell Gallagher points out that nationalism and racism are two of the sins of man threatening to plunge the world into atomic warfare. He writes:

The second great world-wide immorality which threatens to bring atomic war is racism. "The sin of man," said the Oxford Conference, "asserts itself in racial pride, racial hatreds and persecutions and in the exploitation of other races. . . . The deification of one's own people is a sin against God." The sins of nationalism and of racism, which breed the sickness of our age in the cesspools of civilization, must be treated like the immoralities they are. But to turn away in revulsion and piously to affirm that God wills the end of human life because of man's sinfulness is hardly short of blasphemy. Repentance, not self-righteousness, is in order.[12]

In personal as well as in social life the consciousness of guilt is one of the primary requisites for release from the dominance of sin. It is quite clear that the spiritual forces of our time must bring the awareness of the sins of racism upon the consciousness and consciences of the people. Especially must the Christian church recognize continuously and increasingly its own sins and failures in this area. Doubtless Jesus himself would be outraged if he were to witness in the flesh some of the un-Christian and undemocratic practices of the institution and people which bear his name.

The Christian doctrine of man assumes that human nature is capable of transformation. Without this belief, our teaching and preaching are in vain. To be sure, this transformation is much slower than we want it to be. But an examination of the history of the race reveals that human nature has been modified through the centuries of man's ongoing development. Progress can be seen in the development of refinements and tastes, and in the reduction of the sum total of man's inhumanity to man. Despite the fact that each new war has brought with it the development of some new instrument of death and destruction more terrible than the last, it is true that there has been a slow but growing tendency in the direction of outlawing war as a means of settling international and interracial disputes. Education, both secular and religious, can be directed to sharpen unequivocally the issues involved in the principle of all men living as brothers and point men to a way to constructive participation in a democratic society. This will inevitably result in a modification of human behavior in the area of race relations.

The law of self-preservation is undoubtedly a factor, though

[12] Buell Gallagher, "Annihilation Is Evitable," *The Christian Century*, LXIII (1946), 1310.

a negative one, which will act as a force making for the development of a co-operative society. In a very real sense, we are beginning to see that it is either "one world or none." From the process of working toward the unity of the nations should come a wider appreciation of various groups within nations such as our own United States. Certainly without the development of a genuine sense of self-preservation and community of interests the realization of the dream of a really democratic society will long be delayed.

The explanation of many of the difficulties we face in race relations is deeply rooted in economic competition and the desire for security, which has back of it the fear of insecurity. This plays a significant part in the tendency of social groups to seek their welfare at the expense of the welfare of other people. There is a growing recognition on the part of some of the less privileged groups in America that their fortunes and misfortunes are inextricably bound up with those of the underprivileged in other races. The fact of the interracial tenant farmers' union in the South, along with the increasing recognition of some other unions, that labor cannot succeed in reaching its goals under a policy of segregation and discrimination, is an indication that some of the fear of economic competition is losing ground. In addition, there is to be observed a growing liberalism with respect to racial justice on the part of enlightened and emancipated leaders in the southern region. These leaders have sponsored, often at the risk of opprobrium by their fellows, movements designed to improve the welfare of all the people. They have seen that neither a nation nor a region can exist economically half slave and half free. There is, in the conviction of this writer, a real ferment in process in the South, which may be the beginning of a more genuine democracy than that region has ever known.

Some grounds for hope are to be seen in the increased amount of enlightened social legislation which has been passed in recent years, along with some liberal interpretations of the Constitution of the United States by the Supreme Court. The Fair Employment Practices Commission established by executive order of the President during World War II did much to focus attention on the inequalities existing in employment practices and, although it was allowed to die by Congress, paved the way for the enactment of similar legislation by two or three states in the country. Moreover, the movement for increased educational opportunity and the equalization of the salaries of teachers has had an encouraging measure of success, although what has thus far been accomplished is only a fraction of what is needed to achieve the full measure of equity which the principles of Christian race relations demand. It is sometimes said that we cannot legislate men into goodness; but it is possible to provide the legal framework within which justice and democracy can begin to grow. In this way the law itself becomes an instrument of education for justice. Some decisions of the Supreme Court of the United States with reference to race relations in recent years have resulted in just this process being established.

Other examples of progress in various organizations are noted in the discussions by other writers in this book. These instances are to be taken as indicative of the possibilities for good on the part of people working consciously toward the ideal of human brotherhood. Every success by any such organization strikes a blow at racial exclusiveness.

Finally, it is difficult to conceive of Jesus teaching the doctrine of the Kingdom of God and not believing that man can actively and realistically share or enter that Kingdom. Although the standards of the Kingdom are definitely high, Jesus evidently felt that men should endeavor to reach them by the grace of God. The Kingdom of God may properly be defined as the rule of God in the hearts of men. It appears that Jesus felt that men were capable of achieving this possibility. In his own day, his teaching of the Kingdom brought a new hope to men. In the subsequent history of the Christian church the ideal of the Kingdom of God has served to inspire countless followers of the master Teacher to love and serve their fellow men. Today that ideal can still be the goal which gives meaning and direction to all worth-while enterprises. For those who take it seriously and thoughtfully, it certainly involves a society in which universal brotherhood under a common Father is recognized.

Moreover, the ideal of the Kingdom of God is basic for the development of the sense of community and fellowship. If it is true that one of the most serious aspects of sin is the rupture of fellowship, it follows that the re-establishment of mutuality is an indispensable basis for the renewal of the spiritual and social life. Niebuhr has stated the necessity for the sense of community in convincing terms:

> The obligation to build and to perfect communal life is not merely forced upon us by the necessity of coming to terms with the rather numerous hosts, whom it has pleased an Almighty Creator to place on this little earth beside us. Community is an individual as well as social necessity; for the individual can realize himself only in intimate and organic relation with his fellowmen. Love is therefore the primary law of his nature; and brotherhood the fundamental requirement of his social existence.[13]

It is not to be expected, however, that on this planet there will be achieved a state of complete perfection. Some struggle and tension are probably inevitable among us. As long as man is man we may expect conflict of will with will. Jesus urged his followers to be perfect as their Father in heaven is perfect. But this doubtless means that the Christian who has placed himself under the rule of God is to act with complete justice toward all men, even as God gives his rain and sunshine to the good and bad alike.

If the Christian church can deepen among its constituents a sense of sin and guilt and inspire them to be loyal to the highest sense of community and brotherhood implied in the religion they profess, we can expect a revolution in our social relations. This will be a constructive upheaval, making for peace among all the children of God. To this end the church may work for the elimination of deep-seated fears which keep men apart. The fear of persons differing externally from ourselves, the fear of economic competition, of what is called "social equality," and,

[13] Reinhold Niebuhr, *op. cit.*, II, 244.

behind all these, the fear of insecurity can all be effectively attacked when the church makes bold to be God's church. Let the Christian people give themselves systematically to the analysis and breaking down of such fears and their causes, and the ideal of God's Kingdom, the realm of mutual and active respect for personality, will be realized among us in much fuller measure. This is our hope for the Christian way in race relations.

INDEX